P9-DDM-934

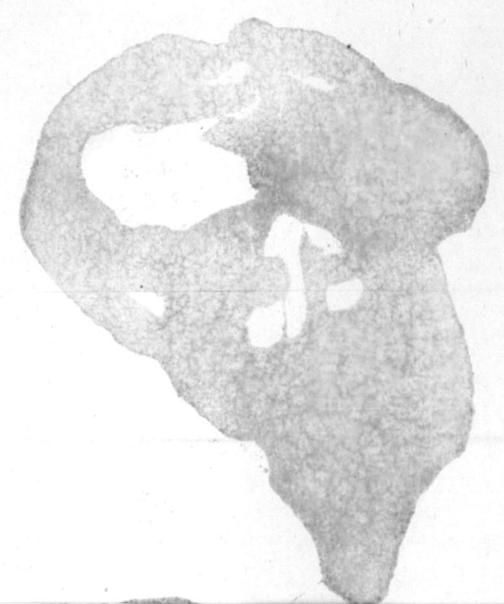

RIVERSIDE CITY & COUNTY PUBLIC LIBRARY
0 00 01 1504703 7

ALSO BY EDNA BUCHANAN

Carr: Five Years of Rape and Murder
The Corpse Had a Familiar Face
Nobody Lives Forever

NEVER LET THEM SEE YOU CRY

NEVER LET THEM SEE YOU CRY

More from Miami, America's Hottest Beat

EDNA BUCHANAN

RANDOM HOUSE • NEW YORK

 Published in the
United States by Random House, Inc., New York
and simultaneously in Canada by Random House
of Canada Limited, Toronto.

Portions of this work were originally published in *The Miami Herald*.

Library of Congress Cataloging-in-Publication Data

Buchanan, Edna.
Never let them see you cry: more from Miami, America's hottest beat / by Edna Buchanan. — 1st ed.
p. cm.
ISBN 0-394-57552-0
1. Buchanan, Edna. 2. Journalists—Florida—Miami—Biography.
3. Crime and the press—Florida—Miami. 4. Crime—Florida—Miami.
5. Murder—Florida—Miami. 6. Police—Florida—Miami. 7. Miami (Fla.)—Biography. I. Title.
PN4874.B793A3 1992
070′.92—dc20 91-52682
[B]

Manufactured in the United States of America
98765432
First Edition

Book text set in Times Roman
Book design by Debbie Glasserman

For Quinn and Callie Cagney,
and every little girl
with big dreams

CONTENTS

PART III: THE HEROES

PART IV: THE STORIES

INTRODUCTION

I had never planned a crime before. I usually arrive after, or during, the action.

Speed and surprise would be the most important elements: Strike swiftly, give witnesses no time to react. Don't seek approval from the people in charge—ask bureaucrats for permission to do anything out of the ordinary and they either say no or launch meetings to consider the question until long past your deadline.

On a leave of absence from *The Miami Herald* to write two books, I had begun to teach a crime-reporting class at Florida International University. At first I was unenthusiastic about teaching. An accidental journalist who had never studied the subject or attended college, my only qualifications were a 1986 Pulitzer Prize, a book called *The Corpse Had a Familiar Face*, published in 1987 and now in use at some journalism schools, and thousands of stories on Miami's police beat. But the offer to teach was one I could not refuse. Journalism had been very good to me, and pay-back time had arrived.

The class took only one night a week—no problem, that would leave ample time to write my books.

Wrong.

I became hooked on teaching. The term was exciting, the students terrific. We dialogued with experts from the police beat and took a field trip to the county morgue. We posed with the chalk outline of a corpse, surrounded by police crime-scene tape, as Pulitzer Prize–winning photographer Brian Smith shot our class picture.

And I plotted a perfect crime.

No guns, I decided. It was unlikely that any of my eager students would come to class armed, but this was Miami, a city like no other, unpredictable and stranger than fiction.

Ann and D. P. Hughes, the friends recruited to be the perpetrators in this piece of street theater, were uneasy. "I don't want to have to hurt anybody," D.P. muttered. The tough and savvy chief of operations at the Broward County Medical Examiner's Office, Daniel P. Hughes is also a lawyer and a certified police officer. Ann is his wife. Should you fall grievously ill or injured and spot her sweet face at your bedside, you are in serious trouble. In her soft and soothing southern accent she will talk you, or your next of kin, right out of your vital components. At the very least, she wants your eyes, skin and bones. Your heart, liver, lungs and kidneys would be ideal. Arranging the harvest of human organs and tissues is her job, for the University of Miami and Jackson Memorial Hospital. A woman who smiles freely and laughs often, Ann is dead serious about her work. She is as dedicated to tracking down the right parts for people who need them, as D.P. is to investigating how and why some stranger died.

While we conspired, I pointed out to my uneasy friends that these college seniors were not aspiring cops or Marines but would-be journalists: At moments of high excitement they take notes, not action. But I promised to shout "Nobody move! Stay in your seats," the moment D.P. burst through the classroom door. "Don't worry," I insisted. "It will all happen so fast, they won't know what went down. They'll freeze in their seats."

Wrong again.

Midway through my lecture on good cops–bad cops, Ann made her entrance as planned, through a door behind me. She frantically scanned the students' faces. "Where is my son? Isn't this the journalism class? You've got to help me. There's been a terrible accident, I have to find my son and take him home."

She was good. Very good. Tearfully, she tugged at my arm, skillfully maneuvering me around, drawing me back toward the door she had entered. Remember, this is a woman who can talk you out of your vital organs. She was so convincing that even I, the architect of the scheme, was suckered in.

I missed my cue.

D.P. burst through another door, snatched my black leather handbag off the desk and took off running. I never saw him. By the time I turned around, he was out the door, two students in hot pursuit. Scuffling sounds made me spin back toward Ann. She too had fled—or tried to. Before she could escape, a petite woman student had seized her belt from behind and was now scaling her back like a Sherpa ascending Mt. Everest.

Outside the classroom, D.P. reached for the police badge tucked in his belt. His pursuers momentarily fell back. Miamians, they assumed he was drawing a firearm. The rest of the class surged forward, a human tidal wave scattering furniture in its wake.

Finally I remembered my lines.

"Freeze! Nobody move!" I flung my arm at the wall clock. "You're on deadline. You have fifteen minutes. Write what just happened. Give me a lead, quotes and descriptions, height, weight, clothing."

Thirty-four astonished young men and women froze in disbelief. Nervous, adrenaline-charged laughter rippled through the room. Several students stared accusingly. They had been had. A burly young man, big as a linebacker, was too shaken to grasp a pencil.

The lesson, of course, was the fallacy of eyewitness identification, so beloved by juries, so consistently inaccurate.

The written accounts, from these alert young observers who saw everything under excellent conditions, were widely divergent.

Ann is lanky and fashion-model tall, with shoulder-length dark hair. She wore a green print jumpsuit. One earnest would-be reporter described her as a "petite blonde in a miniskirt." D.P.'s height estimates ranged from five feet six inches to six feet two inches. Ann's attire was described as a leopard print, D.P.'s as a dark, "FBI-style" ensemble. Neither was correct.

An excellent lesson. Hopefully they will never forget it when encountering eyewitnesses. The experience was revealing. Two of the three students quick and courageous enough to chase the "criminals" were young women. That one of them put it together fast enough to pursue Ann without hesitation astonished me.

The students' reactions demonstrated how violence and crime have changed people since I first began to cover the police beat two decades ago. We react faster and more aggressively. Perhaps that is why television shows on unsolved mysteries and wanted fugitives are so successful. Viewers jam telephone lines calling in tips, turning in their neighbors. We are all fed up with crimes unsolved and missing children never found.

Crime fighting has become a participatory sport.

A few years ago who would even have envisioned a journalism course specializing in crime reporting? Teaching it remains a fond memory, but I will never do it again. I became too fond of my students to replace them with a room full of strangers. My time is better spent reporting and writing.

The term ended, and before saying good-bye, I made them promise to always observe the journalist's three most important rules:

1. Never trust an editor.
2. Never trust an editor.
3. Never trust an editor.

It was difficult to part with them, tougher than covering rapes, riots, plane crashes and more than five thousand violent deaths. So was embarking on a book tour. A lifetime of cops and crooks was nothing compared to *Oprah, Late Night with David Letterman*, and the *Today* show and trudging down long, cold airport concourses in strange cities with sunless climates. The temperature was twelve the night I arrived in Boston, with the wind-chill factor twenty to thirty degrees below zero, the coldest night in Boston in one hundred years. "Where's your coat?" cried the publicist who met me at the airport.

Leaving Miami is like leaving a lover at the height of the romance. The city is an enigma that constantly unfolds, and I don't want to miss a moment. But authors, it was explained to me, must introduce their books to the world. I asked my friend, mystery novelist Charles Willeford, what I should to know about the book tour. He did not hesitate: "Never miss a chance to take a piss." *Men*, I thought, sighing impatiently, disappointed and frowning at Charles. *Why must they always be crude?*

Soon after, departing a Pittsburgh radio show during the book tour, I told the publicist who had me in tow that I intended to stop at the rest room before leaving. "No way," she said firmly, pushing me aboard an elevator. "We're behind schedule already."

Charlie was right.

Another radio and one TV show later, my keeper consulted her schedule. "You can go now," she announced, "but make it fast." Authors on a book tour are like prisoners of war, with better accommodations.

The hotels are not bad, but I hate airplanes.

After too many years of covering crashes, I am always sure that the man in the cockpit is under the influence of cocaine, about to suffer a major coronary, or simply suicidal. Snowstorms made my flight to Minneapolis five hours late. The waiting publicist, impatient at my delayed arrival, drove us at ninety miles an hour at one A.M. in her tiny car over icy roads through snow and sleet. No food seemed to be available at that hour in Minneapolis, and although the bellman said he turned on the heat in my room, it never worked. I piled all my clothes on the bed and huddled miserably beneath them. Exhausted, but too cold to sleep, I thought I was freezing to death. My only goal was to survive long enough to escape.

The publicist arrived at dawn. Her first question was, "How

can you *live* in Miami?" How? My toothpaste was frozen, it was too cold to take a shower, and she wondered how I could live in Miami? I prayed that the approaching blizzard would stall long enough for me to fly out on schedule late that afternoon. For the first time in my life, I was eager to board an airplane.

I scrambled out of her car at the airport so hastily that the sleeve of my borrowed coat dragged through a slushy black puddle at the curb.

There was something unreal about the Twin Cities airport. While waiting, I realized what it was. The only language heard was English, and all the strangers seemed to be light-skinned, fair-haired—and even polite.

After a one-hour delay, we soared into blinding snow. In front of me, a little boy about eight years old became violently airsick, screaming, retching and vomiting all the way to Washington. Nobody could be that sick and live. I feared he would not survive the flight. Was there a doctor aboard, I wondered, or would we be forced into an emergency landing to save his life? As we filed off the plane, in Washington at last, my knees trembling, I heard the boy, who appeared near death minutes earlier. "When can we get something to eat?" he eagerly asked his parents. He was starved, he announced. Children are so resilient. It took me three days to recover.

I was scheduled to appear on a radio show twenty minutes later. The station was thirty minutes away, under good driving conditions. A stranger hustled me to his car, careened like a madman through ice and snow and delivered me just before air time, my knees still shaky.

Not until the wee hours did I finally arrive at my hotel, longing for sleep, haggard and weather-beaten, my makeup long lost in some far-off city, my belongings crumpled and disorganized at the bottom of a battered garment bag. A message was waiting: A newspaper photographer would arrive to shoot my picture at dawn.

There were many other unforgettable moments, such as the routine takeoff from New York's Kennedy Airport, quickly followed by the emergency landing at LaGuardia, ten miles away.

Little wonder that the sight of soft pink and gray mists rising off the great swamp as we swept in over the Everglades to land in Miami brought tears to my eyes. Little wonder that the usual cacophony of noisy, rapid-fire talk in half a dozen exotic dialects was music to my frostbitten ears. Little wonder that I was delighted to come home to the police beat, covering life and death on the steamy streets of the city I love.

On the job a few days later I encountered a perfect eyewitness to murder. Smart, talkative and tough, he was accustomed to violence. Trouble was, he was only three years old.

As I canvassed a tough Miami neighborhood, piecing together the story of a brutal murder, I knocked on a strange door. Michael peeked out from behind his mother's skirt. He wore little red shorts and a *Marathon Man* T-shirt. He had never met the dead tourist, a millionaire who summered in a Montreal mansion and wintered in Nassau. Major heart surgery three months earlier had won the man a new lease on life.

The lease was canceled in Miami.

The millionaire had come from Canada for repairs to his yacht. Lost en route to the boat show, one of Miami's fine winter events, he stopped his rented car to seek directions.

Of all the strangers on all the streets in all the city, he chose a twenty-year-old with a gun, a rap sheet and no conscience.

The tourist stopped at the curb and rolled down his window. The younger man seized the opportunity, wrenched open the car door, piled into the front seat, hit the tourist in the face and drew his gun. "Drive," he said.

The stunned Canadian obeyed. His unwanted passenger took his money and his gold Rolex wristwatch, then shot him in the chest. The gunman grabbed the wheel, steered the car down an alley, shot the wounded man four more times, shoved him out and drove away.

Michael, who had been playing in his backyard, watched all

this through a chain-link fence. A young Miami policewoman arrived. He watched her, on her knees, urgently questioning the dying man. Michael appeared perplexed, but suddenly, during the victim's final, terrible moments, he understood. "Mama," he cried, tugging at her skirt. He pointed at the Canadian. "That's Toby!"

She calmly continued to remove her newly washed laundry from the clothesline. "No, baby, Toby got killed last week."

Toby had lived and died at the crack house a door away. The man who shot him also drove off. Michael's confusion was understandable. The three-year-old had just witnessed his second murder in two weeks.

Soon after, I arrived, seeking witnesses. Michael was shy until he recognized the face on my wristwatch. "Charlie the Tuna!" he cried. His eyelashes were long and curly, his smile a winner. We had a pleasant chat.

The killer cruised the neighborhood, displaying the blood-spattered rental car to friends, until police caught him. He had pawned the dead man's $15,000 gold Rolex for $95 and had tried without success to spend his Canadian currency.

Homicide detectives wanted an explanation. "I just shot him," the suspect said, flashing a goofy grin. Somehow it made sense to him.

Months followed, with more stories, more murders, more witnesses. I did not see Michael again, though I wanted to go back. Bright and beautiful, he belongs in a Montessori school somewhere, not in the Beirut he lives in. One reason I did not return was the impulse to snatch him and run, somewhere, anywhere, to a safe and secure future. But in my business the rules are clear:

Do not get involved.

Remain objective and professional at all times.

Keep a stiff upper lip.

Take notes.

Above all, never let them see you cry.

I cover the police beat for *The Miami Herald*, daily circulation

427,954. Over eighteen years I have covered thousands of crimes, most of them violent, and talked to thousands of witnesses: cops and convicts, little children and old ladies. Some are doomed, some deadly. A few, like Michael, I cannot forget.

This book continues the story of life and death in Miami—the place and the people, in my world as a police reporter in this treacherous, dazzling and dangerous city.

Part One

THE JOB

Chapter 1

PUTTING IT IN THE NEWSPAPER

Truth is such a rare thing, it is delightful to tell it.

—EMILY DICKINSON

People ask if I am callous and cold after years on the police beat. Quite the contrary. You cannot grow calluses on your heart.

If I have become anything, it is more sensitive, because I now know the truth: The victim will most likely be victimized again, by the system.

How can I do this job year after year? they ask. Why would I want to? The question always surprises me. How could I *not* do it?

In a world full of bureaucracy and red tape and social agencies that do not respond, this job can be a joy. A story in the newspaper can slash through red tape like a razor. Sometimes it can help bring about justice in cases where it would never triumph otherwise. Cops' hands are often tied. Judges are often inept, corrupt or incompetent.

Sometimes, we are all the victim has got.

A half-million informed readers can be a far more effective force for good than a few overworked, indifferent or preoccupied cops.

Sometimes you feel like Wonder Woman, or Superman, going to the rescue. Reporters can find missing kids, lost grandmothers and misplaced corpses. We fish out people who fall through the cracks. Publicity rescues people tangled in the hopeless mazes of government and bureaucracy. We recover stolen cars and priceless family heirlooms. A story in the newspaper can secure donations of blood, money and public support—and occasionally that rarest gift of all: justice.

A brutal fact of life and death is that a crime with media attention is better investigated—and better prosecuted. Police stories often make a difference—the difference in whether the crime is solved or not.

A good reporter can be a victim's best friend. How could one *not* do the job, even when it is unpleasant?

We all must do things we don't want to do. Heart in my throat, I approach the bereaved spouse or parent. For each who is not, a dozen are eager to share their story. A reporter's arrival often validates their tragedy, assuring that the terrible event that befell them does matter and that the rest of the world does care.

A young man who lived with his grandmother was murdered while I was away on a book tour. Only a brief paragraph appeared in the newspaper. Finding myself in the neighborhood weeks later, I stopped by to learn more. I knocked, introduced myself and said I wanted to talk about her grandson's death. The woman stepped back, swung the door open wide and welcomed me inside. "I wondered why you never came," she said.

No one had, except a policeman to tell her that the boy she raised was dead.

How could one *not* do this job?

The good news is that putting it in the newspaper works, even for me. The bright spot in a bleak childhood was my seventh-grade English teacher, Edna Mae Tunis. She changed my life when she said: "Promise you will dedicate a book to me some day." Decades later, I kept the promise. She never knew; she died when I was in the eighth grade. But I wanted someone to know that I remembered. Mrs. Tunis had a little girl, but I had no luck finding her. Little girls grow up, marry and change their names.

During the book tour I told the story to a reporter in New Jersey. He included it in the article he wrote. The newspaper hit the street. His telephone rang. Mrs. Tunis's daughter was calling, and she was crying. Grown up, married and, as I suspected, an English teacher like her mother.

Putting it in the newspaper works.

When his picture appeared in *The Miami Herald* it posed a problem for Maurice Edwin Darden.

The caption said: SUSPECT.

A bank surveillance camera snapped the photo during a stickup. Darden was the man in dark glasses, holding the gun. My story quoted the FBI as saying that they believed he was the same man who had been robbing banks and fast-food restaurants all over Dade and Broward counties.

Darden, age thirty-four, stared at his own face, staring back at him from *The Miami Herald*, and pondered what to do. He even considered surrendering. As he tried to make up his mind, the FBI saved him the trouble. They surrounded his house.

The feds had been flooded by calls fingering Darden after his photo appeared in the newspaper. His mother and three sisters wanted him off the street, too. His sisters joined the FBI agents outside the house and talked him into stepping out with his hands up. His girlfriend also emerged, clutching a copy of the newspaper article, which she handed to a detective.

Everyone had seen it. They all had been trying to talk him into giving up.

Putting it in the newspaper works.

Some people are unaware that they are missing or in trouble unless thcy rcad the newspaper.

Retired New York City Police Captain Alexander Kneirim, age ninety-five, mugged by two youths, was treated for head injuries and released from Miami's Jackson Memorial Hospital. Still disoriented, he staggered into the path of a patrol car six hours later and was rushed back to the emergency room. Four days later he stumbled and fell while chasing a bus. He again visited the emergency room and was again sent home. Next morning he was back, and doctors agreed he needed placement in a care center. But when they turned their backs, the captain vanished. Still frisky for a nonagenarian, he had marched out of the ER to conduct some business at his bank. He returned to the hospital several hours later and was admitted to the Happy Home Care Center.

That was Friday.

When he did not come home, his alarmed landlady notified relatives. They called the police. My friend, Missing Persons Detective Sandy Weilbacher, checked hospitals, the jail and the morgue. She found no trace of him. On Tuesday, she called fifteen numbers at Jackson Hospital, requesting that medical records, the emergency room, crisis intervention, the outpatient clinic, placement and patient information double-check, in case his name had been misspelled. Still nothing. His relatives sobbed. Sandy feared the worst.

After six days, grim Miami police stopped the search for an old man and began looking in alleys and under expressways for a body. Then the story and a picture of the missing captain appeared in the newspaper. The staff of the Happy Home Care Center recognized him at once, of course, and called the police, who found him watching television.

"I spent hours stomping around under bridges looking for a body," Sandy groused, her freckles and red hair pulsating as her blood pressure soared. "Everybody's time and effort was wasted."

The captain was also nettled. No one had come to visit him. He had no idea he was missing and presumed dead. If not for his picture in the newspaper, he might still be lost.

People *do* slip through the cracks. Putting it in the newspaper does work.

Sometimes it is the only way to shake the truth out of the system. A young wife, seven months pregnant, had feared for months that she had cancer. Busy doctors had performed tests and a biopsy. They told her only that her condition could not be treated until after she gave birth. Convinced she was suffering a malignancy that endangered her unborn child, she became deeply depressed. Her husband tried to reassure her, but after he dozed off one night, she swallowed some pills, then vanished. For two nights and a day she wandered in a disconsolate daze.

She returned safely after seeing a newspaper account of her family's anguished search. Hospital officials also saw the story, checked records and said her medical problem was not cancer. She gasped at the good news. "Are you sure?" she asked me. "I was so depressed. They kept taking tests. They did a biopsy. They told me to come back. They wouldn't tell me a thing. So I knew I had it."

But she didn't.

Total strangers sent messages of support and hope. "People were concerned about me," she said, choking back tears. "It made me feel good. I thought nobody cared."

Given the straight story, people *do* care.

Frail and sick, an elderly widow called the Dade tax assessor's office, complaining in tears about her increased property tax assessment and pouring out her problems. Not only was she poor, she said, she had been too weak even to change her sheets for a month.

Vickie Nevins, clerk-typist, took the call. "I can't do anything about your taxes," she said, "but I can do something about your sheets." Nevins, a thirty-four-year-old, eighty-nine-pound divorcée, fixed dinner for her two children that night, then drove to the home of Minnie Wheeler, a lonely seventy-year-old heart patient, changed her sheets and visited for two and a half hours.

The widow Wheeler was astonished. "It's like an angel dropped out of heaven."

I wrote about Vickie Nevins's kind deed. Mrs. Wheeler had said that she had no money left to pay her rising property taxes. Her husband was dead and "his illness took everything." Hospitalized twice recently herself, she had found life "a terrible thing for old people." She had no transportation, so the only time she saw a doctor was when taken to the hospital as an emergency. She received $176 a month from Social Security. Her home was in dire need of repair. Her mortgage payment was $72. Now her taxes had increased from $85 to $112.

"She called at ten minutes to five, crying her heart out," Nevins said. "It's heartbreaking. I can't help her financially. I'm in a bind myself. But I'll do anything else I can for her." Minnie Wheeler had proudly shown her visitor a prized possession, all her favorite old hymns on a long-playing record sent by her minister the last time she was hospitalized. She had never heard it. She had no record player.

"I'm looking around for a small turntable," Nevins told me. "I feel so sorry for her. She's just a very sweet little old lady trying to make it all by herself."

The brief story about a stranger's compassion produced immediate results: Three businessmen offered to pay Minnie Wheeler's taxes. Readers wrote checks. A medical clinic offered free services. People called with gifts of record players, friendship and assistance.

It works.

I wish I could write stories about every poor and lonely little old lady, but helping one is better than nothing.

Putting it in the newspaper works especially well if you are seeking a long-lost person. Always attracted to stories about lost people, I wrote about four sisters and a brother tragically separated as children, forty years earlier. Their father was killed working undercover in a police bootlegging investigation in 1932. The widow remarried. The children recall their stepfather fondly, but a malicious relative filed a false complaint telling the local sheriff that the couple was not legally married. Police arrested the stepfather. His wife took her four youngest children with her to the jail to find out why. She too was arrested, and the children, ages five through eleven, left on the sidewalk. The oldest girl took them to a relative, where authorities found them and took them to an orphanage.

Charges were dropped two months later and the parents freed. Too late. The thirteen-year-old had been released to an aunt, but the two youngest girls were gone, already adopted by strangers. The boy had also vanished, taken by foster parents. The eleven-year-old girl had been transferred to an out-of-town orphanage and would spend the next five years with families in St. Petersburg and Fort Myers. She ran away at age sixteen and made her way back to her mother and sister. The trio never stopped searching for the other children. It took them eleven years to find the boy. He joined the navy shortly after they were reunited and was killed in a car crash outside Jacksonville. He was twenty-one. Then their stepfather drowned in a boating accident off Tarpon Springs. The search for the two youngest girls continued.

Orphanage officials agreed to release the records only if the new parents granted permission. The adoptive mother of one girl refused. The other family could not be located.

The sisters pressed their search with even greater determination as their mother lay on her deathbed. She died without finding her missing children, but her daughters never gave up. The reluctant adoptive mother relented after being contacted a second time by a social worker. When the long-lost little girl, now a woman of forty-five, returned home that night, her husband said, "Your sisters have called eight times." The joyous reunion brought a new resolve to find Dorothy, the last missing sister.

I wrote that Dorothy would now be forty-seven. When last seen she was age seven and wore her light brown hair in a Dutch-boy cut.

"If she sees our picture or hears about us," one of her sisters said, "we want her to know that if she can't get to us, then for God's sake, let us know where she is. We'll get to her."

No results, at first. But eventually the Miami newspaper story arrived in Detroit. When it did, we found Dorothy, a widow with five children. After forty years, the sisters wasted no time. The reunion took place at a Florida airport twenty-four hours after the first telephone call.

Putting it in the newspaper works.

Some results are unexpected, but often you know at once how readers will react.

At Miami Beach police headquarters on other business, I could not help but notice Rose Goldberg. She sat sobbing on a hard wooden chair. "I have no home! Where can I go?" she cried.

That got my attention.

Wearing a torn white sweater with two one-dollar bills—all the money she had—folded neatly in the pocket, she was homeless, evicted from her South Beach hotel room because she was ten days late with her $150-a-month rent.

It was Saturday, the day before Mother's Day.

Her trembling hands clutched her cane and a crumpled green paper sack, her heart medicine and hairpins inside—all she had been able to salvage before a Metro deputy, summoned by the hotel owner, locked her out of her room on Friday. She sobbed to police officers who tried to help that she would rather be dead than homeless and indigent.

Once a wife and mother, she was now alone. European born, she had no brothers and sisters. "Hitler killed them," she told me. She had come to this country and married. Her only son had eagerly counted the days until he was old enough to join the navy. He was killed in 1945. Her husband, a Brooklyn carpenter, died a year later, in 1946.

On Saturday, she had promised the hotel manager that she would pay the rent on Monday. She did not. Her Social Security check had failed to arrive. Miami Beach Police Lieutenant George Morgan tried to intervene, but the landlord refused to let her live out her $150 security deposit because she had violated her lease by failing to pay on time.

I confronted the hotel manager. The man was not exactly all heart. "I don't want this kind of customer in my hotel," he said. "She doesn't want to pay the rent."

I asked if he planned to return her deposit. "Talk to my lawyers," he said.

Sympathetic police had taken Mrs. Goldberg to another South Beach hotel Friday night. But she left on Saturday because kosher dietary rules, to which she had adhered all her life, were not observed there. At her other hotel, she had fixed her own meals in her room.

Unwilling to leave her on the street with nowhere to go, Morgan and officers Dennis Ward and Patricia Evans spent hours trying to comfort Mrs. Goldberg, negotiate with the man who had evicted her and work out a solution to her problems. They did so, at least temporarily. The Jewish Family and Children's Service agreed to pay for her weekend at a kosher hotel. Annie Lefkowitz, owner of the Granada Hotel, said Mrs. Goldberg would be welcome.

But Rose Goldberg still wept. Dennis Ward, a husky Irish rookie whose father and uncle were also cops, tried to stop her tears. "You'll have a nice bed and a room. You can take a nap. And you'll have three kosher meals a day," he promised.

"I'm ashamed to go like this." She stared down at her red house slippers. "I gave away my best clothes because I never go anywhere."

"You look fine," said Officer Evans, holding her hand.

Saturday night Rose Goldberg rested in a room at the Granada. Sunday morning, Mother's Day, her story was in *The Herald*.

For me, the anticipation mounted, like Christmas morning, waiting for the newspaper to hit front lawns. What would the good readers do? They never let me down. It is almost as though we share a secret conspiracy.

Rose Goldberg was remembered on Mother's Day—for the first time since 1946. Well-wishers kept the telephone at the Granada busy all day. Someone brought flowers. Someone else brought perfume. Strangers came to visit. A Lincoln Road shopkeeper sent two dresses.

Sunday afternoon she dined on vegetable soup, stuffed cabbage and roast chicken, marble cake and tea.

For me, best Mother's Day I ever had.

How can you *not* do this job? It may not always be fun, but when it works, it works.

Chapter 2

NEVER TOO YOUNG, NEVER TOO OLD

Only the dead have no troubles.

—Leonard Louis Levinson

People who look for trouble never fail to find it. Maybe it is too many soap operas, too much testosterone or the need for attention. Other people never look for misfortune, pain or woe, but it finds them just the same. Age is no barrier. Nobody, it seems, is ever too young or too old to step into trouble big time.

Take soft-spoken and grandmotherly Lilly Pender, age sixty-three.

"I'm a nervous person," she told me. That news came as no surprise. We were discussing a job-related incident. Hired as a security guard to protect a county garbage dump, she had used her .38-caliber revolver to kill a Boy Scout leader who had tried to discard unauthorized items.

Why armed guards must patrol Miami garbage dumps is another story.

Buster McCrae, sixty-nine, collected Social Security and cooked, cleaned and cared for his blind wife. He too worked as a security guard. He got in trouble for killing a fourteen-year-old avocado thief.

Some people take their jobs too seriously.

Following those cases, and others, the state took over security-guard licensing and instituted training including a one-hour program on "When to Use a Gun."

On the short side of the generation gap is Miami's youngest murder suspect, age two and a half. He looked like a fine little boy to me, though perhaps a bit hyper. Strikingly handsome, he was bright-eyed and big for his age. When I came to visit he was clad in T-shirt and shorts, with red, white and blue socks and shoes, racing about his mother's immaculate apartment with a toy truck, shouting "Vroom, vroom!" He cried, "Night-night, night-night," flung a blanket onto the floor and flopped down. Seconds later he was darting about in a new game. His favorite television show was *The Incredible Hulk*. He loved talking to strangers and vigorously waved "bye-bye" when I left.

He had battered a twenty-two-month-old playmate to death, police said, pounded his head on the floor, then slammed a heavy glass vase over his skull.

"He's not mean," his mother said. "He's a little rough."

Her thirty-eight-pound son pushed the smaller boy down several times, she said, so she separated them, then left the room. She later found her son straddling the victim, brandishing a large glass flower vase over the baby's battered head, saying: "Bad boy, bad boy . . ."

Police bought it. So did her best friend, the mother of the dead toddler. A working mother, she had left her only child in this woman's care. "I'm not angry," the bereaved mother said. "They were good babies, both of them. Sometimes they were buddy-buddy, kissy-kissy, and the next minute they were fighting or fussing over a toy. He is two and a half years old—I don't think he did it deliberately. He's a good boy. I love him."

The child had too limited a vocabulary to dispute the case against him. "He doesn't realize what happened," said a homicide detective, father of a small boy himself. "How can you expect a two-and-a-half-year-old to know he wasted another kid? He's a pleasant little boy—a little tornado, but he's pleasant. It's a very sad, sad case."

Prosecutors refused to charge the tot with a crime but did

instruct the Department of Health and Rehabilitative Services to "determine if the child is delinquent."

Psychiatrists called the tot the youngest perpetrator of murderous violence they had yet encountered. One urged that he be evaluated in terms of impulse control and tested by a pediatric neurologist.

"Most two-and-a-half-year-olds do not murder other children or hit them over the head with flower pots with such force or violence," a doctor said. "I'm sure something is going on with this kid. His level of aggression is excessive, with poor controls."

Right the first time: Most two-and-a-half-year-olds do not murder other children. This one didn't either.

He was framed.

Police acknowledged eighteen days later that the tot was innocent and announced they had a new suspect.

It was not hard to figure out who that was.

"They think I did it," his mother told me. "You have to ask the police why."

I did. They had become aware of the similar death of another child, an eighteen-month-old boy, left in the same woman's care five years earlier. She claimed that that child's fatal injuries were caused by a fall. No one else could take the blame. Her son had not been born yet.

Miami Homicide Sergeant Mike Gonzalez studied both cases and found it likely that the same person was responsible for both deaths.

There was not enough evidence to arrest the mother. She did submit to a lie-detector test administered by internationally known polygraph expert Warren Holmes. His conclusion: "This woman has got no business baby-sitting."

The news clearing the toddler was a relief. That left a five-year-old as Dade County's most dangerous child.

The smiling youngster deliberately pushed a three-year-old playmate five floors to his death off a Miami Beach bayfront condominium.

Police thought the fatal plunge was a tragic accident, but when they talked to the five-year-old he readily confessed. His six-year-old cousin corroborated his story, saying that the boy had returned to the family apartment and confided that he had just shoved the other child off an outside stairwell.

The boy shocked detectives. "He doesn't think he did anything wrong," Detective Robert Davis told me.

"He said he pushed him. He watched him fall. He heard him scream when he hit the ground and then he went for help. It's horrendous. He doesn't show any remorse. He was smiling when he was telling the story."

The husky seventy-pound preschooler wolfed two slices of pizza, a garlic roll and a banana after his confession.

Children without conscience can be frightening and deadly creatures. A seven-year-old with a fatal fascination for fire touched off a blaze in which a young woman and her baby perished. He put a match to alcohol because he liked the blue color of the flames.

Or take the curly-haired seventh grader, caught behind the wheel of a stolen Miami Beach Water Department car. The boy lived across the street from police headquarters and had stolen enough equipment to outfit a small law-enforcement agency of his own. "I wish he'd leave us alone," whined a detective. "We have so little equipment as it is."

The boy took three guns, all expensive Magnums, 398 rounds of ammunition, hollow-point bullets, several boxes of .38-caliber cartridges, a hand computer, half a dozen walkie-talkies worth one thousand dollars each, five electronic beepers with battery chargers, cylinders of Mace, sets of handcuffs, nightsticks and other gear.

"I've been to court three times, and I always get out," the thirteen-year-old bragged.

"He's nervous," the boy's mother told me tearfully. He did not look or sound nervous to me. "Take me to Youth Hall," he razzed a detective. "I'll get out. I always do."

His favorite pastime was hurling big rocks through the front door at headquarters, trying to hit the desk sergeant.

The boy broke into the city water department on a Saturday night, snipped a chain with cable cutters, pried a gate and a padlock hasp, removed five jalousies, broke into the office, and stole four walkie-talkies and the keys to a Plymouth. Before driving away, he rewired the gate so the crime would go unnoticed until Monday. A city employee, however, discovered the thefts at one A.M. on Sunday. A policeman spotted the deftly camouflaged car parked on a South Beach street at ten A.M. The thief had spray-painted over the city seals on the doors and replaced the city tag with a stolen license plate.

Cops staking out the vehicle saw a small figure with a walkie-talkie climb into the front seat and drive off. The youngster had to push the seat all the way forward in order to peer over the steering wheel. He swore someone had sent him for the car. Police assumed an adult was involved and asked him to hand up the guilty man. He led the cops to a park and pointed out a startled stranger.

The boy, who carried a pilfered police badge in his pocket, had actually stolen the car to escape the city and an upcoming date in Juvenile Court.

•

So many stories involving the very young and very old are unutterably sad. How do you forget the shabbily dressed gray-haired grandmother who tried to rob a Miami Beach bank by threatening to explode a "bomb" in her handbag? The tattered purse held no bomb—or money—just a pair of spectacles and some crumpled tissues. She said she was starving.

Domestic violence or love gone wrong is sad at any age, but for some seniors it is a tragic conclusion to otherwise unblemished lives. A Miami man's first marriage endured for sixty-two years. His second ended after six days when he beat his petite bride to death with a claw hammer. She was seventy-six. He was ninety.

The bridegroom, a great-grandfather of ten, was charged with murder. The arrest was his first. The fatal argument erupted over the honeymoon cruise. Suitcases stood by the door. She wanted to go; he had second thoughts.

When a sixty-nine-year-old woman savagely beat her eighty-nine-year-old husband to death, the murder weapon was a urine bottle. They had been married for forty-eight years.

One couple was married in Brooklyn in 1920. Sixty-three years later, in Miami Beach, he beat her to death after a vicious argument. "I wouldn't wish her on my worst enemy," he told police.

One is never too old to be among America's most wanted. Old people are rugged and resourceful, the toughest desperados, especially when they feel they have nothing to lose. In gunfights, Miami police have killed an eighty-three-year-old great-grandfather with a pacemaker, and a seventy-nine-year-old man in bib overalls. Both fired at police first.

Joseph Thomas still eludes police. He is eighty-five and wanted for murder.

He accused Sadie Sheffield of being unfaithful and ended their twenty-eight-year relationship with a bullet. Sadie was seventy-three. The romance was always stormy. "They feuded most of the time," Miami Homicide Detective Louise Vasquez said. "They never got along."

After a bitter argument over his suspicion that she was seeing another man, Thomas went to his apartment, came back with a gun and shot Sheffield in the face. "He just walked out, got in his car and took off with the tires spinning," Louise said.

The case did not seem like a tough one. In such homicides, the shooter usually shows up shortly, conscience-stricken and full of remorse. Not this one.

When Joseph Thomas raced away in his old and faded green car, it was July 1978. He was seventy-two. The search for Joseph Thomas has stretched into one of Miami's longest manhunts.

Norman David Mayer, sixty-six, did not die like a typical Miami Beach senior citizen. He did not die like anyone you and I ever knew.

He worked as a handyman at a beach hotel and wore a pigtail

held by a rubber band, a baseball cap over his balding pate and flowered Hawaiian shirts with yellow trousers.

Norman David Mayer had a cause. He was the founder—and total membership—of an organization called "Number One Priority." He had been arrested twice for handing out leaflets on college campuses. He sold death's-head emblems urging "As an Act of Sanity Ban Nuclear Weapons . . . Or Have a Nice Doomsday." A tireless antinuclear activist, he waged a one-man ten-year crusade to ban the bomb.

Nobody listened.

Mayer bought a used Ford step-van and converted it into a rolling bomb shelter, reinforced by steel and stocked with dried food and an anti-radiation suit. When the world blew up he wanted to be the one to see how it looked afterward.

Before leaving Miami Beach for the last time, Norman David Mayer told his only close friend, an auto repair shop owner who had known him for thirty-three years, that he would not be back. "It's over now. There's nothing more to be said. I've had enough."

The aging activist called later, bragging that he had distributed five thousand leaflets in Washington, some on the steps of the Capitol. For thirty-five days, he protested in front of the White House from eleven A.M. to six P.M. He told people that he had been arrested twelve times for his cause.

Still, no one listened. "You have to do something," he declared.

So he did. On his last day he donned a dark blue jumpsuit and a black Darth Vader–style helmet with a visor. He raced his van up to the east face of the Washington Monument at 9:15 A.M. and threatened to blow it up with one thousand pounds of dynamite unless his demands were met.

Everybody listened now.

He insisted that every governmental agency and private organization join a national dialogue on the dangers of nuclear war. He refused to negotiate with a team of FBI agents and police.

We heard about the threat at *The Miami Herald*, and I got a local tip that the man holding the Washington Monument hostage might be Norman David Mayer. The FBI was dubious, doubting that the terrorist in the taut standoff could be a senior citizen. The cool, quick militant in the dark helmet appeared to be about thirty years old, but an FBI spokesman conceded, "We don't know who he is." He suggested that more than one person might be inside the van.

The owner of the Miami Beach hotel where Mayer had worked flew to Washington at FBI request, to help negotiate. He was too late. At about 8:30 P.M., after a tense ten-hour siege, Norman David Mayer decided to drive away.

The barrage of police gunfire that killed him overturned the van at the foot of the Washington Monument.

There was no one else inside—and no dynamite. Only Norman David Mayer, age sixty-six, and his leaflets.

He had a cause.

If Wayman Neal had a cause, nobody knew what it was. He did, however, have a nasty habit.

Wayman Neal did not look like one of Miami's most dangerous men. He looked like a nice, sweet, docile old gent—somebody's grandfather—until you put a knife in his hand. The last time Miami police arrested Wayman Neal he was attending a prayer meeting. They charged him with murder—again.

The bloody knife was in his pocket.

He did not run or resist. He could not run or resist. He walked slowly—with a cane. He was either seventy or seventy-four years old, depending on which records are correct. In court he was humble, sober and soft-spoken. He wore a blue baseball cap, a Grateful Dead T-shirt and bib overalls.

The saga of Wayman Neal is a story about our criminal justice system: how it works, how it malfunctions and what happens when a criminal is poor and black and his victims are the same. It is a story of half-hearted prosecutions, frightened witnesses and forgiving victims.

The criminal record of Wayman Neal begins with murder in

St. Petersburg, Florida, in 1938. Forty-two years later, in Miami, in 1980, it was murder again. This time there was a difference: The victim was white. All the others had been black, like Wayman Neal.

No one is sure how many victims there are. In just four years in Miami he was charged ten times.

"He has stabbed strangers he never met before in his life," Miami Homicide Detective Bruce Roberson told me in awe.

Wayman Neal failed to finish grade school. As a young man, he left his father's farm in Quitman, Georgia, to seek work. Unemployed laborer or bricklayer was the occupation he listed on arrest reports. His family heard nothing from him until his 1938 "trouble" in St. Pete.

"We got the news that he cut a man, and the man died," said younger brother, Peter Neal, sixty-two. "He's quiet when he's not drinking. But when he drinks . . ."

Few records remain of the 1938 murder. A jury in St. Petersburg agreed that "on the 16th day of April, 1938, Wayman Neal did inflict mortal wounds in an assault on Willie Williams with a knife." Willie Williams was black, unmarried, about thirty. On his death certificate both birthplace and relatives are listed as unknown.

A judge sentenced Wayman Neal to twenty years. Richard Patrick Moore, the 1980 victim, was three years old at the time.

Neal was paroled in 1943. Parole revoked, he was sent back to prison in 1947. He was released in 1955, then arrested for larceny in 1958. He served sixty days for assault in 1960, was acquitted of robbery in 1961 and then arrested again for shooting a thirty-year-old woman in the foot. "Just horseplay," he explained.

A St. Pete policeman wrote in a file: "He has been known to claim that he has killed before and wouldn't mind doing it again."

Wayman Neal never married, but there was a woman. Her name was Gladys Harris. They lived together in St. Petersburg until a day in 1966 when Gladys and her friend Beatrice Scott, fifty-four, locked him out of the house. Enraged, he sliced open the screen with a knife and stepped inside. Gladys got away.

Police found broken furniture, blood on the walls and Beatrice Scott—stabbed nine times in the back.

She survived. Neal did three years in prison.

On January 19, 1970, Neal walked up to Willis Harvey, sixty-seven, on a St. Petersburg street, according to police, and carved a wicked six-inch gash through his upper lip. They found a Kutmaster hollow super-edged knife stashed in Wayman Neal's right shoe. Harvey failed to appear in court, and prosecution was dropped.

That summer of 1970, Wayman Neal walked into St. Petersburg police headquarters and asked to be jailed for his own protection. He said a woman named Mary wanted to shoot him.

An agreeable police officer locked him up for vagrancy, noting that Neal was "just somebody with no money and no place to stay—or a mental case."

Despite forty-two years of violence, no judge ever ordered a psychiatric examination for Wayman Neal. He walked into a police station asking to be arrested again in 1971. Police obliged.

Wayman Neal was first noticed in Dade County at 4:35 P.M. on October 18, 1975.

Peter Roy Rivers, fifty, sat with Neal, quaffing cool ones on a wooden bench at the Store Porch, an aged row of peeling bars and shops. Claiming the man snatched his drink, Wayman Neal rose and pulled two knives.

"He was stabbing, with a knife in each hand," a witness said.

Police found Rivers bleeding in the gutter. Bystanders said the attacker, wearing a blue cap, had strolled into a bar across the street. Inside, wearing a blue cap and holding two blood-stained knives, stood Wayman Neal.

An ambulance rushed Rivers to a hospital in critical condition, his scalp nearly severed. Four stab wounds had pierced his back and two his chest. A long slice to the side penetrated his intestines, liver, spleen and pancreas.

He survived.

Wayman Neal was charged with assault with intent to commit murder. Rivers failed to appear at a preliminary hearing.

The prosecutor said the man was out of the hospital and had been notified. A judge dismissed the charges for lack of prosecution.

Less than a month later, Wayman Neal angrily confronted two policemen, demanding to go to jail. They said they had no reason to arrest him, so he gave them one by shouting and threatening to hurt people.

On May 18, 1977, Neal sent a pal on an errand. J. B. Williams returned with a bottle of wine and change from a five-dollar bill. Neal insisted he had given the man two five-dollar bills. They fought. Williams was stabbed. Neal was arrested a block away. That case was dropped after Williams signed a paper stating he had no wish to press charges.

On April 3, 1979, Neal snatched a table knife in a Miami rooming house, witnesses said, and plunged it into the neck of fellow boarder William Fry, fifty-six. Another boarder, Curtis Driggers, fifty-three, stood up to protest. Neal stabbed him, too, and slammed him over the head with a chair.

The injured men went to the hospital. Wayman Neal went to jail—but not for long. When I asked the prosecutor why, he could not recall the case, even after reviewing the file.

"It must have been fairly insignificant," he said, because he had reduced the charges to a misdemeanor. Neal was sentenced to time served: sixteen days in jail.

Stabbed next was Donald Darling, thirty-nine. Without provocation, according to witnesses, Neal slashed Darling's face and left arm with a razor-sharp Barlow knife on July 13, 1979. Darling required plastic surgery on his nearly severed lip.

"I didn't cut him bad enough to die," Neal indignantly told police who arrested him. "I wish I had cut him on the neck."

The maimed victim failed to appear at three pretrial conferences. He telephoned the state attorney's office to leave a message. He was in the hospital "next to the jail" and unable to attend. The prosecutor did not find him listed as a patient at either of two hospitals near the jail. His home phone had been disconnected, and he failed to reply to two Mailgrams. Charges were dismissed.

Wayman Neal was back on the wooden bench at the Store Porch at eight P.M. on September 7, 1979. The victim: Moses Shands, seventy-six. The knife blade laid open eighteen inches of thigh. Shands pointed Neal out to police. They found a knife in his pocket. Shands went to the hospital. Wayman Neal went to jail—briefly. Three weeks later: case dismissed. The victim "failed to appear in our office for the third straight time," a prosecutor explained.

At nine A.M. on November 3, Wayman Neal stood on a downtown Miami street corner, mad as hell about his Social Security check. It was missing, he said. He blamed James Yancey, fifty-four. He stabbed him in the back and cut his left arm and right wrist.

Again the charge was reduced from felony to misdemeanor and later dropped.

Wayman Neal was arrested four times that December, for sleeping on public property and loitering in a park. Judges released him each time, often the same day.

For two months Wayman Neal was not arrested for stabbing anyone.

When he was, the victim was white. The charge this time: first-degree murder.

Downtown Miami at dusk, January 22, 1980. Wayman Neal had been drinking. He accosted a stranger outside the Miami Rescue Mission. "You're wearing my coat!"

"No, it's my coat," the startled man said. He was telling the truth. Neal angrily swung his wooden cane twice at the man.

On a ledge outside the Mission sat Richard Patrick Moore, forty-five.

"He was a good man, down on his luck," his brother Jack said later. "He always liked to be a peacemaker."

Moore grew up on a tobacco farm in Upper Marlboro, Maryland. Once he had worked hard, but his father suffered a stroke and sold the farm, then his wife divorced him, and Richard Moore took to drinking and drifting.

On Miami's skid row, far from the farm and the family he had not seen in eight years, Richard Moore, the peacemaker, snatched away Wayman Neal's wooden cane as he raised it again to strike the man in the coat.

Moore walked around the corner with the cane, drawing Neal away from the target of his anger. Neal followed, looking like somebody's grandfather in a jaunty baseball cap. Moore peacefully handed back the cane, then walked away casually. He stepped off the curb and headed across the street.

Everything was over. Everything was fine. Then it happened.

Wayman Neal threw the cane down and darted into the street. Police said Moore did not see him until it was too late.

Witnesses said they saw Wayman Neal raise his hand and stab Moore twice. The knife pierced his heart.

Richard Patrick Moore, the would-be peacemaker, stumbled down the street and collapsed in front of a run-down rooming house.

Wayman Neal strolled back across the street, entered the Mission and joined the prayer service in progress.

A witness ran to a nearby firehouse for help. Paramedics worked frantically, attaching Moore to the "thumper," a machine that performs mechanical cardiopulmonary resuscitation—squeezing the heart against the backbone, pumping out the blood and forcing oxygen into the lungs. Delivered to the hospital at 7:17 P.M., Moore was pronounced dead at 7:30 P.M.

A witness accompanied police into the Mission, where fifty men were participating in the service—a requirement before receiving a bed for the night. He pointed out Wayman Neal, seated four rows from the front. His prayers were interrupted.

"I stabbed him, but I don't know why," he told detectives. The bloody knife was in his pocket.

A grand jury indicted, charging first-degree murder. Premeditation seemed evident; the confrontation between the men had ended before the attack. Yet a judge reduced the charge to second-degree.

"That last murder was an unnecessary death, a murder that shouldn't have happened," said Daniel Insdorf, a detective who had turned in his badge, disgusted by the system. "I don't think it's entirely Wayman's fault. He's not stealthy. What more can a person do to get himself locked up? All the cases were dropped because nobody took the time or the effort to advise or assist the victims. They were indigent, they were injured, and they were ignorant of the criminal justice system. They don't have carfare. They don't even know where the courthouse is."

"If someone doesn't want to come in and testify, we can't convict anyone," a prosecutor countered.

"Wayman Neal shouldn't have been out walking the streets," said Jack Moore, who took his dead brother home to Maryland. "If he gets out on the street again, he will stab somebody else. He will kill somebody else. He should be put away where he can never get out."

The trial date was set, reset and postponed, month after month. Neal gained weight behind bars. He seemed robust and alert. A neighbor forwarded his Social Security and welfare checks to him at the Dade County Jail each month.

Many of the delays were due to plea negotiations. A public defender said he would plead guilty but was seeking an institution other than prison for Neal. Facilities for alcoholics declined to accept the defendant because of his advanced age.

The trial date was finally set for December 15.

But no trial took place.

The witnesses had disappeared. "They're just not the type of people you can hang on to," the prosecutor said. "Other than the body, there is no physical evidence."

The charges were dropped.

Wayman Neal walked out of Dade County Jail a free man.

After eleven months of forced sobriety, he seemed to be thinking clearly. He acknowledged problems in Miami and agreed to return to Georgia, where his brother lives. His public defender raised enough money for a Greyhound ticket—one way. Wayman Neal thanked his lawyer politely and departed.

"I just hope he stays in Georgia," the young lawyer said. "I hope he stays there and goes fishing, like he said he was going to do."

The dead man's nephew, in Upper Marlboro, Maryland, did

not understand. "It proves all the stuff I've read in the papers about Miami," he said.

Interested in how Wayman Neal was faring, I telephoned his brother Robert, who lives in Quitman. Wayman, he said, had gone away, to Valdosta.

Last time he had seen Wayman Neal, Robert Neal said, "He'd been drinking."

Chapter 3

LOVE KILLS

Murder is always a mistake; one should never do anything that one cannot talk about after dinner.

—OSCAR WILDE

The person most likely to murder you sits across the breakfast table.

Your nearest and dearest, the one who sleeps on the pillow next to yours and shares your checking account, can be far more lethal than any sinister stranger lurking in the shadows.

Love kills.

Caught with another woman, a Miami man quarreled with his wife, cried "I'm going to kill us both!" and slammed his car into a concrete support column at fifty-five miles an hour. She survived; he did not.

A local electrician delicately attached wires to the wrist and ankles of his sleeping wife and killed her with a massive jolt of electricity.

The spark had gone out of their marriage.

Haven't these people ever heard of divorce?

Men are the usual suspects when love explodes into homicidal hatred. Women may experience similar pain, but they rarely resort to deadly violence.

There are exceptions. One Miami housewife stopped coloring

eggs and shot her husband in the heart on Easter Sunday morning as he whispered to another woman on the telephone.

A prim retired schoolteacher hired two hit men to put her husband of thirty-four years out of her misery.

A policewoman fatally shot her husband's sweetheart and was killed as she struggled with him over the gun.

But most often it is men who hound, torment, terrorize and stalk. They pursue parties they once promised to cherish and protect, with machetes, rifles, shotguns, sledgehammers and firebombs. They even try to run them down in fake hit-and-run accidents. Some cases are so volatile that lawyers and judges hit the floor as irate spouses pull guns in divorce court.

What is wrong with these people?

Waving a gun will not force somebody to love you. Quite the contrary.

Where is Prince Charming? What ever happened to happily ever after? Why is it that a man who is unhappy with a woman—a man who may neglect, abuse or abandon her—cannot bear to see her happy alone or with someone else? That manner of macho is decidedly unattractive.

No wonder I have become a conscientious objector in the war between the sexes.

Others would rather fight. For weeks, perhaps longer, Jose Umberto Mejia, fifty-seven, stalked his ex-wife with a pair of binoculars. No one is sure when he bought the .357 Magnum.

Maria Estelita Mejia Kossakowski, forty-three, and her ex-husband were in litigation. Mejia had left her four years earlier and returned to his native Mexico. She divorced him soon after. Estelita had married Jose when she was fourteen, and had given him six children; in return she got twenty-five stormy years.

After he left, she supported the children by operating a small schoolbus service.

Two years later she married IRS agent Ronald Michael Kossakowski. Her children called him daddy. "He was more a father to them than a stepfather," a neighbor told me. "The children adored her and her present husband. They were a wonderful family, heartwarming and giving."

They were happy for the first time.

Then Mejia returned to Miami and was not pleased at what he found. He claimed he had never been properly served with legal papers and was unaware he was divorced. He was shocked, he said, to find his wife married to an IRS agent.

He wanted the divorce decree set aside. He wanted half the home and half of her schoolbus service.

His ex-wife insisted that he knew of the divorce.

"She seemed concerned," her attorney said. "Not for herself, but for the happiness and safety of the children." She asked a judge to keep Mejia away from the house and the youngest daughters, eight and fourteen.

The judge sent them to mediation counselors.

"He was agitated that the case was not progressing more quickly," his lawyer said. "He had a very hot temper. I think he was disturbed at not being able to see his two youngest children."

"Mejia didn't want to accept the fact he had lost his family," Metro Homicide Detective Rickey Mitchell later said.

Family members spotted Mejia lurking near their home several times. "A relative spotted him hiding in the trees across from the house," Mitchell said. "They were alarmed."

One night the family watched *Fatal Vision*, a TV movie about a doctor convicted of killing his family. One of the children spoke fearfully of her father. "It's like something he would do," she said, with a shudder. His wife walked in, and Kossakowski switched off the set.

On Tuesday he told their attorney that he and his wife were eager to end the legal bout with Mejia.

Estelita Kossakowski worked three jobs: driving the schoolbus, working part time with a travel agency, and serving as a data processor on a four-to-eleven shift at Financial Federal Savings and Loan in Miami Lakes.

That Tuesday evening she telephoned from work to tell her husband where to find the Cabbage Patch Kid doll they sought for the eight-year-old daughter's Christmas present. He went out to buy the doll and hid it on the yellow schoolbus parked outside.

Something happened when Estelita Kossakowski emerged from

Financial Federal shortly after midnight. Police suspect that Mejia was hiding in her white van and abducted her. They do not believe she willingly went with him.

The van pulled away. A short time later it ran a traffic signal, then stopped. Estelita was seen running away. Mejia leaped from the van and chased her. She fell and was shot, time after time.

The killer drove the van to the family's home in Hialeah, just two minutes away. Kossakowski, forty-one, had been jumpy, friends said. He probably would have been more cautious, but he saw his wife's van and opened the front door.

"Bingo, he was shot immediately," Detective Mitchell said.

Shot three times at close range, Kossakowski fell dying. His body lay there, sprawled in the open doorway until dawn. Neighbors heard the shots at about 12:30 A.M. Nobody called police. "You know how people are," Hialeah Homicide Detective Lorenzo Trujillo explained.

The killer drove away in the white van.

Through the night, Metro detectives investigated the murder of the unidentified woman found dead in the street. They learned her name through fingerprints once taken when she had applied for a job. At dawn they drove to Hialeah to perform a police officer's most difficult task. They were going to tell Estelita Kossakowski's husband that his wife had been murdered.

The Metro homicide detectives found the residential street blocked off by Hialeah homicide detectives, who told them that Estelita Kossakowski's husband had been murdered.

The fourteen-year-old daughter had awakened at 6:24 A.M. She had overslept. She dashed out to see why her stepfather had not awakened her as usual.

He lay dead in the doorway, in a pool of blood. She woke her seventeen year old sister. The two froze, staring at the body. Eventually they called for help.

Hialeah and Metro detectives gently interviewed the children. They learned about Mejia.

The detectives found Estelita's white van parked at Financial Federal, her purse inside. They launched a manhunt for the killer.

It ended quickly. Passersby waved down the investigators to report a body, in a car, in a nearby parking lot.

It was Jose Mejia.

He had shot himself in the head. They found the .357 Magnum, extra ammunition, and the binoculars. He left no suicide note—only legal papers on the backseat. Mejia and his ex-wife were scheduled to meet in his lawyer's office the next day. The meeting, of course, was canceled. All the principals were dead.

"He wouldn't wait for the courts, I guess," his attorney said.

Love kills.

Another vengeful killer fled Miami to elude capture, then returned to continue stalking his wife's terrified family.

Enraged when she left him and filed for divorce, Francisco Serra, twenty-seven, pounded on the door of her parents' home demanding to see his wife. Police arrested him. He was wearing a bulletproof vest, armed with a .38-caliber Smith and Wesson revolver and a pocketful of hollow-point bullets.

None of the above seemed to concern authorities, who immediately released him on bond. Serra insisted on speaking to his wife. She refused. So he took a shotgun to the grocery store where her younger brother worked part time. He blasted the sixteen-year-old high school student, then dragged the bleeding youth to his car and forced him, screaming, into the trunk.

All this in front of shoppers.

Serra drove off, then telephoned his wife's family. He taunted her mother. "I've got your son. You'll see him when I talk to my wife." Police launched a frantic search, hoping to save the wounded boy. They found the car abandoned the following day, the boy still in the trunk. He had bled to death.

The elusive killer tormented the family and evaded police for eighteen months. He was finally arrested, as he slept in a car before dawn.

Even when the system and individuals within it respond, it is often impossible to save someone stalked by an obsessive lover. Sometimes good people get involved and are lucky to save themselves.

Haasen Zock, twenty-five, a Lebanese-born Burger King management trainee, and his German wife, Heide Marie, twenty-one, suffered serious marital difficulties. Alone in this country and unable to support herself, she continued to live in the same house with Zock, though they were estranged. One night he tied her arms and legs to the couch on which she slept. He raped her while holding a knife to the throat of their son, Mohammed, age three. She called police when he fled with the child. Zock threatened by telephone to kill the boy unless his wife spoke to him. She refused.

Police traced him to a Broward County pay phone. He shouted curses, pushed the barrel of his loaded gun into the child's mouth and drove away. The frantic pursuit involved police from two counties. Zock paused long enough to take another prisoner, a Miramar police sergeant, a hostage negotiator who tried to talk Zock into surrendering. Instead of giving up, Zock held a cocked revolver to the head of his little son and forced the sergeant to chauffeur them away in a squad car.

At another pay phone, the father took the gun from the boy's head long enough to dial his wife's number. The sobbing child was rescued when the hostage cop and other officers wrestled Zock's revolver—bought for $139.95—out of his hands.

The *Herald* published a photo, Haasen Zock surrounded by police officers as they permitted him to kiss little Mohammed good-bye. Hauled off to jail, Zock did not stay there long.

Judge Ralph Person appointed psychiatrist Lloyd Miller to evaluate the prisoner. Two days later, at the Dade County Jail, the good doctor found Zock "rational, coherent . . . and competent." He did not deem him dangerous.

Zock's attorney, Louis Jepeway, asked for his client's release on bond.

Prosecutor David Markus objected. He wanted another opinion and the police officers present if a bond hearing was conducted.

The prosecutor said he was never notified of a later hearing at which Zock's attorney called the events preceding his client's arrest a mere "family argument."

Judge Person released Zock on a five-thousand-dollar bond.

Both parents went to Youth Hall four days later for a hearing involving the custody of little Mohammed.

Markus, twenty-four, and another prosecutor, Gregory Victor, twenty-six, were at Youth Hall on another matter. Heide Marie Zock approached Markus. She had wavered about prosecuting her husband on the rape charge. Now she was terrified. Her husband had already left the building. He had bought another gun, she said, and threatened her again. Now she was frightened enough to press charges.

Eager to take Zock off the street, Markus agreed to take Heide Marie directly to his office at the Metro Justice Building to swear out an arrest warrant.

They climbed into Victor's two-year-old Toyota. Victor was totally unaware. When Markus and a woman he had never met climbed into his car, he simply assumed she was someone who needed a ride to the Justice Building. As he drove his Toyota out of the parking lot, Zock pulled up in his aging brown Chevrolet Impala. He spotted his wife in the car with the two prosecutors.

"I knew as soon as I saw him there was going to be trouble," Markus told me later.

Heide Marie ducked. "My husband! Get me out of here!"

"Greg!" Markus exclaimed. "Let's get out of here. I know he's got a gun and he'll kill us."

Victor could not believe his fellow prosecutor. "Why would someone have a gun, and why would he be after us?"

He believed it when the young woman in the backseat began to scream hysterically.

Zock waved a gun, shouted something they could not hear and tried to force them off the road. Neither prosecutor was armed. Victor speeded south through dense rush-hour traffic at fifty miles per hour, making a run for Metro-Dade police headquarters. The prosecutor tried evasive action but a lumbering Metro bus blocked their flight, then wheezed to a stop in front of them. Zock rammed into the driver's side of the Toyota, disabling the smaller car and forcing it to the curb in front of a Cuban cigar factory and a coffee shop.

Zock ran to the passenger side of the Toyota, ordered Markus out at gunpoint, leaned into the car and leveled his gun at Victor. The young prosecutor raised his hands. He said nothing.

"Get out! Get out!" yelled Zock, struggling with his wife and trying to pull her out of the backseat.

She was screaming. "Don't let him get me. I don't want to go!" Terrified, she planted her feet against the door frame for leverage.

Unable to drag her from the car, Zock shot her there. Twice, at point-blank range, in the face. She died instantly. Zock turned and pointed the gun at Markus, staring him right in the eye.

"Don't kill me," said the young prosecutor, due to be married in ten days. "I'm not going to do anything to interfere with you."

Zock turned away, put the gun to his left temple, pulled the trigger and crumpled dead to the pavement.

Ray Cullinan, fifty-seven, operated a Philips 66 station across the street. He saw the young prosecutors waving their badges in the air and shouting for somebody to call police. "They were scared men, plenty scared," said Cullinan, who dialed 911. "I would have been scared myself." Cullinan had witnessed violent death in the South Pacific for three years during World War II. "But that," he told me, "was for a reason. These people are crazy. I'd like to see gun control in this town—maybe in the whole state. I can see a gun in your home or business, but not on your person or in a car. It's too easy to grab and start shooting."

Oddly enough, Haasen Zock agreed.

When I routinely asked homicide detectives what they had found in Zock's car, they exchanged glances. A suicide note? Not exactly. He had left two handwritten letters. Addressed to?

The Miami Herald.

Since I represented the newspaper at the murder scene, I wanted my mail—*now*—before deadline. Detectives are far more accommodating when the guilty party is dead, and they foresee no courtroom disputes with his lawyer.

Like so many letters to the *Herald*, these were irate. In one Zock condemned American divorce law. "Who is a judge to change what God brought together?" he asked piously. Marriage, he wrote, is when "you commit yourself to spend the rest of your life with your partner. In the good or bad and you take a vow to 'till death does us part . . .' " He meticulously listed character references: friends, neighbors, former employers. He urged *The Miami Herald* to inquire about him. He predicted what they would all say: "I am a hell of a person, always trying to do his best for my family."

So far, his best efforts had orphaned his only son at age three.

His second letter to the *Herald* quite accurately pointed out that everything in the story I was about to write was made possible by Broward County's gun laws—or lack of them. "Twice I was able to acquire guns instantly." He waxed indignant.

> If there was a cool-off period, I would have calmed down and not have done things impulsively because I was upset.
>
> In Broward you may walk into a gun shop at any time and purchase a hand weapon. Why? What purpose does it serve, except giving a mad person or a criminal the capability of possessing a weapon in the shortest most convenient time . . . ?

Why indeed.

> People get mad at times and lose their temper. Making it easy for them to get a gun is a crime in itself.

The letter from a dead man closed with a plea:

> Stop the killings. Help people, don't kill them. You could have saved lives. But it is not too late. It is all up to you.

Made sense to me.

Obsessive love can kill innocent bystanders. Sometimes they're not even in the way—they are merely the means to an end.

Miami police greeted a tanned and handsome young couple as they disembarked from the cruise ship *Sun Viking*. The polite, all-American boy and the pretty, small-town girl he had loved since junior high school had cruised the sparkling waters of the

Caribbean first class—to Jamaica, the Cayman Islands and Cozumel, Mexico.

Detectives said the romantic seven-day odyssey had been financed nine days earlier by a night of murder that had stunned the sleepy gulf town of Destin, Florida.

Boy loved girl, boy promised girl cruise—and boy had to deliver.

He had been trying to impress her for a long time, but he was financially embarrassed, already three payments in arrears on his flashy customized van. So he robbed a popular seafood restaurant after closing time. He did not deny it. When the night watchman shouted at him, he lost his cool and shot the man. That made the woman cashier-bookkeeper scream and run, so he shot her too. Then he and the twenty-two-year-old woman he loved, she unaware of the murders, drove off to Miami for their cruise. Even murder-weary Miami cops who assisted the out-of-town police were disbelieving.

"He is an all-American boy," Lieutenant Robert Murphy said, "such a polite young gentleman. His love for this girl must have been overwhelming. I look at this handsome, absolutely clean-cut young guy and it's scary. It makes your blood run cold."

Love does that sometimes.

Love and hate intermingle and do strange things to people. Strong men go weak, and weak men become raging monsters.

A man showed up with a birthday cake to surprise his sweetheart, caught her with someone else and killed them both.

A Metro Transit Authority bus driver who had won awards for safety and courtesy emptied a gun at the wife and three daughters who refused to fix him breakfast.

A bruised and irate waitress picked up a rifle and went hunting for the boyfriend who had abused and battered her. Police found her before she found him. When she would not drop the gun, they shot her.

If this is love, I'll pass.

Some people grow radiant in love; others become downright scary. Most frightening are the lovers who refuse to let go. Couples from hell who hate living together but cannot bear to live apart. Each feeds some twisted need in the partner's psyche. Their lives are inextricably tangled, and each torments the other, literally, until death do them part.

Maria Papy Cunard and her ex-husband, Joseph, loved and hated each other. Blond and beautiful, she was a former airline stewardess and the cousin of a prominent South Florida politician.

Married only three months, they had been divorced for three years. They had no children, nothing held them together, yet somehow, they could not remain apart.

Maria, age thirty, was last seen at four A.M. one morning, by her ex-husband. He had dragged her out of his car, scratching and spitting like a wildcat, he said, after one of their many quarrels. She had scratched his hand and arm in the struggle. He drove off and left her about three miles from her home. Neighbors remembered a man's angry voice and a woman's screams.

Joseph, also thirty, said he saw his 110-pound ex-wife walk down the street into the darkness. No one ever saw her again.

A search of surrounding woods yielded nothing. Cunard, a skilled medical technician who operated a heart-lung machine for a surgeon, refused to take a lie-detector test. "We're very disappointed," Miami Homicide Sergeant Mike Gonzalez said carefully, in an understatement, "because we're trying to be selective about what area to pursue in this investigation."

They asked Cunard if crime-lab experts could examine his Lincoln Continental Mark IV, his white Triumph sports car, and a twenty-three-foot motor sailboat moored at his home.

Cunard's lawyer said his client was "thinking about it."

A prosecutor denied police a search warrant, saying they had no probable cause to believe that a crime had been committed.

His client admitted he was thc last person to see Maria, Cunard's attorney said. If she had walked into trouble that night and been raped or mugged by a stranger, she should turn up. He suggested something far different: that the woman had engineered her own disappearance "out of malice or a vendetta."

Police discounted nothing. A hoax would be especially cruel.

Maria, an only child, was close to her parents. They were sick with worry at her disappearance.

There were other ominous possibilities.

Maria had changed her apartment locks on Thursday, saying that two youths had tried to break in the night before. When her father drove her to work that day she had given him her mink coat and expensive jewelry for safekeeping.

The summer before, a serial rapist had stalked the neighborhood. Maria had been accosted by a stranger who fit his description. She had helped police prepare a composite drawing of the suspect, who was still at large. Police looked at everything, including her ex-husband.

Maria was a cocktail waitress at the Mutiny, a swanky Coconut Grove private club. Thursday night after work she had asked a co-worker to drive her to her husband's home, a guest cottage at the bayfront estate of his heart-surgeon employer. Maria was upset, insisting that she must see her ex-husband, according to the co-worker. She said she saw them drive off together.

Maria had a date with a pharmacist Friday night. She failed to show up. She also failed to appear for work Saturday night. Friends, co-workers, neighbors and the building manager became concerned. They took her apartment door off the hinges.

Lights were on, the stereo was playing and the two pampered pet cats that she loved were hungry, unfed for days. Maria never neglected her pets, including a large turtle, which was roaming the apartment. None of her personal possessions were missing.

The co-worker said that Maria and her ex-husband drove off in his white Triumph sports car. Cunard insisted that he drove Maria away in his Lincoln. He still refused to let police examine either automobile.

I talked to the man. Why wouldn't he submit to a polygraph test? "I know it looks bad not to," he said, "but it looks worse if you take it and fail." Made sense. But why did he think he might fail?

"My only question about taking the test is that I'm frightened out of my mind that she'll turn up in a ditch somewhere or be another Amy Billig [the missing Coconut Grove teenager who has never been found] and cast suspicion on my head the rest of my life."

Why wouldn't he allow police to examine his cars?

"My attorneys say I shouldn't do anything," he told me, reluctant to discuss the matter. He was eager to discuss their short and stormy marriage. Marriage to Maria had forced him into bankruptcy, twenty-five thousand dollars in debt, he said.

He had been wrongly arrested after she maliciously filed an assault complaint against him, he said. Police said he had broken her arm.

Months earlier, he said, Maria had given him her expensive gold wristwatch, then filed a police report accusing him of stealing the timepiece, a gift from her parents. Police had recovered the watch from Cunard's sister.

He said that Maria's phone calls and harassment had wrecked his romances—including a ten-month live-in arrangement with a National Airlines stewardess.

"My entire relationship with her has been a mess," he told me. About that night he said, "I don't know why I opened the door. I don't know why I didn't call her a taxi."

Instead, he said, "I got dressed and we got in my car. I backed out, went up the street, and she started screaming, ranting and raving that I didn't have the consideration to call her on New Year's and that I didn't give her a Christmas present."

He stopped the car and ordered her out, he said, exasperated. She refused. "I took the keys out of the ignition, went around, opened her door, pulled her out by the arms, locked and slammed the door, ran around the car, got in and drove home."

He last saw Maria "standing in the street, ranting and screaming and pointing her finger, yelling, 'You'll be sorry!' "

He went home, he said, locked his car and his doors and "waited for a brick to come through my window."

It didn't.

He had been talking at length to Maria's mother. "She gave me a lot of faith," he said. "Her mom believes Maria is alive out there somewhere. I didn't physically harm her. I'm innocent. I know I'm innocent. I'm scared. I'm frightened. I am in a very serious, precarious position. I'm going through more than any man should go through. She threatened to put me in jail. At first I thought this was one of her pranks. I felt she was still alive, playing hide and seek. Now I'm beginning to doubt it. It'll look bad until she turns up. If this is her idea of a joke, it's a sick joke."

He sounded sincere, but men have lied to me before.

Maria's mother stayed strong. "I have a devout faith that she's going to come home."

Mothers always have faith, whether it makes sense or not.

The search for Maria continued. Because of the embarrassing publicity, Cunard and his surgeon boss agreed that he should move. Several times after he did so, the doctor asked Cunard what he planned to do about his Triumph. The sports car, draped with a heavy canvas auto cover, was still parked about a hundred feet from the surgeon's home, about thirty feet from the guest cottage where Cunard had lived.

On a Saturday morning in February, six weeks after Maria's disappearance, Cunard appeared at the doctor's posh home. He said he would return that afternoon to take the Triumph, parked there since January.

A short time later, two pretty young women, one of them the doctor's daughter, the other his girlfriend, detected a foul odor. Laughing and joking, they cried: "What if it's Maria? What if it's Maria?"

One of them playfully lifted the white Triumph's unlocked trunk lid and gasped. It was Maria. She had been there the entire six weeks. Strangled, her body wrapped in plastic, under the tools, the mud flaps and the junk. The coverings, plus cool weather and the fact that the car was not parked in direct sunlight, kept the smell from being obvious sooner. She was discovered at 12:45 P.M.

Cunard arrived to take the car at two P.M.

Police were waiting.

■

Looking for love can be as lethal as finding it. So many of us are lonely in the midst of city crowds.

Anita Babette Greenstein was the only person to bring along her own life jacket on a sailing outing. She also carried tools in her car, in case of trouble. Though lonely, she never frequented bars or talked to strangers. A cautious career woman, she subscribed to a computer dating service.

Police suspect it sent her a killer.

They believe that the man who robbed and strangled the well-known commercial photographer, then drove her body 170 miles north on Florida's Turnpike and dumped it near Yeehaw Junction in Osceola County, was referred to her by a computer-style dating service.

"I feel so sorry for her," Miami Homicide Detective Andrew Sundberg told me. "She was looking for Mr. Right."

At forty she was in a hurry.

Anita Babette lunched with her parents one Tuesday in August. She mentioned no date that night. In fact, she said she planned to work late in her darkroom to complete a major project. Among her commercial accounts were restaurant chains and shoe manufacturers.

Police believe that the next day, while an unidentified man drove her tan station wagon to drive-in tellers at three banks and cashed checks drawn against her business account, Anita Babette was bound and gagged, lying helpless in her home.

Unable to reach her by telephone Tuesday night, Wednesday or Thursday, her worried parents went to her house. They found it ransacked, pictures removed from the walls, even kitchen cabinets searched. If the killer was seeking something specific, it is unknown whether he found it. Expensive cameras, photographic equipment and other valuables remained. Some small cameras and a TV were missing, along with her handbag, wallet and credit cards.

Late that same day, at Yeehaw Junction in upstate Florida, a turnpike employee noticed what looked like a "bolt of multicolored cloth" thirty feet off the pavement. When it was still there the following day, he stopped to investigate and found the body of a barefoot woman clad in underwear and a striped bathrobe. The unidentified woman was five feet two inches tall and weighed ninety pounds. Deputies sifted through statewide missing-persons reports and stopped at one from Miami.

Anita Babette had been found.

Her station wagon was discovered back in Miami, clean and undamaged, abandoned just off the Palmetto Expressway. Police were puzzled. Why did the killer drive Anita Babette, bound and gagged, possibly still alive though probably already dead, nearly two hundred miles north to Yeehaw Junction? It would have been simpler and far safer to leave her in her house. If what the killer sought was a headstart on police, why then did he drive the dead woman's car back to Miami?

In her big house—both home and studio—detectives found lists, the names of more than one hundred men referred to Anita Babette by half a dozen dating services.

"There are a lot of women like her in Dade County," Homicide Sergeant Mike Gonzalez said. "They outnumber the men. They get lonely." He hoped other lonely women would help him catch the killer.

"We believe that if he went so far as to keep her prisoner, take her car and cash her checks, that he has victimized other women. We want to talk to anybody who has ever had a problem with a computer date who tried to get money from them in any way.

"I think we have his name," Gonzalez said of the killer, "but there are just too many to properly investigate each one."

Many of the men declined to cooperate.

"They are all a little embarrassed," Gonzalez said. "I don't think they want it known that they even used a dating service."

Sundberg said many were "losers, introverts, quiet conservative guys. They resist coming in to talk to us." The detectives found the typical man registered with the dating services to be a "middle-class, private person. They're average. They're not brain surgeons, they're not street sweepers either. Maybe they're a little shy. They're not your Dale Carnegie–type people."

Anita Babette, highly regarded in the field of photography, had been eager to meet professional men of similar education, background and interests. She told friends she was disappointed. Many of the purported professionals referred by the dating services were not what she expected. Some even lacked high school diplomas. Several had criminal records. A few were married men.

Most said they had talked to Anita Babette on the telephone but had never met her. A few said they had dated her. A few submitted to voluntary fingerprinting.

Asked how potential dates were screened, a spokesman for one Miami firm said, "They're not, really."

His firm had sent the names of many men to Anita Babette. "I know nothing about her. I'm not interested in discussing her or us," the spokesman said, and cut me off.

Members of a singles boating group missed her, but to most she was just a name and a number. She was also remembered by the operators of an outing club. She took a bicycling trip and went sailing with them. The family man who had organized people who love the outdoors recalled her "as a cautious person. We were very sad when we heard about it. We'd like to see whoever it was get caught."

During a long and intense investigation the detectives came to understand Anita Babette and other women like her.

"In her earlier life she traveled all over the world photographing everything," Sundberg said. "It was always her career. Footloose and fancy free, a girl-and-her-camera type of thing. Then she was forty and thought, 'I've got my career, but I've got nothing.' She wanted the right man."

We hoped another lonely woman somewhere in the city might supply an answer, but none did.

The ultimate Mr. Wrong, the man who killed Anita Babette is still out there.

Somewhere.

Another innocent who died for love was a Miamian, kidnapped, robbed and brutally murdered as he moonlighted to buy a birthday present for his wife. As the killers tried to bury the corpse in a backyard, neighbors called police. A year later, five days before the first anniversary of her husband's death—and her twenty-sixth birthday—the widow swung her son, age two and named after his father, over the edge of the roof at the federal courthouse. Then she let go.

Even puppy love will sometimes go horribly awry. Two high school sweethearts told friends they could not face a summer apart. The girl was being sent to Italy. The boy was to start summer school. Both were sixteen. The Italian trip was designed in part to separate the pair, in love for three years. They had asked permission to marry, but were told they were too young. They wanted to become engaged, but were told they were too young. They were also too young to die, but when the girl said, "I'd rather be dead than in Italy," the boy believed her. He took a gun from a house where she babysat and shot her five times. Then he shot himself.

"They were such sweet little children, childhood sweethearts," a shocked neighbor told me.

Love makes some people crazy.

The death of Lance Christian Anderson is a perfect example. An airline pilot, as handsome as a movie star, he wheeled his brand new champagne-colored Mercedes Benz into his circular driveway, where a ski-masked killer waited in shadowy ambush.

This is a story of a love triangle and sudden death. The scenario is pure Hollywood, the stuff movies are made of. Beautiful people, illicit romance, money and murder—even, indirectly, an Academy Award winner. The assassin was an Eastern Airlines pilot. So was Lance Christian Anderson. Both loved the same woman. She was an Eastern Airlines stewardess, married to the victim.

The murdered pilot, forty-two, was stalked and killed with his own gun.

The victim and his killer scarcely knew one another, yet they had a great deal in common. Both were New Englanders, both had resettled in Miami, both loved to fly, and both wanted the same thirty-nine-year-old flight attendant, Kathleen K. Anderson.

Her husband, Lance, born on the Fourth of July, was well on his way to becoming a millionaire. A whiz at business, he owned boat, marine-supply and seaplane firms. A natural athlete, a crack shot and an expert sailor, he was at home on the water and in the sky.

"There was no façade about Lance," said Jeane Kates, who lived with her husband, Jack, next door to the Andersons' ranch-style home on two and a half acres. "He was what he appeared to be." Lance thought it "terrible" to keep a bird in a tiny cage. He once drove his parents' new puppy all the way from Miami to their Bradenton home rather than see it endure an airline flight.

"He was a classy sort of person, always thinking of ways to improve things," said retired Commander Richard Jaffee, Lance's superior in the Coast Guard Reserve. "He was such a good-looking guy, he could have been a movie star."

Lance was twice invited to escort Miss USA contestants at the pageant in Miami Beach. That was before he married—and before another man fell in love with his wife.

The man in love with Lance's wife, Kathi, was Gerald John Russell, thirty-nine, a boyish former Air Force captain who had won two commendations for bravery in Vietnam, one of them for landing a burning aircraft. He had a degree in psychology from the University of New Hampshire and moonlighted as a home contractor. He is the son of a famous man, the only actor to ever win two Oscars for the same role.

His father, Harold Russell, seventy-seven, a handless World War II veteran, won the awards for his classic 1946 performance in *The Best Years of Our Lives*. He went on to become a successful executive and chairman of the President's Commission on Employment of the Handicapped.

He once confided to Hollywood gossip columnist Louella Parsons that he had adopted his wife's tiny son by a prior marriage. "He's ours now," he told Louella proudly.

Lance and Kathi married in June 1966. Their only child, Lisa, was seven at the time of his murder. Shortly before his death, Lance bought a matched pair of Mercedes; his a station wagon, hers a four-door sedan with a KATHI-K personalized license tag.

The marriage survived a separation in 1980. At about the same time, Jerry Russell and his wife, his next-door childhood sweetheart, were divorced. His famous actor father flew to Miami half a dozen times to persuade the couple to stay together. "It was one of the failures of my life," the father said.

The romance between Jerry Russell and Kathi Anderson began in 1978 and continued after her husband moved back into the house. Although Kathi lived with Lance, she and Jerry attended concerts and plays and dined at fine restaurants. On Valentine's Day, Jerry sent Kathi and her daughter roses and took them to dinner. The child signed Kathi's valentine card to Russell. While Lance piloted an Eastern flight on Thanksgiving, Jerry cooked a turkey for Kathi and her daughter.

Russell's father met Kathi at that family dinner. "She seemed like an airline stewardess, a girl in a uniform who serves the drinks and is nice and polite." At his son's request, he autographed for Kathi a copy of his latest book, *The Best Years of My Life*.

Jerry's friends knew about his obsession with Kathi. Perhaps her husband also knew. Relatives said that for a time, Lance had a private detective "monitor" his wife's relationship with Jerry.

Though his marriage was troubled, Lance's businesses flourished. His brother Erik, forty-seven, had sold his Alamonte Springs funeral home and intended to move to Miami to be a partner. Erik admired his brother's cool-headed style. In January they were aloft in a small plane when the single engine quit. Lance smoothly glided the aircraft into a pasture, repaired a clogged fuel line and off they soared again.

After delivery of his new Mercedes on February 16, Lance decided to put a gun in the car for protection. He discovered his .357 Magnum missing from his study, an employee said. "He thought maybe Kathi had borrowed it, or he may have mislaid it."

The weapon was the third of Lance's guns to apparently go astray in recent weeks. The first, a .38 Arminius Titan revolver he had owned for years, seemed to have disappeared from his car, parked in the Eastern employees' lot. The second was a derringer. He did not report the guns stolen, believing they were just misplaced. He took another two-shot derringer, which he had bought for Kathi, and placed it in his briefcase.

On Wednesday, February 24, 1982, the day of the killing, a friend of Kathi's skirmished with her husband, a Delta Airlines pilot. He ripped the phone out of the wall and left for work. So after a dental appointment, Kathi drove her new Mercedes Benz to Jerry Russell's townhouse, and together they went to the Delta pilot's home. Jerry repaired the phone, then took Kathi to lunch. Lance was at work, exhibiting marine supplies at a boat show in Miami Beach.

From seven to nine P.M., Jerry played tennis with the usual Wednesday-night crowd at the Biltmore Hotel in Coral Gables. In a foursome with insurance agent Alex Soto, a real estate agent and a travel agent, Jerry played his usual game.

"He's a hacker," said Soto, thirty-three, "but he played a pretty good game, for him." Jerry appeared to have been drinking, but not enough to affect his game. "He was kidding around, very calm, relaxed, a typical, average, laid back, normal individual. He was not plotting or planning a murder that night—or I know nothing about human nature."

After the boat show, Lance picked up Frank Armstrong, twenty-one. Armstrong had recently moved to Miami from Bradenton to work for Lance. He was staying in an office-study in a barn behind Lance's house. They headed home. "We were joking and talking and having a good old time," Armstrong said. "Lance was telling me how well the boat show went for him."

Earlier that night Jerry was at his own home with his sixteen-year-old daughter, Wendy. She heard her father take a telephone call in his room with the door closed. Then Jerry Russell went out. His TV was left on. So was the garden hose, which would run all night, flooding the lush green lawn he prized so highly. "Not like a precise pilot accustomed to checklists," his bewildered father would say later.

By 11:20 P.M., Lance and his passenger were almost home. A

ranch-style wooden fence stretches 166 feet across the front of the property. Lance spotted something unusual out of the corner of his eye as they passed. A blue bicycle leaned against the east end of the fence. Lance stopped the Mercedes on the roadway and backed up at an angle, lighting up the bicycle and his front lawn.

"That's when we saw the guy in the yard," Armstrong said. Someone was lying in the shadows, next to a large bush. Something silvery and box-shaped lay next to him. "Maybe it's a bicyclist who's just going to sleep there for the night," Armstrong suggested.

Lance reached into the backseat for the derringer. He knew his wife was home. Perhaps he feared something had happened to her. Lance drove through the gate, into the driveway, onto the lawn, "and angled around the bush where the guy should have been lying. But he wasn't there," Armstrong said.

"Lance put it in park and we were about ready to get out to look for him, when he came walking around the bush."

The man wore a burgundy-colored jogging suit and a ski mask. "His left hand was on the mask. I think he just pulled it down," Armstrong said. The eye holes had been enlarged. "He was holding a blue steel revolver in his right hand."

Three feet from the car the gunman opened fire. A bullet shattered a bone in Lance's upper left arm.

"Oh, dear God!" Lance said, and shot back. They were his last words. The gunman kept coming.

He was about a foot from the side window when he shot Lance twice in the face. Armstrong saw part of Lance's jaw disintegrate. Another bullet struck Lance under the eye, snapping his head back.

Then the gunman, "who never uttered a word, swung the gun in my direction," Armstrong said. A bullet grazed Armstrong's shoulder.

He bailed out. "I knew Lance was dead. I wasn't thinking about anything at the moment but saving my own skin."

Three more shots thudded into the ground behind him as he

scaled a fence and scrambled into the room where he had been staying. Panting, he pawed in his suitcase for his own gun, then sat, terrified in the dark, waiting. The motor of Lance's car had been racing. He heard someone switch it off. No footsteps approached on the gravel, so he sprinted out the door, hurdling three fences in headlong flight. Spattered with Lance's blood, stained by his own, his clothing and flesh torn from the fences he'd leaped, he pounded on a neighbor's door for help, still clutching his own gun.

The frightened family refused to open the door, but called the police.

The gunshots had routed neighbor John Kates from his bed. He heard sirens and saw police cars skidding into his neighbor's drive. He and his wife hurried to the Anderson home.

Lance sat dead at the wheel of his Mercedes, the tiny two-shot derringer still clutched in his right hand. The bullet fired into his face at close range had left powder burns on his forehead. Kathi never stepped outside to see what had happened. She was not alone. Her daughter was asleep, and fifteen minutes before the ambush, another of Lance's business associates, Thomas Sloat, had arrived at the house from the boat show.

Sloat heard the shots, found the body, turned off the engine, and told Kathi to call police.

They found the murder weapon, Lance's missing Arminius Titan revolver, near the fence. The silvery box-shaped object also lay in the yard: a homemade silencer, fashioned from a section of air-conditioning duct, altered and taped.

Six minutes after the shooting, Jerry Russell's telephone-equipped pickup truck smashed into a pole eight blocks from the crime scene. He was slumped unconscious over the steering wheel, bleeding from a bullet wound. The single high-velocity .22-Magnum bullet Lance had managed to squeeze off from the derringer moments before his death had caught Jerry square in the chest.

A ski mask lay on the seat beside him. On the floorboard, a set of Smith and Wesson handcuffs and empty bank money wrappers in one-thousand- and five-thousand-dollar denominations. Detectives speculated that Russell intended to make the murder look like a drug killing. In the back of the pickup was a bloodied blue ten-speed bicycle, owned by his teenage daughter. Critically wounded, Russell told police he had been shot while taking a walk.

Police asked Kathi if she knew Russell. She said she did. The Kateses drove her that night to make a formal statement at Metro police headquarters.

"I know who killed Lance," she told the couple. "It was Jerry Russell."

She told police she had met Russell on a flight three years earlier. A part-time contractor, he soon began to build a house across the street. She invited him over. She admitted an affair while separated from her husband, but swore that since the reconciliation her relationship with Russell had continued "on a friendship basis only."

"How did Jerry Russell feel about you?" a detective asked.

"He loves me. My friends and his friends tell me, 'He is absolutely crazy about you. And this is just killing him. It's absolutely destroying him.' " She repeated their conversation over lunch after he fixed her friend's telephone.

RUSSELL: Well, what are your plans for a divorce?

KATHI: No plans. I have no plans for a divorce.

RUSSELL: Well, is money that important to you?

KATHI: I'm not so sure that money is the issue.

RUSSELL: Money has to be the issue. You can't, the way you're talking—the way you felt about him when you were separated, you just can't . . . A person doesn't change their feelings . . .

KATHI: Well, he's my husband and, yes, I can change my feelings.

RUSSELL: I still find it very hard to believe the two of you can make anything out of your life. I fully believe money is the only thing keeping you there.

She said they talked by telephone again that night around 9:15 or 9:30. Two hours later Russell was lurking in the shadows outside the house. Kathi denied knowing her husband was about to be murdered. Calm and cool, according to police, she said she and Sloat, her husband's associate, watched the eleven o'clock news on the giant-screen television Lance had bought her for Christmas. They saw the headlights from Lance's new Mercedes station wagon—then they heard the gunfire.

Harold Russell was asleep at his daughter's Cape Cod home when the telephone rang at 1:18 A.M. His son, on his way to surgery, said, "I've been shot." Before boarding the next flight to Miami, his father and sister learned the shooting involved a man named Anderson.

During the flight it occurred to the father that Anderson was the name of the woman he had met at Thanksgiving. "It's so insane and unbelievable," he said later. "So many crazy things are happening. I hate guns. I've always hated guns."

Lance's mother was bitter. "When I heard those three terrible words, 'Lance is dead,' I could not accept it," Erika Anderson said. "It is too horrible. I would have preferred that Lance be killed in a plane crash."

Homicide detectives with a search warrant took 78 spent cartridges, more than 150 rounds of ammunition, scissors, fibers, thread, two rolls of duct tape and photographs from Jerry Russell's home. They also found papers in a white envelope marked KATHI and a Valentine's Day card.

Russell, shackled to a hospital bed, was charged with first-degree murder.

Lawyers estimated the net worth of Lance's estate at $1 million. He was insured for more than $200,000. His widow was the beneficiary.

Kathi hired a lawyer and declined to take a polygraph test. "She is not a suspect in anything," her lawyer explained.

Prosecutor Roy Kahn agreed. "The poor woman," he said, "has suffered enough."

Kathi later changed her mind and, without telling police, submitted to a private polygraph test. "She felt there were certain implications and innuendos," her lawyer said. "She passed with flying colors." He did not know the precise questions, but said, "Whatever you think is relevant, she passed."

The top-flight Miami criminal defense attorney hired by Russell's father was not impressed. "I've seen people pass polygraph examinations they should have flunked," said Joel Hirschhorn, "and I've seen other people fail tests they should have passed. The results are not acceptable in court because too much depends on nonscientific matters." He questioned whether the state's initial investigation was "as thorough as it should have been."

But prosecutor Kahn pronounced the case solved.

Executrix of Lance's estate, Kathi collected his $201,485 life insurance and sued her former sweetheart for shooting her spouse. She asked for damages, citing funeral expenses, mental anguish and the loss of Lance's support.

Jerry Russell's ex-wife sued also, asking to have his assets frozen to assure her $600-a-month child support. Eastern fired him for shooting a "fellow pilot" and creating "unfavorable publicity" that reflected on the airline's reputation.

Russell disputed his dismissal, on grounds that his "alleged misconduct" occurred "off duty" and not on Eastern property. Kathi, president of a flight attendants' organization, was not fired.

Eastern officials remained tight-lipped. "We never comment on the personal lives of employees," a spokesman said. Russell added to the airline's grief by pleading insanity. Pilot of a jumbo jet just three days before ambushing Lance Anderson, Russell's defense was that he was such a severe alcoholic that his brain was addled. Hirschhorn said his client had been drinking and could not remember why he was outside the Anderson home that night. He said Russell was hopelessly addicted to both alcohol and Kathi, who had shared a carafe of wine with him at lunch on the day of the crime.

One of Russell's friends, top aide to an assistant Miami police chief, had tried to talk Russell out of his dead-end romance with a married woman. Russell refused to listen. "He was absolutely infatuated, enthralled," Donald Warshaw said. "It reached the point at which I think he was somewhat embarrassed about the fact. He would lie to his friends and say he was staying home—when he was really seeing her."

"I think most people who have been in love understand the power of that emotion," attorney Hirschhorn said. "It all really goes back to when Eve offered Adam that first apple."

The dead man's mother stopped speaking to her daughter-in-law, who had refused to pay the $5,418 owed for Lance's funeral. The mother wrote to then–Eastern chairman Frank Borman: "Your employees are liable for our losing Lance. He left your employ unwillingly, as he left his life."

Borman did not reply.

To Dade State Attorney Janet Reno, she wrote: "My fine young eagle should still be flying."

Reno did not reply.

Erika Anderson wanted a first-degree murder conviction and the death penalty—nothing less. "Can Lance be allowed to be second-degree dead? Like only on weekends?" she asked. "He is one hundred percent dead."

The week-long trial on the fourth floor of the Justice Building played like a hit show to a packed house. A sign outside the courtroom announced NO SEATS AVAILABLE. Crowds waited to be first in line after luncheon recesses.

Circuit Judge Joseph P. Farina, a boyish workaholic, urged jurors to bring sweaters because of the building's runaway air conditioner, to stand and stretch often, called them "folks" and worked them hard. Marched off to a nearby hospital cafeteria for suppers, they labored through ten-, twelve- and thirteen-hour days.

Prosecutor Kahn waived the death penalty. Defense attorney Hirschhorn, almost breaking into song, warned prospective jurors that the case dealt with "hearts full of passion, jealousy and hate." Anyone involved in a love triangle, he said, might find the testimony "too uncomfortable." He suggested they speak up before being chosen.

Nobody did.

Russell, pale and thin, listened intently, occasionally jotting in red ink on a yellow legal pad. His sister, stepmother, sixteen-year-old daughter Wendy, and his father were all present in court. The elder Russell, heartsick, said that the murder pained him more than the loss of his hands in World War II.

"As one who has been flying for forty years," he questioned, "just how much psychiatric testing is done by the airlines to ensure that the men who fly these planes carrying millions of passengers have the mental and physical capacity to do so?"

The grim parents and brother of Lance Anderson were also present. The mother, a stately blonde, wore black every day.

"Was this murder one of premeditation, first-degree murder?" asked prosecutor Kahn. He said it was, that Russell was neither crazy nor alcoholic, but was cold-blooded. "This man was prepared to kill. He had the intent."

Hirschhorn said that Kathi Anderson, a "woman loved by two dashing airline pilots, wanted the best of two worlds. She had a husband who was a superlative provider and a lover who could satisfy her sexual needs." While her husband bought her a new Mercedes and planned their future, she continued seeing Russell, who wanted to marry her. "Like a carrot before a rabbit, she dangled her personality and her body before Jerry Russell."

Driven mad by jealousy and frustration and manipulated by the woman he loved, his client, he said, arrived at the murder scene drunk, pedaling a bicycle and toting a bulky air-conditioning duct that police identified as a crude silencer.

Kathi testified for the prosecution. Wearing a modest high-necked white blouse, her blond hair in a prim Dutch-boy cut, she admitted lying to police and to the prosecutor. In earlier statements she had told them she met Russell in 1979. During questions from Hirschhorn she conceded that she had comforted her lover the day his mother died—in 1978. Both were married when they met. Earlier she said she began the affair with Russell while she and her husband were apart and ended it when they reconciled. Now she acknowledged that their intimacy began long before the separation and continued afterward.

"Why didn't you terminate your relationship with Russell when your husband moved back into the house?" Hirschhorn asked.

"I didn't want to," the widow coolly replied. Unruffled after grueling hours of cross-examination, she gazed dry-eyed at her former lover, who stared back.

Russell was the friend her husband was not, she said, but lacked ambition. She had no idea, she said, that he would kill Lance.

"You saw nothing wrong in living with your husband and having Valentine's Day dinner with Russell?" asked Hirschhorn.

"What's wrong with that?"

She admitted dining with him at nearly twenty fine restaurants and accompanying him on trips to Boston, Cape Cod and Toronto. Her daughter, Lisa, she said, "liked Jerry very much, he made her mother happy, and she had seen her mother unhappy."

She was neglected, she said. Lance was "never home," because of business. She added that she saw nothing unusual about Russell's drinking habits, although he once crawled into the backseat of a car and fell asleep after they left a restaurant.

Hirschhorn asked about Russell's former wife, Judy, who had called Kathi before the divorce, pleading to save her marriage.

He asked Kathi if she felt the slightest "moral concern for that woman's feelings about her marriage." Kathi asked him to repeat the question. Twice she said she did not understand it.

That, the lawyer said, was his answer.

Kathi did once consult a lawyer about her rights if she divorced Lance, she said. "I was concerned about what would legally be mine."

"You are now suing Mr. Russell for every penny he has?" Hirschhorn asked.

"Correct," the widow said crisply.

Gerald Russell took the stand in his own defense.

"Did you shoot Lance Anderson?" Hirschhorn asked.

Struggling to speak, Russell began to weep. "Yes," he whispered.

"Why did you shoot him?"

"I don't know," Russell said, shoulders shaking as he began to sob.

"How do you feel about Kathi Anderson today?"

"In my head, I feel like I was used," he said, tears streaming. "But when I saw her the other day, my heart said I still feel the same way. I had some very, very strong feelings when she walked in here."

The eyes of five female jurors were swimming. One, a divorcée, wiped away tears.

The day Kathi testified against Russell was the first time he had seen her since the day of the murder. She had come to his home the morning of the murder, he said, and they had made love.

He went to her home that night and made her a widow.

It all began when he invited her for a drink, he said. He was nervous. "I had never asked a flight attendant out before." Eventually he neglected his contracting business, divorced his wife and built his life around Kathi.

They kept the secret from their spouses. They spent even more time together after Kathi and Lance separated. But then Lance, a success with four thriving firms, moved back into his home.

"Our relationship took a step backward," Russell testified. "We had to work our schedule around when he was there."

He waited, he said, frustrated and unhappy. "Kathi said she was protecting family finances. She was very concerned about getting her share of the money, what was due her from her marriage." She feared Lance might hide his assets. So when he was away on flights, the lovers regularly raided Lance's car in the Eastern employee parking lot, he said, searching for papers relating to Kathi or her husband's money. They found Lance's .38-caliber revolver in the car, and Kathi seized it. "Here, take this, so we don't get shot," she said, according to Russell. He took it.

Russell even knew the secret combination to Lance's locked briefcase: 7–2–7. The dead pilot's brother covered his eyes during that testimony. The combination was correct.

Russell wanted to get married, but Kathi insisted they wait until "the time was right."

In evidence were stacks of greeting cards from Kathi, including her last one: *The two of us together . . . All I want. Love on Valentine's Day and Always, Kathi.*

Russell read aloud a three-page memo he wrote himself nearly a year before the murder. Methodically listed were the facts of the tortured affair and his options. Murder was never an option. He choked with emotion as he read his feelings, "very much in love with her. Worship her."

While he remembered watching Kathi and Lance ride arm-in-arm aboard an Eastern Airlines float during Miami's New Year's Eve Orange Bowl parade, he could not remember driving to their home the night of the murder. Only nightmarish snatches: "Headlights, shining on me. A really bad pain"—when he was shot. "I think I remember firing a gun three times." Then, at the wheel of his pickup truck, saying aloud, "I'm passing out," moments before the truck crashed into a pole.

He admitted feeling guilty about the affair and about Lisa. From age four she had shared their secrets. "Kathi would tell her not to tell her father. I thought it was bad for her to learn whatever she was learning from this double life."

Harold Russell trembled at his son's testimony. "She put the gun in his hand and the idea in his mind. She killed Lance Anderson even though she didn't pull the trigger. I'm bitter. I never met Lance Anderson, but I understand he was a fine man. If there is any way I can sue her for every penny she has, I will, for the children. She has destroyed so many lives."

Outside the courtroom Wendy Russell sobbed in the arms of a friend. "I tried not to cry," she said, "but he started to cry . . . and he's my dad."

Several jurors wept during closing arguments for the defense. "He was addicted to Kathi Anderson," Hirschhorn told them. "He might as well have been mainlining heroin."

Prosecutor Kahn remained unemotional. "Nowhere in this country is adultery or love a defense for first-degree murder. You may have a license to fly, but you don't have a license to kill." Kathi Anderson, he acknowledged, "is not a nice lady," but, he pointed out, she was not on trial. "Kathi Anderson, the adulteress—let's make her out to be the worst person in the world, but she had nothing to do with the murder." He instructed jurors to "catch yourselves" if overwhelmed by emotion.

They listened. After six hours of often loud and angry deliberation they returned with more tears and a verdict: guilty of murder in the first degree.

Russell stood stoic, facing life, which means a twenty-five-year mandatory term. He will be old enough for Social Security by the time he is eligible for parole.

"It was a nightmare to me," said juror Juanita Wilson. "He is so sorry it happened, but he can't undo it. I did what I had to do."

"Some of the jurors really cried," said juror Bertha Mustafa. "We had to quiet each other down. Going by the letter of the law is a very hard thing. We constantly had to remind ourselves to put emotion aside. Everybody wanted to make the right decision."

"The men took it a little better than the women," said foreman Howard Dorfeld. "There were only three men and we sort of had to stabilize the women."

"When there's premeditation, there's premeditation," said juror Robert Matthewman. "He's not a criminal. The woman had a lot to do with it, but he did premeditate it. A couple of women were very adamant for second degree, but their reasons were illogical. We made them see they had to go by the law."

Matthewman, the younger brother of two policemen, was as sympathetic as any juror could have been. He had been involved in a similar love triangle. He buried his face in his hands when they delivered the verdict. "My heart started racing. I was hyperventilating and my stomach was churning. I know how he felt about her. I know what a woman can do to you."

Matthewman's own love triangle ended without violence.

All swore they would never sit on a jury again.

Sentencing was a formality. There were no options. Hirschhorn called it a death sentence. "It will be 2007 when he is paroled. Chances are minimal that he will survive those twenty five horrible years. His life has come to an end."

Throughout the trial, the families of both pilots had occupied opposite sides of the high-ceilinged courtroom. First they avoided each other's eyes. By midweek, they exchanged hesitant words. By the time it was over, they had joined forces.

"We are working on a plan of action," the elder Russell said. "The Andersons are fine people. We will work together to make sure the children are taken care of, that Lisa is taken care of."

The Andersons hired private detectives to investigate the widow.

Before he was sent to state prison, I visited Jerry Russell in the county jail. He tried to joke, but could not smile. He felt like Rodney Dangerfield, he said. "I get no respect." When he told them he was a killer and demanded some space, his cellmates jeered. Guards did not even take the trouble to strip-search him after visiting hours.

Even the woman he loved showed no respect.

Kathi agreed to talk to me, after refusing for months. "I hope no man ever loves me like that again," she pouted.

Both still asked themselves why.

"If Jerry Russell had not been wounded and had not been caught, there is no way I ever would have been convinced that he did it," she said. "You have no idea the nights I have paced my living-room floor, trying to figure out what Jerry planned that night. I really do not think that love had anything to do with it. It was one of two things: greed or revenge."

Jerry too seemed in the dark. "I killed a man I didn't know. If I had planned it and blown it, going to prison would be easier to accept. But I don't know why I did it. I stepped out of my life and all the things I believe in and did a monstrous thing—and I don't know why."

He hoped to talk to Kathi one last time. The affair was over "but I would like to clean up the loose ends and wrap it up."

"He did a super job of wrapping things up himself," Kathi blurted. "I am scared to death of him. If I saw him a mile away, I would head for the nearest police station. The thought of him ever being out on the street terrifies me."

The twenty-five-year minimum mandatory is not harsh enough, she said. He deserves death. "It was a cold-blooded, brutal murder. You have no idea how I miss Lance," she said, voice quavering.

The lovers each accused the other of lying.

"Why did he say I was in bed with him that day?" She insisted that all they shared the day of the murder was a lunch date and wine. She heard Russell's kiss-and-tell testimony during an evening newscast. "You have no idea what a crazy person I was. I was throwing things at the TV."

Both disliked the news coverage. It made their "gentle and loving" affair seem sordid, he complained.

Kathi accused reporters of making her appear unsympathetic. She was angry at Hirschhorn for saying she hated Lance. They were happy, she said, and she loved him. I asked if she thought their marriage would have endured forever. "What's forever?" she answered. "I have lost a lot of faith in forever. I can't even bring myself to date. How could I ever trust another man? You don't know how many times in the heat of the day, with the mosquitoes, I have sat by my husband's grave."

Russell worried about his future parole. "I don't know what I'm going to be like when I'm sixty-four. I don't know what kind of job I can get. I don't want to depend on my sister or my kids when I get out."

Kathi worried about "trying to make a life for a little girl. I don't know how I'm going to fly, run my husband's business, keep house and be a mother." Because she had received threats, she said, she spent each night of the trial with different friends. A surprise awaited her on the day the defense accused her of "dangling her body in front of Jerry Russell like a carrot before a rabbit."

"You need this more than I do," that evening's hostess declared, presenting Kathi with a huge stuffed carrot that had decorated her kitchen.

"It was funny," Kathi said. "You have to admit, it was funny."

Eight years later, in 1990, I looked up and saw a familiar face at a library fund-raiser on Florida's Gulf Coast. Erika Anderson, still elegant and stately. I asked how she was. "Angry," she said.

All the legal efforts have accomplished nothing. Erika Anderson has not seen her granddaughter, Lisa, for years.

Lance is dead.

Jerry is behind bars.

But for those left behind, it is never really over.

Chapter 4

THE TWILIGHT ZONE

The middle ground between light and shadow . . . it is an area we call the Twilight Zone.

—Rod Serling

Into the daily life of reporters and cops seeking only the facts come occasional events that defy rational explanation. They are more chilling than a man with a gun.

How do you explain the premonitions, the dreams, the ironies and otherworldly occurrences? Specifically, how do you explain them to an editor, in his brightly lit and high-tech tower? His eyes invariably narrow as you report that the story you are writing involves a voodoo curse come true or a dead man apparently returned from the grave.

Mamie Higgs opened her door and screamed. The visitor was Alex Monroe, her father. The last time she saw him he lay in a coffin. He had been murdered four months earlier, and she had identified the corpse. She had paid for his funeral. The entire family had attended the open-coffin services. Now he was alive at her door.

Even as they embraced, she looked to see "if there was any graveyard dust on him." The man in her father's grave was somebody else.

The man in her father's grave was Alex Monroe—the *other* Alex Monroe.

There were two Alex Monroes—both sixty-two years old, both

five feet nine inches tall, both 140 pounds. Each Alex Monroe had a scar on the left side of his face. They lived six blocks apart in Miami.

They had never met.

Mrs. Higgs had identified the Alex Monroe shot dead during a fight in a grubby downtown neighborhood as her father. "The scar was in the same place, from the temple to the cheek. He had the same small ears, the same salt-and-pepper hair."

Now her father had returned months later from a stay in North Carolina. As he strolled down a Miami street a passing friend slammed on her brakes, shrieking, "You're dead!"

He denied it. "I'm not dead," he said. "I just came from North Carolina."

Mamie Higgs had borrowed from her credit union to bury her father. Now that he wasn't dead, she wanted her money back.

Made sense to me.

I tried to mediate, calling the funeral home in her behalf. The director was adamant. "We simply carried out a service."

A compromise of sorts was finally worked out. Mrs. Higgs was promised free services when her father really does die.

People do not come back from the dead, but if they don't, how do you explain Earl Allen?

Earl Allen did not feel well. He had suffered dizzy spells for two weeks and had a severe headache, but not severe enough to make him stay home instead of going night fishing with Charlie Fletcher and two other chums. They took Charlie's twenty-two-foot boat into the Intracoastal Waterway.

Allen complained about his terrible headache, suddenly stood up and pitched overboard, headfirst. His companions were not sure whether he fell or dove into the water.

They saw him come up swimming, against the tide, toward the shore, but suddenly he disappeared about thirty feet from some mangroves. That's when they began yelling for help.

A security guard at a nearby high-rise heard their cries and called police. It was 12:49 A.M. Metro-Dade Officer Bart Cohen and his partner arrived one minute later. They radioed for the Coast Guard. An Indian Creek Village police boat arrived first, sweeping the area where Earl Allen was last seen. The dark water, lit only by their searchlight and a three-quarter moon, yielded nothing.

"There was nobody swimming, no calls for help," Officer Cohen said. A Coast Guard eighteen-footer arrived an hour and a half later. Cohen climbed aboard, and close to where he was last seen, they spotted Earl Allen, fifty-nine, floating facedown beneath the surface, 150 feet away. Cohen radioed that they were about to recover the victim's body. As the Coast Guard boat came alongside, the "body" appeared to lurch toward the boat. The policeman assumed it was the movement of the water. A Coast Guardsman snagged the back of Earl Allen's shirt and maneuvered him to where Officer Cohen could grab his arms and pull him into the boat. He did, and then the "dead man" began to move.

"He's alive!" gasped the disbelieving cop, his own pulse pounding. "Nobody could believe it," said Cohen, a six-year police veteran and a former lifeguard. "It totally amazed me. He had definitely been underwater, facedown."

Earl Allen spit up water "like a fountain."

When they delivered him to waiting paramedics, Earl Allen sat upright on the stretcher to look around him. "It's unbelievable," Police Sergeant John Cini said. "Nobody can stay underwater an hour and a half and live."

His theory was that Earl Allen had been drinking and perhaps that's what saved him. He could have been so intoxicated that "he went into a coma and didn't require the same amount of oxygen."

Made no sense to me. Police regularly blame drownings on victims who were drinking.

Hospital officials declined to advance any theories. "Generally speaking," said assistant Dade County medical examiner Dr. Erik Mitchell, "for a person underwater, it's just a matter of a few minutes until brain damage and death."

Examined at the Veterans Administration Hospital, Earl Allen had suffered no apparent ill effects and was released twelve hours later. He had no other means of transportation, so I drove him home. We talked on the way.

Earl Allen was not brain damaged, though he did seem sort of loose and happy-go-lucky. He said he had stood up in the boat, caught his foot in the carpeting and tripped. He remembered "hitting the water." His next recollection was the policeman dragging him into a boat as he wondered, "Where am I?" He vaguely recalled being treated by the paramedics.

Earl Allen denied being drunk. He only had about eight cans of Old Milwaukee, he said, during the entire outing, which had begun in late afternoon. "It takes more than that to get me drunk," he said. He had experienced no long tunnels or bright white lights, nor did he seem surprised by his own survival. A World War II veteran of the navy, he had survived thirteen major battles, including a "torpedo coming right for the ship—it went under the bow" and kamikaze attacks. "When the Japs start diving into your ship, now *that's* nerve wracking," he said matter-of-factly.

We were exiting the expressway at that moment and my car suddenly went dead on the ramp. When it wouldn't start, we hiked to a nearby house to call for help. While we waited, I tried it again. This time the engine started, and I took my passenger on home. Standing in the afternoon sunlight, slightly stooped and grinning, he waved a casual good-bye as though all that had happened was nothing unusual.

Just another day in the life of Earl Allen.

And what about the precognitive dreams? Like the young policeman's nightmare that quickly became reality.

Rick Trado, twice honored as Miami Beach's most outstanding cop, was cited as a hero for freeing the unconscious driver of an overturned truck that gushed gasoline.

The dream came eighteen months later.

"I woke up in a cold sweat," he told fellow officer Thomas

Moran as they carpooled to headquarters that Sunday morning at dawn. "I had a dream. I stopped a car, and the guy got out and shot me." Nearly an hour later, Trado stopped a car.

The guy got out and shot him.

Officer Trado had stopped a speeder on the Julia Tuttle Causeway stretching between Miami and Miami Beach. The motorist routinely stepped out, then charged the patrol car, firing a .357 Magnum. As Trado reached for his service revolver, a bullet hit his right hand, shattered the wooden stock of his gun and slammed into his biceps. The gunman shot out the front tires of the patrol car and fled.

Simultaneously, the wounded officer's radio began to broadcast reports of a robbery that had just occurred and a description of the suspect. Officers were warned to use caution, the robber was armed.

Trado already knew that.

Pandemonium broke out, as it always does when a cop is shot. The shooter had escaped. A huge manhunt was under way. I raced out to the scene, then to the hospital emergency room. The atmosphere was one of relief. The wound was not life threatening. Hit in the hand, Trado was about to go to surgery, but everybody considered him lucky, all things considered.

I found Rick Trado lying on a table in the emergency room, pale and in pain, his right arm swathed in blood-soaked bandages. It is always shocking when a cop is shot, more so when it is a cop you know, a cop with a toddler son and a pregnant wife.

"I felt so helpless," he said. "When the bullet hit me, I couldn't control my fingers." He lowered his voice. "Edna, you won't believe this. I dreamed this this morning. I dreamed I stopped a car and the guy shot me."

Back out on the street, an army of 150 police from at least eleven agencies sealed off an eight-block area, using dogs and helicopters to track the suspect. During the confusion I spotted Tommy Moran. His first words: "Edna, you won't believe this. On the way in, Rick told me he woke up this morning in a cold sweat. He dreamed he pulled over a car and the guy shot him."

The bullet wound was more serious than it first appeared.

Hundreds of tiny fragments, splinters from the shattered wood, were embedded in the nerves, bones and muscles of his hand, causing massive infection and complications. He nearly lost the hand. Extensive surgery never restored its full use.

The injury ended his career prematurely, a loss to us all. The man who shot him was captured, declared insane, hospitalized, "cured" and released.

Dreams do come true. Unfortunately many of them are terrifying.

Connie Thomas, troubled by bad dreams in the night, pleaded with her husband, Meldren, not to take the blue boat he had named *Sea Breeze* out the next morning. He reassured her, even delayed his departure long enough to fix her a hot breakfast. Then he and his brother-in-law, W. L. Gavins, set out for a day of fishing. It was Saturday, the day before Easter. Their wives knew something was wrong when the men did not return at dusk. Gavins was to sing "When the Gates Swing Open, I'll Walk Right In" at sunrise services in the morning.

His worried wife drove to the Crandon Park boat ramp and found her husband's old pickup truck still parked there. She called police, who took the report, assuring her that it would be forwarded to the Coast Guard. The sisters prayed through the night. At five A.M., with still no word, they called the Coast Guard. Their call was the first notice rescuers had of a missing boat. The policeman had left the report on his desk to be reviewed by a sergeant the following Monday morning. If approved, it would then have been forwarded, through proper channels, to the Coast Guard. Petty officials had struck again, blinded by their own bureaucratic routine and red tape. Always frustrating, this time they were deadly. Now it was too late.

Easter Sunday afternoon the crew of a fishing vessel spotted Gavins, floating facedown. The second corpse was found hours later. The men had taken life jackets, but neither wore one. Whatever happened to them happened fast, like something out of a bad dream.

Some dreams, if heeded, are providential.

Henry Sims, seventy-two and many times a grandfather, slept in his Miami home, dreaming of a fire twenty-five years earlier in Live Oak, Florida.

His brother-in-law had been at work in a field. His wife joined him to pick peas. When she looked back, the house was burning. A wood stove had ignited the wall. Other men had to hold back Henry Sims's brother-in-law as the blazing house caved in. The oldest boy and the baby perished inside.

This night in Miami twenty-five years later, Henry Sims saw it all again in his dreams. "I was dreaming about them. I never dreamed nothing like that before." The dream so moved him that he awoke, a sob in his throat.

He opened his eyes and could still smell the smoke. It was 4:20 A.M. He sat up in bed and realized that the smoke was real.

He jumped up, thinking first of the children. He opened a door and saw nothing but black smoke. His hand clamped over his mouth and nose, he made his way to their room. He led his handicapped daughter Marie, forty-five, and granddaughters Sheila, thirteen, Kim, twelve, and Jaklin, sixteen, to safety. His shouts awoke his grandsons, Nathaniel Williams, twenty-two, and Anthony Sims, fourteen, and a visitor, Bobby McGredy, twenty-two, in another bedroom. Williams needs braces and crutches to walk. His teenage cousin Anthony snatched him up and carried him outside.

Henry Sims's wife was still away, at the hospital where he had also spent the evening with an eighteen-year-old granddaughter, Louise, a dialysis patient. At ten P.M. he had decided to go home for the night. Their home and possessions were lost, but had Sims not been there the loss would have been far greater.

Sometimes the warning is far less explicit, but no less ominous.

Three young women and a teenage boy died in a bloody wreck on U.S. 27. Two other boys were critically hurt. Two of the dead women were elementary school teachers. The third had joined the weekend outing, to an Optimist League football game in Tampa, at the last minute, to replace Maria Zarabozo, twenty-six, who had suddenly refused to go. She had had a premonition.

A school secretary and close friend of the two teachers, Zarabozo had accompanied them on many vacations. All three wore identical silver rings, souvenirs from a trip to Peru. But this time, she told me, a dream the night before had changed her plans. The identical dream had come in the past, always signaling death and tragedy. In the dream, she walks down a path and encounters a strange small boy in white. "Every time he comes into my dreams I know that something bad is about to happen, either to me or to somebody close to me."

She told her friends. They insisted she accompany them. She refused.

"Don't pay attention to premonitions," one of them scoffed. "If something is going to happen, it'll happen."

She saw them off. "I hugged and kissed each one good-bye," she told me, weeping. They had laughed.

"Do you think you're not going to see us again?" one asked.

She shrugged. "Maybe."

The woman who died in her place agreed to go at the last moment, to help with the driving. Nine miles north of Andytown and five miles south of Bean City in Palm Beach County, a southbound tractor trailer, hauling frozen vegetables to supermarkets, sideswiped a Dodge towing an airboat on a trailer. The huge truck swerved out of control, crossed the northbound lane, slammed into the guardrails, careened back onto the road and crashed head-on into the young teacher's car, which burst into flames. The burned bodies were identified by the identical silver rings that matched their friend's.

The small boy in white first began to haunt Maria Zarabozo's dreams in Cuba when she was seven—before an aunt's fatal accident. She wishes she had never seen his small pale face. "I wish this didn't happen." she said tearfully. I believed her, but she was alive.

Other nightmares are dead right and need no interpretation. A Miami man's dream of death solved his own murder and led police to his killer. Rafael Gonzalez, owner of a wholesale fish and poultry market, had a terrifying nightmare one Friday. He told employees that in his dream he was robbed and shot by a former employee named Roberto Alvarez. The vivid dream was so chilling that when the former employee appeared on Sunday, asking to buy shrimp, Gonzalez refused to open the door.

Tuesday night another knock came. The next morning a customer saw blood seeping from beneath the locked door of the market. Gonzalez had been shot three times. The cash box was empty. Police had no suspects. A shocked employee told detectives about the dead man's dream. Cops and reporters are skeptical at best about dreams, premonitions and psychic phenomena, but this was at the height of Miami's 1981 murder epidemic and detectives were crime-weary and overworked.

"It's spooky," Homicide Sergeant Richard Napoli told me, "but I'll take help from anywhere."

Dubious detectives, who had no other leads, visited Alvarez, who agreed to be fingerprinted. Then police found a witness, a neighbor, who had seen former employee Roberto Alvarez leaving the market around the time of the murder. Crime-lab experts matched Alvarez's fingerprints to those found on the cash box and the dead man's car. Confronted, he confessed.

Some people know they are about to die.

James Edward Jenrette, eighteen, told his brother he dreamed he would be shot down by police. He was.

Soon after the dream Jenrette's girlfriend complained that a man had slapped her. Jenrette took his brother's gun to seek justice. He and the man were fighting when police arrived in the neighborhood on an unrelated call. Jenrette saw them and ran, but he still had the gun. They ordered him to halt. He did, but when he turned, still holding the weapon, they shot him down.

"I won't be seeing you again," a regular customer told a Miami barmaid. He said he had just purchased a cemetery plot and asked her to "put a Schlitz on my grave." Just the whiskey talking, she thought, as he waved and walked out the door.

Moments later he was dead, hurled a hundred feet by a car as he crossed the street.

The sense of déjà vu is palpable as I cover story after story of history that repeats over and over. Almost as though there is a cruel lesson to be learned, a fateful pattern that, if somehow deciphered, would all make sense.

At age seventeen Ruth Betty Porven, who loved music and played the piano, survived the car crash that killed her date. Her injuries were critical. Ten months later, Ruth Betty Porven, now eighteen and still recovering, went on a date with a nice boy with a new car. There was another crash. This time Ruth Betty Porven and her date were both killed.

Robbers murdered Serafin Lopez, seventy-three, shot him in the head and stole the money from the family supermarket. I covered the killing and interviewed his daughter-in-law. Four years later, almost to the day, robbers murdered the dead man's son, Jorge Lopez, forty-nine, shot him in the head and stole the money from the family supermarket. I covered the killing and interviewed the same woman, now widowed.

A twenty-two-year-old Dade County Jail prisoner died in his cell, hanged himself with strips of bedsheet. Eight years later, his twenty-two-year-old brother, a Dade County Jail prisoner, died in his cell, hanged himself with strips of bedsheet.

Milton Facen was never tried for killing a man in an argument over a crap game. The week before his trial he was killed in an argument over a crap game.

A jury acquitted Glen Watkins, twenty-one, of drunk driving. He went out to celebrate and died in a crash, driving drunk.

I don't believe in Big Foot, the Bermuda Triangle or UFOs, but how do you explain the helicopter that slammed upside-down into a huge, water-filled rock pit in northwest Dade County—the precise location of a mysterious cargo plane crash exactly two weeks earlier?

What *is* this? What the heck is going on here?

And how is it that some people just can't seem to be killed?

A suicidal youth, age nineteen, threatened to leap from the ninth-floor roof of a Miami Beach apartment house. As two Miami Beach policemen edged toward him in a desperate rescue attempt, he flung himself off the ledge to certain death. He plummeted nine floors and splashed into the building's small pool, sending a geyser of water high into the air. He emerged from the shallow end and trudged to a waiting ambulance. He had missed the paved patio by inches, a feat no trained stuntman would dare.

The gunman who shot King Dixon five times in the head at close range was astonished. He had emptied his gun into Dixon's skull but Dixon, forty-six, still stood, staring at him in shocked surprise. The startled gunman finally succeeded in decking Dixon by slamming him over the head with the empty weapon. Then he ran, along with everybody else in the bar. A passing patrolman witnessed the stampede and asked why they were all running. "A man's been shot in the bar," somebody cried.

"Who shot him?" the cop asked.

"I did," burst the shooter, still unnerved.

The cop locked the man in his patrol car and ran inside. Dixon lay on the floor bleeding from multiple bullet wounds in his head. The cop took one look and radioed for homicide. But then the wounded man sat up, staggered to his feet and began to complain to the cop about what had just occurred.

Not one of the .22-caliber bullets had penetrated his skull.

Dixon was treated at a hospital and sent home, where I talked to him the next day. "My ears are still ringing," he said. "The gun was right at my ear. Those shots were really loud." Other than that, he felt fine. "I guess you have to ask the good Lord why I'm still alive."

But the bullets did kill him. I found King Dixon at the morgue eight years later. Since the shooting he had suffered seizures, and one of them killed him.

The medical examiner blamed the old bullet wounds and ruled the death a homicide.

King Dixon became Miami's only murder victim in 1984 killed by bullets fired in 1976.

Three days before Christmas a robber shot college student Barry Williams in the face, at point-blank range, at the gas station where he worked nights: cold-blooded murder, but Williams did not die. He did not even fall down. The startled robber squeezed the trigger again. That slug grazed Williams's hand. When the robber leveled the gun a third time, Williams fought back. The gunman fled. The first bullet had penetrated the skin, then stopped—no fractures, only an Excedrin headache.

"It's a miracle," said Homicide Detective Luis Albuerne, a man never given to exaggeration. "It must have been old ammunition."

Some people seem impossible to kill, yet innocent bystanders die suddenly, struck by stray bullets that fall from the sky.

Such anomalies always remind me of my friend D. P. "Book 'Em" Hughes, former cop and chief of operations at the Broward Medical Examiner's Office. Book 'Em's Blackboard Theory: "There must be a big blackboard in the sky. If your name is on it, you're gonna die today. If it ain't, you ain't."

Take the Chicago fireman who retired to North Miami for the good life and was killed by a bullet that hurtled straight down out of the sky as he stood outside his home. Police theorized that the slug may have been fired into the air three quarters of a mile away. They never learned who fired that one, or the bullet that wounded a fifty-five-year-old carpenter during a springtime stroll. The bullet entered his upper back, trajectory straight down. "It dropped out of nowhere," he said, nervously eyeing Miami's wide and innocent blue sky.

Some things bigger than bullets seem to tumble out of nowhere and appear in unexpected places. The strange case of Sevanda Margarita Hernandez Pacheco would have mystified Rod Serling himself.

Her last afternoon was spent happily. She and two friends talked, fished and cooked hamburgers on Watson Island, until a cloudburst ended their pleasant weekend picnic. The three women piled into their car as the rains came. Sevanda sat in the right rear seat of the two-door Chevrolet. The other women sat in the front. Turning left to leave Watson Island in a heavy downpour, the driver pulled into the path of a Lincoln driven by a Miami man. His car hit theirs, just behind the driver's door.

A Miami Beach city employee saw the accident. He notified Miami police and medics at 7:42 P.M. and gave first aid to the two women in the Chevrolet. The driver of the Lincoln, stunned by the crash, also saw only two women. They told rescuers that their friend had been in the backseat. Puzzled police could not find her.

At 7:58 P.M.—sixteen minutes later—a caller to Miami Beach police reported "something lying in the street." An unidentified woman lay dead in an intersection at Lenox Avenue and Fourth Street.

A car had run over her body, leaving tail pipe and muffler burns.

The day after the Watson Island accident, Sevanda's niece reported her missing. Her aunt was found at the morgue, listed as a Miami Beach accident victim. The puzzle is how she traveled from the scene of the accident to the place where she was found, minutes later, in another city, 2.2 miles away. The body had not been dragged. Where did she die? Was she Miami's forty-sixth auto fatality of the year, or Miami Beach's twenty-fourth?

Maybe she was ejected out the car window on impact.

Maybe a passing motorist picked her up, panicked and dumped her when she passed out or died. But why would anyone pick up a victim at an accident scene and drive her away?

Maybe she landed atop a passing car or truck headed to South Beach where she rolled off. But wouldn't any motorist be aware of a body on top of his or her car?

Maybe she was scooped up into the undercarriage of a large truck and later disengaged at the spot where she was found.

None of the theories makes sense.

"It's unreal," the Miami investigator said.

"It's very weird," the Miami Beach investigator said.

"We're not going to charge anybody with anything. We just want to know how she got there," one said, issuing a public appeal for the answer. None came.

So many mysteries go unsolved.

Who is buried in James E. McCoy's military grave? And who collected his death benefits?

McCoy died of natural causes in a Miami VA hospital. His widow's attempts to bury him in a military grave, however, were rejected. The burial site had already been used and his death benefits collected eight years earlier. The name, serial number, Social Security number and dates of military service were identical. The first man was obviously not the real McCoy.

Who *was* he?

And why would a Miami Beach fireman strip naked and ride his high-powered motorcycle at speeds in excess of eighty-five miles an hour at 10:45 A.M., roaring through a toll booth, off an expressway ramp, through a red light, crashing, his body bouncing off the autos of four horrified motorists? He wasn't even wearing a helmet.

What is going on here?

A powerful explosion with green flashes, a white glow and a green fireball shattered the upscale home of a Miami realtor, nearly killing his two college-age sons. Floor beams were blown out, the front door hurtled onto the lawn, and windows, still in their frames, landed in the treetops. First theory was a gas leak, but truth was that the blast was triggered when one of the boys plugged in a television set and turned it on. He lost his right leg and an eye, and was burned over 90 percent of his body. His severely burned brother had stolen the TV set from a parked car. The set was rigged—booby-trapped.

Investigators first suspected that "somebody got tired of getting ripped off and set it up for a thief," but that theory faded in light of the bomb's complex construction, a sophisticated combination of high- and low-order explosives that rained a never-identified silver dust down on the wreckage. Was the deadly device built to retaliate against thieves? Or did the boy steal it before a bomber could deliver it to its intended target? Were the plans of some international terrorist thwarted by a petty thief?

We have all walked into buildings where we felt at ease, comfortable and at home, and we have all walked into places where we did not. Perhaps it is design, decor—or perhaps, the history. Such as the Miami Beach high-rise constructed on a historic and troubled site. In a relatively young city, only seventy-five years old, few addresses conceal such secrets and stories. Carl Fisher, the eccentric, far-sighted millionaire who founded the city, chose the oceanfront site to build a home for his teenage bride, Jane. Finished in 1915, their elegant mansion, The Shadows, surrounded by green lawn and blue sea, was the hub of high society. As Fisher's workmen literally tore a city from a morass of worthless swamp, the finest house in all of Florida was alive with music, laughter and grand parties.

But things went wrong, and the splendor faded. Jane left him. Fisher died a broken man, down to his last $400,000. Jane died destitute, in New York.

They never knew that the deserted beach, where Fisher built his mansion out of love, had an earlier, violent history. Startled workmen unearthed the secret when Fisher's dream house was demolished in 1965 to build a twelve-story apartment building. Earth-moving machinery turned up an ancient cannon and parts of a sailing ship. Other items, including pieces of eight, were reportedly pocketed by construction workers. The cries of drowning sailors and the death of a ship wrecked on treacherous shores had been long buried by shifting sands. Instead of preserving the site and excavating the ship, it was lost forever. The builders refused to delay construction and poured concrete over all of it.

But things went wrong. A two-year zoning tangle erupted in the fall of 1967 when the city discovered that the project had too many units and too few parking spaces. Daily summonses were issued. The owners were convicted in city court, but a higher court overturned the conviction. The veteran building inspector who issued the certificate of occupancy was forced out of his job. The builder, a Beach city councilman, dropped out of politics.

Apartments in the building filled quickly, but strange things began to happen. Benjamin Weinstock, seventy-five, was first, found near the pool, wearing only his underwear, his skull so shattered that no one recognized him, until his wife called from their tenth-floor apartment to report him missing. He had been in good spirits, she said, waiting for her to return from shopping with his favorite pastry.

Maybe he was dizzy, police said, and accidentally fell over the balcony railing.

Next was Tola Lishner, fifty-one. Her husband and a porter were in the sixth-floor apartment when it happened. She suddenly began to pace between the living room and bedroom, they said. When she did not return from the bedroom, they followed. She was no longer in the room. She was standing out on a ledge. They ran to the window—too late.

Ann Ganz, sixty-three, followed from the eighth floor, less than a month later. She left a kitchen step stool beneath her open bedroom window. Her stunned husband said nothing was wrong. They had just eaten lunch together, and he had returned to work.

Six months later, Dolly Raz, seventy, joined them. An employee at a nearby hotel saw her at 7:30 A.M., wearing a pink bathrobe, standing astride the sixth-floor railing. She let go once, screamed, then grasped the rail. About a minute later, she let go, the fourth resident to plunge from the building in sixteen months. I know of no other Miami Beach structure with such a record—or such a history.

Many Miamians are dead serious about voodoo hexes and Santeria curses. One man, age thirty, maddened by the belief that he had been rendered impotent by a voodoo curse, emptied a gun into the man he accused of placing the hex.

Perhaps it cured him, but now he suffers the curse of life in prison.

Evidence of Santeria rituals is everywhere. Bowls of blood, sacrificed animals and graveyard desecrations by people who claim freedom of religion. When a police officer stopped a couple sneaking out of a cemetery at dawn, a human skull fell from beneath the man's shirt.

Sometimes I accompany homicide detectives on the midnight tour of duty, a time like no other to see the city I love. One night we took a routine call, the natural death of a man in his forties. The victim worked nights at a restaurant. He had come home and collapsed while climbing the front stairs to his apartment. Death came suddenly, with no warning. Up until then, his evening seemed routine. He was carrying a Cuban sandwich and a newspaper home with him.

His apartment, virtually empty of furniture, was not routine. A letter written in Spanish, in a feminine hand, lay in front of a decorative gold-framed mirror in the foyer. Pennies were scattered across the pages.

The man's sweetheart had moved out a week earlier, furious after an argument. She took the furniture and left the letter. A young Spanish-speaking police officer translated. Sergeant Mike Gonzalez, Detective Louise Vasquez and I stared at each other as he read it aloud. The writer was bitter and had cast a Santeria curse on her former love.

"You will die," she had written in closing.

He did, of course, within days.

And Rod Serling would have loved the two little girls, both twelve, one a weekend guest—home alone at midnight—who outdid each other telling spooky stories. They scared each other so badly that they fled the house with all its ominous creaks and shadows. As the frightened youngsters ran to seek refuge with a neighbor, they saw heavy black smoke curling from the house next door. They pounded and kicked until they woke the sleeping occupants. The house was filled with smoke. The cord on a new air conditioner had overheated, setting drapes and carpeting on fire. The couple who lived there never would have awakened had it not been for two little girls scaring each other in the dark.

The Twilight Zone—sometimes I think I've been there.

Chapter 5

BETTER THAN REAL LIFE

Reality has come to seem more and more like what we are shown by cameras.

—SUSAN SONTAG

Bullet-riddled bodies, orphaned babies, grim police controlling the chaos with yellow ropes: murder in Miami—as usual.

But this one had something no murder scene in Miami ever had before: a movie star.

Hollywood had come to *The Miami Herald* to shoot *The Mean Season*, a movie starring Kurt Russell and Mariel Hemingway, with Russell portraying a police reporter. Some scenes would be shot at the newspaper, and the director had asked me to take Russell out on the police beat to prepare for his role.

It would be a learning experience for us both.

I was not thrilled. I like working alone. This is not entertainment, I told myself, this is real life, serious business. In addition I had little faith in Hollywood's dedication to reality. When scenes for *Absence of Malice* were filmed at the *Herald* years earlier, Sally Field had accompanied a reporter on a story to prepare for her role. Sally quickly became bored and departed. We never saw her again, except on the big screen.

So I was surprised and slightly annoyed one afternoon when Kurt Russell called and asked to come by the newsroom. Sure, I said, warning that if a story broke I might be gone before he arrived.

A short time later a stranger appeared at my desk. "Hi," he said, "I'm Kurt Russell."

He looked rumpled enough to be a reporter: gold-rimmed spectacles, faded blue jeans, tennis shoes and a T-shirt from a small-town Colorado bar.

I had only seen one of his films, *Silkwood*, and clearly remembered the scenes with his shirt off, but I would not have recognized him now. Not only was he fully clothed, but his entrance was so unobtrusive that no one else even looked up. "Where's your entourage?" I asked. He had none.

Minutes later, as if on cue, a story broke: a double murder. The movie star was surprised that in spite of deadline urgency, we had to fight bumper-to-bumper rush-hour traffic in my nine-year-old car to reach the crime scene. "It never even occurred to me that you have to deal with the stupid everyday things like rush hour."

He was right. Getting there is *not* half the fun.

The neighborhood was residential. A young married couple had been shot to death, murdered in their own home. One eyewitness: their toddler son, fifteen months old. The orphan was found clinging to his mother's body, drenched in her blood and wailing. An older brother, age three, was safe in nursery school. No one had picked up the older child, so school officials notified a relative, who discovered the bodies.

The crowd was mostly neighborhood residents. We mingled with the morbidly curious, the police and the press. The murderer had escaped undetected, but Kurt Russell would not. Since I would not have recognized the actor in a crowd, I did not expect anyone else to. Wrong.

As the star absorbed the real-life drama, the atmosphere began to change. A man in the crowd stared. Some young girls gawked and giggled. An irate young woman, about to slam her door to avoid my questions, paused, eyes fixed on the face over my shoulder. Her expression softened, her lips parted. A middle-aged woman in Red Cross shoes forgot the sheer horror of the crime and trotted after us in hot pursuit of Kurt Russell's autograph.

He had hoped to remain invisible, had even considered wearing a disguise—"big frizzy hair, bushy mustache, big horn-rimmed glasses," he told me later. He does not understand why people seek autographs. "It's not a painting you can admire, it's only a little bit of a trophy."

Gut reaction masked, he pleasantly complied with the request as the woman burbled praise for *Silkwood*. She clutched her little trophy. She had broken the ice.

A cry echoed through the crowd. "Do you know who that is?" Fellow suburbanites slaughtered in their home were suddenly forgotten. A TV news crew caught on. Their camera swung into a 180-degree turn. Dead bodies and babies forgotten, the film crew stampeded after the star, clamoring for an interview. The crowd followed.

Police officers assigned to crowd control at the crime scene looked puzzled. Only moments earlier they had to force people to stand behind the yellow ropes. Now they were no longer necessary. The crowd had run off in pursuit of some stranger. We dashed for the car and made our getaway.

I was surprised. So was Kurt Russell. He had underestimated his appeal. Even if recognized, he had expected to be ignored because of the sensational events at the murder scene. Wrong again.

I thought my job was the real stuff, gritty true life-and-death drama, but to most people what they see in darkened movie theaters, at twenty-four frames per second, is far more compelling. They are fascinated by a re-creation of life, somehow bigger, better and far more appealing than the real thing.

Russell later told costar Mariel Hemingway: "I guarantee you that if somebody was lying in the street bleeding and you came up, they'd forget the emergency. The victim would be crying 'God! Get me help! My leg's been cut off . . . Wait, wait a minute. You're Mariel Hemingway!' "

Later events proved him right.

The crew was shooting a murder scene on the beach at dawn. Coincidentally, a real-life murder was unfolding on the beach that dawn. The scenario began late the night before: A young couple had been drinking wine and cuddling in a car parked near the water. A stranger emerged from the shadows, announced he was a police officer and ordered the young man to step out of the car. When he did, the stranger battered him to death with a baseball bat.

The killer kidnapped the girl. She was raped, driven aimlessly around the city, then left in a strange neighborhood.

Police took her back to the murder scene as they tried to piece the story together. The teenager sobbed inconsolably, with good reason. Her date had been brutally murdered. She had been abducted and violated. A policemen happened to mention the film crew shooting nearby. The victim's sobs subsided. She asked if they thought she could get to meet Kurt Russell. The cops said they would try.

The actor readily agreed, after being told the story. He sat and counseled the girl for some time.

Counseled? Who needs a rape counselor when you have Kurt Russell?

We talked a lot. We both took notes.

I was not hooked on the filming at first. The *Herald* will only permit Hollywood to use the newsroom after midnight, and I am usually gone by then. But one night I worked late on an investigative piece about a police official who had apparently been removing his trousers at elementary school playgrounds and exposing himself to little girls.

As I pounded out the story, I could not help but notice the busy and industrious film crew. They were constructing a railway so the chief cameraman and the director could zoom around the huge newsroom while shooting a chase scene, the one where reporter Kurt Russell hurdles desks and crashes into a copy boy as handsome homicide detective Andy Garcia tries to stop him.

The crew was quick and efficient. They knew what they were doing. It was remarkable how quickly they conceived, constructed and completed the project. Ingenious. I could not help but think of Metrorail, the mass transportation system Dade County leaders had been building for years. They never seemed to finish, and it never seemed to work. Cost overruns were staggering. It is still costing us money. President Ronald Reagan once commented that it would be cheaper to buy each Miami commuter a Cadillac. He was probably right.

Yet this small, unassuming crew swiftly built this miniature Metrorail in no time at all, and it worked perfectly. The difference, of course, was that taxpayers were not footing the bill. Unlike most politicians, these film producers demanded value for money spent. It was exciting to see efficiency and creativity in action, something working right for a change. Deal with government long enough and you forget it can be done.

I finished my story and stayed all night. Next morning I asked for all my vacation time so I could spend the next four weeks watching the film crew work. They have the unbelievable ability and knowhow to turn night into day and day into night. They create their own thunder and lightning—and rain. Real rain does not photograph well, and their rain is better, it looks more real than the real thing. And they can turn it off whenever they like.

Heck, Hollywood *is* better than real life.

ROMANCE

Love is a crime that requires an accomplice.

—CHARLES BAUDELAIRE

Take this job and forget small comforts, such as relationships, romance and a social life.

Working weekends makes sense on the police beat, so my days off are Monday and Tuesday. For a time I dated a lawyer. One night we planned dinner at eight. The timing would be tricky, since I worked until seven, but I thought I could pull it off.

Wrong again.

Minutes before seven, an emergency alert sounded at Miami International Airport: a plane with hydraulic problems limping in for a landing. I snatched up a notebook and raced to the airport. The big jet circled for a long time, then touched down. A perfect, though heartstopping, landing, while emergency crews stood by. I hurried back to the *Herald*, wrote a short and went home, tired, but happy. It was 11:00.

On my front door I found the lawyer's business card. Oh no, I groaned. How could I have forgotten? A single word was scrawled on the back: *Why?*

I don't know why.

I have no explanation for how everything else diminishes in importance when a news story is breaking or how a planeload of people in trouble commands the total focus of my attention, making personal matters such as love and sex insignificant at the moment.

People smarter than I am, with better-balanced priorities, can handle it all. I guess I can't.

A man I loved at the time called one afternoon. On deadline, on my first newspaper job, I snatched up the telephone, eyes riveted to the clock, pressured, pumped up, mind careening in panic between the three stories I had to finish in forty minutes.

The caller casually drawled, "Hi, sweetheart."

"Who is this?" I snapped. In the silence that followed it occurred to me who it was, of course, but I had no time to explain, and the words, already spoken, were irretrievable.

Obviously there is little romance on this job and even less as the years speed by, but no matter. There are small, special moments to savor.

Such as when I called a young Latin homicide detective to talk about a murder he was investigating. "Are you gonna write a story?" he asked.

I said yes. "Good," he said. "I always learn something new about my cases when you write about them."

Neat.

A Metro homicide detective, big, brash and sometimes obnoxious, called to shoot the breeze about his efforts to solve a perplexing murder mystery. "What do you think?" he finally blurted. "What would you do?"

Throwaway lines to them, but they mean a heck of a lot to me.

And then there is Police Lieutenant Arthur Beck, a man I would run away with—if I could mix business and pleasure and he were not happily married. But I can't, and he is. So he's never asked, and if he did, I couldn't go.

Arthur Beck is different than most cops. A wholesome, sentimental man with a goofy sense of humor, all Little League, which he coached, Disney World, where he frequently takes his family, and fun, which he has—except when on a case. Then he is as serious as a stroke.

When we first met he was a new homicide sergeant who had never dealt with the press. It was the weekend, and I was at headquarters talking to him when his radio spit out a shooting in Overtown. We both headed for our cars. I pulled in right behind his unmarked Plymouth at the crime scene, an old wooden-frame rooming house.

Mattie Davis, a seventy-one-year-old woman in spectacles, was the shooter. The man she shot was sprawled on the floor, paramedics working on him. Her niece was nearby, covered with blood, her forehead split wide open.

Mattie Davis owned and operated this old rooming house. Wearily, in the matter-of-fact manner of a woman at the end of her rope, she explained what had happened: One of her tenants, Edward Leon Dukes, age thirty, had turned into a monster out of a nightmare. She had no way of knowing his history of violence when he rented the room, but he quickly began to terrorize and brutalize her and his fellow tenants. He refused to move out.

The problem seemed solved when the tormented rooming-house tenants heard on the street that he was wanted for murder, for shooting a man during a crap game. Somebody tipped off police one night after Edward Leon Dukes came home. Sergeant Beck himself had arrested Dukes.

To the relief of the peaceful tenants, he was gone. For good, they thought, but they never took into account the vagaries of our justice system. Edward Leon Dukes was declared criminally insane and committed to South Florida State Hospital. Four months later, doctors pronounced him competent, and a judge found him not guilty by reason of insanity.

First stop for the newly freed Edward Leon Dukes was his old rooming house. Still seething about his arrest, he bullied and assaulted Mattie Davis and her tenants and kept coming back, again and again. Mattie Davis took out an assault-and-battery warrant. He found out and returned, enraged. He caught her on the second floor, knocked her down and kicked her in the stomach. When Bea Moore, her niece, age forty, tried to stop him, he smashed a bottle across her forehead. As he battered her niece,

Mattie Davis marched downstairs to get her gun. She had never fired the .38-caliber revolver purchased for protection a year earlier.

She ascended the stairs, holding the gun. Edward Leon Dukes saw it and ducked into a room occupied by two other tenants. Mattie Davis squeezed the trigger. A round smashed through the heavy wooden door as she shouted for the frightened tenants to get out. They emerged and stampeded down a back stairway. Dukes peeked out, saw Mattie Davis still holding the gun and slammed the door. He stood with his back flat against it. Her next bullet crashed through the door and into his back.

She handed the gun to the first police officer who arrived.

"I'm glad I hit him. He's a bad man," Mattie Davis told us. Bruised and disheveled, she sighed and sat down heavily in an armchair near an open Bible. A good, church-going woman, she had never had so much as a jaywalking ticket in her life.

The bloodied niece confronted Sergeant Beck. "You should be ashamed for letting a man like Dukes out on the street. I hope he dies."

Beck was not at fault for Dukes's release, but he represented the system. It was only natural to blame him.

I asked Sergeant Beck what he planned to do now.

"Arrest Mattie Davis," he replied.

"How could you?" I whispered, horrified, realizing, of course, that I was not remaining entirely objective.

"I hate to do it," he said, his expression not at all apologetic, "but I have to charge her." He had already conferred by telephone with an assistant state attorney who advised him to make the arrest.

Dukes was a violent man with a violent history. In addition to murder, he had been arrested half a dozen times for assault. One Miami street cop told me Dukes had been involved in at least seven shootings.

Arthur Beck arrested Mattie Davis. The charge: assault with intent to murder. I was worried. If Edward Leon Dukes died, she would face trial for murder. But what if he didn't die? He would surely come back, madder than hell.

I rarely sympathize with people arrested, especially for violent crimes, but this case was different.

Mattie Davis was treated for her beating injuries in the prison ward of the same hospital where surgeons fought to save Edward Leon Dukes, the man who had inflicted them.

The good news was that a judge released Mattie Davis in her own custody. She certainly was not about to run away.

The bad news was that her freedom would end if the charge escalated to murder.

I asked a doctor about Dukes's chances. He was not hopeful. Edward Leon Dukes died less than twenty-four hours after he was shot.

Sergeant Beck's hard-nosed lieutenant showed little sympathy for Mattie Davis. "She will be charged with murder," he announced to the press.

The newspaper story had gone out on the wires. Sergeant Arthur Beck, the good-natured cop who had had little prior contact with the press, began to receive hate mail from as far away as Canada, the Virgin Islands and England. Shame on him, they wrote, for arresting Mattie Davis.

The far-reaching power of the press astonished him, especially when many of the letters were addressed to "Sergeant Arthur Beach Beck." I knew how that happened. Reporters typed stories then on specially treated paper that split into three copies. The pink ones went to the wire service. On first reference to the sergeant I had typed Beach, not Beck. Force of habit. I had worked for five years at a small local newspaper where all the stories were about Miami Beach. I found it almost impossible to type *B-e* without automatically following with an *a-c-h*. My penciled correction did not go through to the pink copy.

We had long suspected the wire services of being lazy. Ditto for many subscribers, radio and TV news people who simply "rip-and-read" stories off the teletype. A *Herald* newsroom prankster had proved the point by typing a story about the discovery of a World War II German U-boat at the bottom of Biscayne Bay, its mummified crew intact. He made it all up of course. The German submarine was top news story on a local TV network affiliate that night. There was hell to pay in the *Herald* newsroom.

My explanation was simple—but Beck did not buy it. His mother's maiden name was Beach. He was now convinced that the jackals of the press were probing his ancestry. Full-blown paranoia had blossomed in a formerly good-natured and easygoing individual.

The state attorney's office, highly sensitive to publicity and public opinion, began to rethink the case against Mattie Davis. "If the facts I have heard are correct," State Attorney Richard Gerstein announced, "it was a serious mistake for anyone [from his office] to advise them to arrest her. It was an obvious case of self-defense, and she should not be charged with anything." He assigned a top assistant to review the facts.

Days later, as irate letters continued to pour into police headquarters, Gerstein made his decision. After hearing accounts from five eyewitnesses, he decided the shooting was justifiable. Mattie Davis would not face a murder charge.

Sergeant Beck, who had taken all the heat for arresting the woman, on advice from that same state attorney's office, was disgruntled. He insisted that Edward Leon Dukes, on the other side of a door, his back turned, no longer posed a physical threat to Mattie Davis and she had no right to shoot him.

The sergeant accused Gerstein of a decision based on "politics." I dutifully scribbled his angry diatribe in my notebook, as he blamed the state attorney's action on the "publicity the case received in the newspaper." In other words, my stories.

Mattie Davis rocked on her rooming-house porch, relieved and apologetic. "I'm sorry. I'm very sorry. But it's a big relief to me and to my tenants that he's gone. I did everything I could to get rid of him," she told me. "I had him arrested three times, and they didn't do nothing but turn him loose. He lived by the gun. It was either him or me. He wasn't crazy. He was just mean."

Made sense to me.

Though all was well, except for Edward Leon Dukes, of course, the case had obviously ended a friendship. It was not the first time, but Beck was a good cop and a decent man. I would miss him and the wacky stories of his misadventures at Disney World.

Surprisingly, the sergeant was not hostile when next encountered at a murder scene. Soon after, he invited me to join him for a cup of coffee. We shared a small table. "I've got a present for you," he said shyly. Ceremoniously, aglow with anticipation, he removed a small square box from his pocket and presented it with a flourish. I knew what it was immediately because of the tell-tale inscription on the lid. Arthur Beck is sentimental, for a cop. So am I, for a reporter. The small box is still on my desk. The bullet inside is flattened and misshapen from slamming first through Mattie Davis's heavy wooden door. I would not trade that piece of lead for one of Elizabeth Taylor's diamonds.

Who says there is no romance on the police beat?

Part Two

THE CITY

Chapter 6

HOME, SWEET HOME

Being born in Paterson, New Jersey, had obviously been a mistake, because I was a Miamian on sight.

Seeing the city for the first time was like coming home, and the love affair endures. The hot-blooded heartbeat of this passionate and mercurial city touches my soul. Palm trees silhouetted against swiftly changing sky and water, towering clouds under full sail, lightning that pirouettes across a limitless horizon and the sheer violence of sudden storms—they all leave me breathless.

Perhaps Hollywood is to blame. As a little girl, the film *Sinbad the Sailor*, starring swashbuckler Douglas Fairbanks, Jr., captured my subconscious and changed my future forever. I realized that recently, when I saw it again on TV. Sinbad sails turbulent Technicolor waters beneath brilliant azure skies, singlemindedly seeking the home of his long-lost father, an island called Deryabar. No one else believes it to bc morc than a myth, but Sinbad searches the seven seas, his quest peopled by monsters and villains, adventurers and beautiful women, until, at last, he finds Deryabar and happiness.

When I saw Miami, its turbulent, Technicolor waters, and its brilliant azure skies, I had found my Deryabar. The color and sweep are identical, the monsters and villains certainly as evil, the heroes as courageous.

Perhaps because Sinbad survived the raging storm at sea, I had little respect for ominous weather when I first moved to Miami. I actually looked forward to a hurricane, fantasizing about wearing new boots and huddling with warm bodies at a hurricane party, where we would gaily lift our glasses, daring Mother Nature to do her worst.

Then I met a real hurricane.

Until then, I had always believed that Mother Nature was on my side. I had no fear of earthquake, typhoon, tidal wave or shark. I had never seen any of them.

As my first hurricane threatened, backtracking across the Caribbean, skirting Florida's coast, sweeping by, wheeling around, then steaming our way, I observed the natives: They took the oncoming storm seriously, boarding, taping and shuttering windows, moving boats and cars to high ground, emptying supermarket shelves of canned goods, bottled water and batteries.

Eager to join the preparations, I stocked up on soup and bought a candy bar. At age eight I read how the Bobbsey Twins survived a blizzard by building a fire, melting a chocolate bar and some snow, and drinking the hot chocolate.

My landlord was more realistic. He urged me to evacuate at once. My apartment, poshly labeled the "Penthouse," was actually a freestanding one-room efficiency on the roof of a Miami Beach apartment building. It more resembled a tool shed than a penthouse. When I called to have a telephone installed, the Southern Bell representative asked my apartment number. When I said penthouse, she tried to sell me half a dozen extensions.

Home was the perfect hideaway. Climb three flights, crunch across a flat gravel roof, and there was my penthouse shed, with its jaunty porthole window. I loved it.

The landlord, my mother and my friends pleaded with me to leave it as Hurricane Betsy swirled her billowing skirts along the Florida coast. I steadfastly refused until the wind began to whistle strangely through the powerlines strung around the penthouse. I fled, forgetting my new boots in my haste. I took my cat, Niña, with me to the lobby of a sturdy beach hotel for some hurricane partying. My mother and some friends were there. So was Billy, a distant and disturbed relative by unhappy marriage. The authorities—school, law enforcement and psychiatric—were constantly on his case. I had never spent much time with him, but he had never seemed all that disturbed. In fact, he seemed fascinated by my cat. I was flattered, until late in the evening, when Billy mumbled, his eyes a glassy stare, "She's so pretty, all pink and white. I'd . . . I'd like to squeeze her." At that moment the lights went out.

Clutching my cat and my raincoat, I decided to take our chances at the penthouse. We drove back on empty streets, through heavy rain. No problem—the hurricane had been scheduled to slam ashore by ten P.M., and it was nearly midnight. Obviously Betsy was not coming. We all had overreacted.

Niña and I quietly climbed the stairs, glad to be safely home. The power was out everywhere, so I lit candles, and we went to sleep. I awoke to what sounded like a chorus of women wailing in my room. The penthouse rocked. Water gushed in. Niña clawed her way frantically to the top of the bookcase, dislodging half a dozen volumes that splashed to the floor—into three inches of water. My battery-operated radio was still dry. Two radio reporters driving a mobile unit into the teeth of the storm shouted that a roof had just landed in the middle of Seventy-ninth Street, a few blocks away. Large objects were crashing onto the roof around the penthouse. Through my porthole I could see the fireworks of fallen wires cascading in the wind.

The high-pitched howl was deafening. Niña ran crazily around the room, slipping and splashing to escape the forces of wind and water all around us. We finally huddled together under a blanket on the bed. My record albums floated by. The candles flickered out. The phone was dead.

We were next.

Suddenly, there was an ominous silence. I knew what that was: half-time. The eye of the hurricane was passing over us. Time to get out of there before the second half of the storm hit. Holding on to Niña, I darted out the door, across the roof—avoiding fizzling wires strewn about like spaghetti—and yanked on the door to the stairwell. It would not open. It was locked, tied shut in fact, from the inside.

My murderous landlord was trying to kill me. What had happened, of course, was that the landlord had seen me evacuate earlier. He did not see me come back and, sometime after I did, he had secured the door so it would not bang in the wind.

I was trapped on a roof in Miami Beach in the eye of a hurricane.

Strangely enough, I felt almost calm, like a captain resigned to sinking with his ship. If my cat and all my worldly possessions were to be blown away, I might as well go with them—quietly. We were so emotionally drained and exhausted that during the fierce and howling second half of the storm, Niña and I actually fell asleep.

At three A.M., I was awakened by my landlord's astonished shout to his wife. "The penthouse is still there!"

He trained his flashlight on my door. I opened it, and he turned pale. "You couldn't have been up here during the storm!" He shone the light on our faces and knew we had been.

The week that followed, without phones or electricity, was anticlimactic. That hurricane, when I was new to Miami, instilled a new respect in me for Mother Nature. As each year's storm season ends, I breathe a sigh of relief. Don't want to see any more hurricanes around here.

New Miamians and people who visit have a notorious disregard for Mother Nature—as they do for almost everything else. Maybe it is the merciless sun, the depleted ozone layer or a grim determination to have a good time, no matter what.

Treacherous rip currents spawned by heavy winds drowned three tourists and left a fourth in critical condition one day. They all had ignored warnings. One was told personally by lifeguards that it was too dangerous to venture into the water. He insisted that he had gone swimming every morning for ten days and had no intention of disrupting his routine.

His body washed up a short time later, disrupting his routine permanently.

You would think that that would scare the rest of the swimmers out of the water. Not in Miami. Determined to have fun or die, they ran like lemmings into the sea, many within sight of the blanket-draped corpses on the beach.

Weary lifeguards rescued nineteen.

Miami's ever-present heat and humidity and the big thunder moon of summer seem to affect human behavior profoundly.

How else can you explain the wealthy young tourist from Brazil? An excellent swimmer and skindiver, he liked to hold his breath under water and would enlist friends to clock the minutes as he sat on the bottom of his condominium pool trying to break his own record. A friend was timing him one August afternoon when the manager strolled by and casually asked how long the man had been under water this time. Told six minutes, the manager leaped into the pool to try to save him. The man from Brazil had apparently removed the grate and placed his body over the drain to hold himself down.

"He couldn't have realized how strong the suction is in these pools," said assistant medical examiner Dr. Garry Brown. "It's like putting your hand over the nozzle of a vacuum cleaner."

The desperate manager tied a hose around the man and tried to drag him out of the pool. But "the entire weight of the water, eight feet above him, was pushing him onto the drain," said chief deputy medical examiner Dr. Ronald Wright. They finally freed him by shutting down the pool pump to break the suction.

By then it was too late.

What could explain the bus driver arrested after fracturing an elderly passenger's skull during a dispute over whether he should pay the twenty-five-cent senior fare or the full fifty-cent fare? The reduced rate for senior citizens went into effect at 6:30 P.M. The passenger insisted the time was 6:32. The driver said it was 6:29. The call for the ambulance was logged at 6:44.

During that same sweltering stretch of summer a naked body

lay ignored on the front lawn of a well-kept home for two weeks.

"I don't know how they couldn't have noticed," complained assistant medical examiner Dr. Stanton Kessler, inspecting the now skeletal remains. "The houses are only twenty to thirty feet apart."

A timid sixty-five-year-old woman experienced a problem with her Chevrolet Nova for an entire week in August. Something was dangling under the car. A white cord trailed from the undercarriage. Her sixty-seven-year-old gentleman friend tugged and yanked at the cord in a crowded supermarket parking lot. When he could not pull it loose, they drove to a service station.

"A bomb," the gum-chewing mechanic announced. Attached to the rear axle. He was matter-of-fact and all business. "Do you want me to take it off?"

The couple decided against it. They drove the car seven blocks to the Coral Gables Fire Department.

The man, gray-haired, slightly built and wearing a little hat, went inside to tell the dispatcher there was a bomb taped to a car. The dispatcher referred them to the police department. "They handle the bombs," he said.

The couple went to police headquarters. "We've got something under our car," the man complained.

Officer Randy Jaques took a look. "It looks like a bomb!" he screamed.

The county bomb squad was summoned, rush-hour traffic diverted, and the streets around headquarters evacuated. Bomb experts gingerly removed the device, carried it to the middle of the empty street and detonated it with a water cannon as a hushed crowd watched. There was quite an explosion. Had the mechanic tried to remove it, he could have lost the entire gas station, the experts said.

The couple had no idea who would do such a thing. Detectives suspected a case of mistaken identity.

Police officials were shaken. "There is a lesson to be learned here," police spokesman Dennis Koronkiewicz said grimly.

"There are bombs out there. And people do place them on cars. This is far more than a prank."

He sternly advised people with bombs on their cars not to drive them "anywhere—let alone to our police station."

The Miami Chamber of Commerce was even less amused when a knife-wielding robber hijacked a busload of foreign visitors bound for Disney World. Their abductor took the distinguished group on a wild ninety-minute ride.

The passengers, including ten members of a tour from Spain, spoke no English. The hijacker spoke no Spanish.

"It's hard times, hard times, man," the robber mumbled. He said he needed money. The crime became a jurisdictional nightmare for police because the hijacker robbed the passengers one by one, as the commandeered bus cruised north, then south, at his direction, across the boundaries of several different police departments.

At one point the driver grappled with the hijacker over the knife as passengers hurriedly stuffed their money into their socks and shoes and the runaway bus picked up speed.

Police asked the rescued tourists if they would return to testify if the hijacker was caught. Only if the United States paid for the trip, they chorused.

More frustrated were Coral Gables police in their hunt for a one-legged man who escaped on foot—literally. His artificial leg was left at the scene of the crime, ripped off by his estranged wife as he attacked her savagely with a tire iron. When neighbors intervened, he hopped off the front porch and made his getaway. "He had to hop fifty to a hundred feet to his car," Lieutenant James Butler said. "If his car hadn't been there we could have caught him."

Some people do not love Miami. A homesick Mariel refugee tried to swim back to Cuba, starting in the Miami River. Police tried to coax him aboard their boat. When gentle persuasion failed they turned to shrimp nets, then grappling poles. Crowds lined the river cheering on the sweaty officers, who finally hauled him from the water with a boat hook. Struggling with his rescuers, he demanded to go home.

He gave as his local address: "wherever I am at the time."

Miami is stranger than fiction, a city where somebody embezzled the tax money intended to fight crime, where thieves armed with axes and cutting torches felled hundreds of three-hundred-pound aluminum light poles to sell for scrap, leaving expressway motorists to careen in the dark; a city where doctors attribute sudden outbreaks of suicide to barometric pressure and where one Halloween became a horror show for police, with thirteen people shot. Officers assigned to the "Pumpkin Patrol" blamed egg throwing that escalated and roving bands of teenagers in Ninja costumes.

Street-smart Miami children, some as young as six, learned how to open parking meters with screwdrivers and looted thousands. A ruthless gang of Mariel refugees bid on old police cars at auction. They shopped for uniforms, guns, holsters, nightsticks, handcuffs, badges and radios at police equipment stores and formed their own "police department." The "officers" robbed, kidnapped and shot shocked citizens who believed they were the real thing. They killed five and were suspects in four more murders before bewildered real cops caught on to the other force, a dark one, out there.

Overhead, Venus, brightest of all the planets, star of the summer night, shines so brilliantly that Miami police are frequently plagued by UFO reports. Observers think they are seeing a star explode, and a confused air-traffic controller once gave it permission to land.

Miami is full of strange and wonderful people—some out of control. As a rookie on my first reporting job in Miami Beach, I covered the predawn exploits of a cherubic young platinum blonde named Peaches. Her real name was Emily, but no one used it. Chubby and fresh scrubbed, from a highly respectable and wealthy family, Peaches persisted in speeding through the city naked at the wheel of her open sports car. Only God knows why, but Peaches loved it.

Other motorists, particularly bus drivers and truckers with more lofty vantage points, would drop their jaws when she pulled up beside them. So would police officers, who arrested her for indecent exposure. She appeared in court, demure in blue and white gingham, and good-naturedly paid her fine, smiling coyly, with lowered lashes, at the handsome young cop who had arrested her. Much to his embarrassment, she sent him roses at police headquarters. Officers arrested her again at five A.M. on the same charge. They accused her of wearing only a Turkish towel—"containing many holes"—as she drove through Miami Beach.

"I'm trying to lose weight, and I was going home from the health studio," Peaches explained. "I always wear just a Turkish towel on the way home."

Made sense to me.

"I think I'm in trouble this time," she confided, though she did not seem unduly concerned.

Peaches lived in Surfside, a small, eight-block-long oceanfront municipality just north of Miami Beach.

"They never arrest me there," she pouted. "They even let me go swimming at night in the nude. They guard the Ninety-sixth Street beach for me. They are why I moved to Surfside."

Surfside police denied ever hearing of her. I believed Peaches. No way she could live in Surfside without coming to their attention.

"The only reason they keep arresting me here," she said, "is because I get so many tickets. I'm a speed trap," she sighed. She slid behind the wheel of her Corvette, blew a kiss to a group of watching police officers and roared away.

A county judge with no sense of humor sentenced her to 120 days in jail and a thousand-dollar fine for four speeding tickets. He recommended she undergo psychiatric evaluation. I could not picture free-spirited Peaches behind bars. I never saw her again. In the press of stories and deadlines, I lost track of her. Though I thought of Peaches every time I saw a speeding sports car, she seemed to vanish from the face of the earth.

A year later I was reading copy off the newswire after a devastating earthquake in Italy. The story listed names, ages, and home towns of Americans killed and injured in the disaster. One leaped out at me: from Miami, a young woman named Emily. It had to be Peaches. First, middle and last name were the same. So was her age, twenty-two. She was among the injured taken to a Rome clinic. Neither her condition nor the severity of her injuries was mentioned.

Our newspaper was so small and impoverished that we were not even allowed to make toll calls, much less overseas to Rome.

I have no idea why she was in Italy, how badly she was hurt, or if she is still alive. If so, she is middle-aged now, perhaps with chubby blond daughters of her own. She remains a symbol, to me, of Miami Beach in its youthful, more innocent days.

I hope Peaches survived the storm and found what she was forever racing in search of: her own Deryabar. And I realize how fortunate I am, to have found my island home, surrounded by turbulent Technicolor waters under brilliant azure skies.

Chapter 7

MIAMI, OLD AND NEW

There is no new thing under the sun.

—Ecclesiastes 1:9

Miami is—and always has been—a city seething with intrigue and tension.

Hot-headed motorists pull guns in Miami traffic. You can buy an Uzi at the five-and-dime, and would-be warriors rehearse for war in the swamps.

The uninformed mourn a paradise lost. How sad, they say, that such a magic place has become so violent—but violence is nothing new to Miami.

A woman and her faithless lover reclined on a blanket beneath the tall, whispering Australian pines at Cape Florida not long ago, listening to bird songs and the sounds of the sea. She waited until he dozed, then shot him in the head.

I drove out to the murder scene, on the tip of Key Biscayne, a strip of beach with an old lighthouse, jungle and pine forest. A homicide detective suggested that this was the first murder at Cape Florida.

Nope. The first recorded homicide at Cape Florida took place at the lighthouse—in 1836. Rampaging Seminole Indians wounded the lighthouse keeper and cornered him in the tower. Overwhelmed, trapped, convinced he was a dead man—the attackers had massacred his assistant—the lighthouse keeper did the only thing that made sense at the time. He hurled a keg of gunpowder down the narrow stairwell, knowing it would explode. He was committing suicide, and he hoped to take a few Indians with him. To his surprise, he survived. The force of the blast generated outward. The Indians ran away screaming, some of them on fire.

Sounds like a Saturday night in Miami in 1991.

The spirit of the lighthouse keeper survives. Modern Miamians, innovative if nothing else, fight back the best they can against marauders who threaten to overwhelm them. In the same week a Liberty City businessman electrocuted a burglar with a booby trap rigged in his oft-looted shop, a Homestead businessman shotgunned and killed a robber after chasing him half a mile in his car, and a middle-aged Miami woman awakened at 1:15 A.M. by the sound of breaking glass investigated and found a man halfway through her living-room window. He proceeded no further. She bashed his skull with an axe handle—twice. Police found him draped over the windowsill.

Headlines and editorials spotlight the current crop of embarrassingly inept or corrupt Dade County leaders, guilty of malfeasance, misfeasance, nonfeasance or all three.

They also are nothing new—they are the wretched legacy of U.S. Army Major Francis Langhorn Dade.

The father of our county was a pompous ass and a know-it-all who led his troops into disaster. His only claim to fame was being massacred.

Dade was a Virginian whose mother's kin hobnobbed with George and Martha Washington. He served in the War of 1812 and with Andrew "Old Hickory" Jackson in Pensacola in 1821. When Spain ceded Florida to the United States, Seminole Indians were scattered across the peninsula. Jackson forced them onto a central Florida reservation.

By the time his old boss became president, Dade was an infantry commander in Key West. White settlers soon coveted the territory the Indians occupied. President Jackson, the old Indian fighter, ignored past promises and ordered Florida's Indians to move west of the Mississippi, to Arkansas. They refused to go peacefully, and a chief named Osceola took leadership in the dispute. Old Hickory was harsh, and trouble was imminent. A deadline was set. The Seminoles were to be rounded up at bayonet point on January 1, 1836. Believers in treaties and justice, the Indians hoped that Washington would relent, but when the government refused to change plans, the Indians made their own.

Fort King near Ocala was manned by a small garrison under the command of General Wiley Thompson. In December, as the deadline neared, reinforcements were sent to back up Thompson and his handful of men. That it was Major Dade who led the contingent of a hundred soldiers was mere chance. The wife of a captain was gravely ill, and Dade volunteered to take the man's place.

Dade had boasted that he could march one hundred men through the entire Indian nation; now he could prove it. They marched out of Fort Brooke, where Tampa is now, on December 23, 1835. The 106-mile trek took them through the heart of Indian country, across rivers and creeks, through swamps and piney woods. Indians stalked them from the start. They would have attacked sooner but Osceola, who engineered the assault, and Micanopy, another leader, were away on other business.

Osceola had hurried ahead to Fort King to kill General Thompson. The grudge was personal: Thompson had thrown him in irons the previous summer. Osceola also wanted to avenge his young wife, the daughter of a slave woman. Slaves' descendants were considered slaves themselves, and whites had seized Osceola's wife. The chief was eager to ambush Dade and his men, but settling the score with General Thompson took first priority.

A seasoned veteran of the military in Florida, Dade had helped build the road between Fort Brooke and Fort King in 1824. He knew the land, and he knew the Indians. He kept advance and rear guards and flankers on the alert for Seminoles, but after crossing the forks of the Witlacoochee River, into open pine and palmetto country, Dade relaxed his vigilance. He withdrew the scouts. Indians had never attacked in daylight in country covered only by scattered pines. The major scoffed at repeated warnings from a sharp-eyed slave who kept pointing out signs of Indians.

The column marched across open land at eight A.M. on December 28. The weather was cold, in the forties, and a chilly rain had fallen. At Major Dade's instruction, his soldiers buttoned their overcoats over their muskets and ammo boxes to keep them dry. No scouts were sent into the low-lying sawgrass, as was usually done on marches. The Seminoles, hidden in the brush among the palmettos and pines, watching the troops trudge by like ducks in a shooting gallery, must have sniggered up their sleeves.

The soldiers were two thirds of the way to their destination when Micanopy arrived. He and two other leaders, Alligator and Jumper, assembled the warriors at Wahoo Swamp, five miles west of the trail Dade traveled, and decided to attack.

Rumors down the century hint that the soldiers had depleted their rum rations and were suffering from hangovers that day. Records indicate that Major Dade also had a fondness for rum and that he had escaped court-martial for drunkenness and sloppy record-keeping only because he was not considered worth the trouble.

Still ignoring the warnings of his slave interpreter, Dade now felt secure. They had left Indian country and were in white man's territory. What he did not realize was that Indian country was anywhere the Indians wanted it to be. Major Dade left the column—only officers were on horseback—to move up and ride point. He shouted out cheerfully as he passed his men, promising them three days' rest and a Christmas celebration at Fort King.

Those were his last words. As he uttered them, Micanopy was taking aim. As Dade reached the advance guard, he was shot dead off his horse. The first barrage killed or wounded half his command. The soldiers fell before they could wrestle their guns from beneath their bulky buttoned coats.

The Indians withdrew to regroup. The captain who had lingered at the side of his gravely ill wife had caught up to the column and took command. During the half-hour lull, he ordered survivors to chop down pine trees and build a fortification—instead of running for the woods, which would have made more sense. The logs were only knee high when the Indians launched their second attack. The last soldier was cut down by two P.M. One hundred and three were dead; five were West Point men. The captain died with them. His sickly wife lived another sixty-one years. The mulatto guide and four soldiers escaped alive. The guide was welcomed into the Seminole Nation. An Indian killed one of the soldiers as he fled toward Tampa Bay, but three survivors made it to safety and reported an attacking horde of 400 to 1,000 Indians.

The Indians said they had 180 warriors: 3 were killed and 5 wounded. The debacle, one of the Indians' most decisive victories over American soldiers, took place four years before the birth of George Armstrong Custer.

That same afternoon, Osceola surprised General Thompson and a lieutenant as they strolled outside Fort King smoking cigars. He killed and scalped them both.

History books refer to the battle as the "Dade massacre." When the army won, it was victory. When the Indians won, it was a massacre.

The shot that killed Francis Langhorn Dade began the Second Seminole War. It was long, unpopular and never won, like Vietnam. The Seminoles battled on for seven bloody years. The United States eventually sent forty thousand soldiers against a Seminole force that never exceeded fifteen hundred. The price was $20 million and fifteen hundred dead soldiers, the costliest, in lives and money, of all our Indian wars.

Osceola led his nation in battle for only two years of the war, but his guerrilla strategy so baffled U.S. troops that his enemies hailed him as a military genius. When the government could neither capture nor defeat Chief Osceola, they invited him to engage in peace talks, under a flag of truce. They guaranteed he would not be arrested.

They lied.

When Osceola arrived to pursue peace for his people, he was seized and thrown into a dungeon. He died there, at age thirty-four. Official cause of death was variously described as malaria, pneumonia, tonsillitis, and a broken heart.

Osceola had refused treatment from the white doctor assigned to his care. His instincts were right. The doctor decapitated his corpse, put the famous chief's head on display and used it to frighten his children when they misbehaved.

Our longest war until Vietnam ended in 1842, without a treaty, but with nearly all the Seminoles relocated beyond the Mississippi. A few hundred hid deep in the Everglades and survived.

The Indians were cheated and lied to by white men whose treaties were masterpieces of double-dealing. The scheme was to force them out west so speculators could seize their Florida property. Those early land-grabbing leaders were no different from the politicos and developers who continue to pillage South Florida today.

Violence did not end with the Seminole wars. The Ashley gang lived some of Florida's bloodiest adventures. John Ashley hunted and trapped in the Florida wilderness until 1911, when he was accused of murdering a Seminole Indian named Desoto Tiger. He showed up in Miami shortly after the slaying to sell eighty animal hides stolen from the dead Indian. On the run for murder, Ashley became the state's most wanted frontier outlaw and bank robber.

Even Carl Fisher, the entrepreneur who would soon build Miami Beach from a swamp, posted a $500 reward for Ashley's capture. Nobody collected. Ashley remained at large. He and his gang, which included his sweetheart, Laura Upthegrove, his brothers Bob, Ed and Frank, and at least four other men, robbed a bank in Stuart. Shot in the eye during the robbery, Ashley was captured and taken to Miami to stand trial for murder.

On a hot summer day at one o'clock in the afternoon, young Bob Ashley arrived in Miami to save his big brother John from the hangman. The sheriff saw Bob Ashley pedal up to the jail on a bicycle. He thought the cyclist was just a local boy who wanted to talk to a prisoner. When the sheriff went to lunch, Bob Ashley rapped on the door of the deputy sheriff's residence, adjoining the Dade County Jail. When Deputy Wilber Hendrickson answered, Bob Ashley shot him in the heart. The deputy's wife grabbed a rifle, aimed it at Ashley and frantically yanked the trigger, but the weapon was not loaded. Ashley snatched the deputy's keys and ran toward the jail. But the gunshot had been heard and men came running. Ashley panicked, dropped the keys and fled. He tried to commandeer a passing delivery truck, pointing his gun at the driver's head. Two Miami police officers overtook him. Officer John R. Riblett, revolver in his hand, tried to take Ashley alive. That mistake was his last. As they struggled, Ashley shot him in the jaw. The officer staggered, Ashley stepped back, took deadly aim and fired again. Struck near the heart, Riblett squeezed off three shots. One went wild, one hit Ashley in the body, the other slammed upward into his jaw and emerged from the top of his head.

His fellow officer rushed Riblett to the hospital. The sheriff quickly arrived and took Ashley there also. His deputy was dead. Riblett died soon after, Miami's first police officer killed in the line of duty. He left a wife and a child.

Despite Ashley's mortal wounds, an angry mob gathered outside the hospital. The sheriff took the dying prisoner to the jail for safekeeping and the lynch mob followed. News reports say that Bob Ashley, frothing red from the mouth, lay on a bunk, in a cell, eyes glazed, "a death rattle in his throat." The grim sheriff visited John Ashley's cell. Was the young man who killed the jailer and the police officer his brother? Was Ashley aware in advance of the attempt to free him? The prisoner denied knowledge of the aborted jailbreak and was allowed to see his dying brother. Too late—Bob Ashley was already dead when his older brother arrived at his side.

Miamians were jumpy. Rumors flew, amid fears that the well-armed gang was planning to swoop down on the city to exact revenge and free their leader. There was talk that the governor would be called upon to send in the National Guard, but calm was eventually restored.

John Ashley won a new trial and the murder charges were dropped. Convicted of bank robbery in 1916 in West Palm Beach, he was sentenced to seventeen years. After escaping a chain gang, the one-eyed desperado and his gang embarked on a three-year spree of bootlegging, rum-running and hijacking, robbing and plundering along Florida's east coast.

Legends grew in dusty Florida boom towns, some that the gang probably never visited. Every unsolved case of robbery and mayhem in the state was attributed to the notorious gang, including a bank robbery in West End in the Bahamas.

John Ashley was captured again in 1921 and sent to prison. Being jailed may have saved his life. His brothers Ed and Frank were lost at sea in a rum-running caper months later. John escaped again in 1923 and continued his lawless ways.

The end for the Ashley gang came the night of November 1, 1924. Police got a tip that the outlaws would be crossing the bridge at Sebastian Inlet. A Model T Ford with John Ashley and three other men, one of them his nephew, stopped at a chain and a red lantern deputies had strung across the south end of the bridge. Too late, they realized they were ambushed.

Deputies said the four outlaws went for their weapons and were riddled by bullets in a wild gun battle. No officers were hurt. Witnesses claimed the gun battle was strictly one-sided, that the shooting started after the four men were handcuffed. None of the gang survived to tell their story, and the cops were cleared after a hasty inquest.

Suspicious police shootings are nothing new in Florida.

Three gang members were buried on an Ashley family homesite. Rumors persisted that $150,000 in cash was buried with them. Looters looking for the money destroyed the tombstones.

Laura, John's sweetheart, committed suicide in the Everglades. Her sad end may be the only real difference between then and now. Today she would write a tell-all book and talk about it on *Geraldo*.

Bank robberies, shootings and jailbreaks, suspected police brutality, a city rife with rumors, and calls for the National Guard to prevent more violence: Miami yesterday, Miami today.

Unsolved mysteries and unclaimed corpses are not exclusive to this generation. In 1923, the early builders of Miami Beach unearthed something terrible where the small oceanfront municipality of Surfside now thrives. In a mass grave, buried in the sand, were the bones of more than fifty and possibly two hundred unidentified people.

The Miami *Daily News and Metropolis* speculated that the remains were those of pirates tracked down and executed. Journalists quoted doctors and anatomy experts who identified the bones as those of Southern Europeans. Many were women and children, even babies, they said. All bore signs of violence: axe marks and holes in the skulls.

One Miami man said he had the explanation: a ship's log. The ship was British and had set sail from Jamaica in the West Indies in 1785, on a mission to eliminate a pesky pirate colony. An accompanying ship's chart supposedly showed the vessel anchored offshore, a mile from the gravesite. But the man who claimed to possess both log and chart was a secretive sort who never shared them. Did they exist? Or were they simply the invention of some early Miamian's fertile imagination?

A charred tree stump and broken cooking utensil unearthed deep in the burial site supported the existence of a pirate camp. The writers also pointed out that had Indians killed the victims they would not have buried them; that was not their custom. One early archaeologist insisted that the bones belonged to Indians, not Europeans. But the pirate theorists pointed out the absence of arrowheads or Indian implements—although a huge conch-shell mound was found south of the grave.

The builders removed the sand surrounding thirty of the skeletons and built a road so the curious could visit the macabre scene. The 1923 residents were apparently no different from the Miamians of today who rush to accident and crime scenes to eyeball the carnage.

One exposed skeleton was that of a man more than six feet tall. Few Indians grew to that stature. A botanist concluded in 1929 that the bones were probably those of aboriginal Indians along with a few white men they had captured.

In the 1930s archaeologists excavated what was left and announced that the bones belonged to long-extinct Tequesta Indians, some perhaps three thousand years old. They crated about fifty skeletons and shipped them by train to the Smithsonian Institution for study. The crate was either lost or stolen somewhere along the way; the Smithsonian claimed it never arrived. The archaeologists maintained that the shipment arrived but was mislaid in the Smithsonian basement.

The mass-grave mystery will probably remain unsolved forever.

People and politics do not change. Miami's first police chief was charged with murder, acquitted and reinstated.

Then, of course, there was Scarface.

Feeling the need to escape the high stress of mob business and blustery Chicago winters for fun in the sun, Al Capone found himself a Miami Beach retreat. The house on Palm Island had been built by Clarence M. Busch, of the Anheuser-Busch brewing dynasty. Capone bought it for $40,000 in 1928 through a "dummy," so residents would not know that their new neighbor was America's most notorious mobster. He installed more than $200,000 in improvements. A wharf was built for his yacht and a tropical garden planted, with a dozen royal palms. He paid $85,000 for the swimming pool alone, the first in Miami Beach with a filtration system adaptable to fresh or salt water. His cabanas were two-story, Venetian style.

The owner's name leaked out fast. Florida authorities and his wealthy neighbors were outraged.

The Capone story was written in bullets and booze.

Bullets cleared his way to the top. Mobsters dropped like flies, cut down from speeding cars. Saloons were sprayed by gunfire. A crusading prosecutor who dared to question Capone about a murder was machine-gunned from a passing car in Cicero, Illinois. Witnesses who saw Capone wield the weapon soon lost their memories. He was never charged.

His reputation grew, and he loved the power as much as he loved money. Arrested for violating the National Prohibition Act, Scarface was released the next day—with apologies. Arrested for a gangster's murder, he had the charges dropped within the hour. When the mayor of Cicero questioned Capone's authority, Scarface kicked His Honor down the front steps of City Hall.

Capone seemed to lead a charmed life. A dozen attempts to kill him failed, he seemed invincible. He wrote his own laws with a "Chicago typewriter"—a portable machine gun.

Florida Governor Doyle Carlton issued an edict to the sheriffs of all sixty-seven Florida counties: *Send Capone a message. He is unwelcome. Arrest him on sight.*

Summoned to the county solicitor's office, Capone and his attorney were told he was to get out of Miami and stay out. Capone refused. He was in Miami to stay, he announced. If pushed, he would take his case to the Supreme Court of the United States.

A lavish spender and big tipper, Capone became a local celebrity. Despite anti-Capone crusades in newspaper editorials, Miamians not only accepted Scarface but applauded when he strutted into a courtroom. The same spectators hissed the mayor and other local officials who sought to banish him, a level of respect Miamians display for their leaders today.

Capone won a federal injunction halting action against him by Florida officials. He sent *them* a message: Even mobsters have constitutional rights.

"I have no interest in politics, neither in Chicago nor Miami," he told a reporter, while puffing on a fat cigar. "I am here for a rest, which I think I deserve. I have done nothing in violation of the law in Miami and will not. All I wish is to be left alone and enjoy the home I have purchased here."

Then he took his young son Alphonse for a speedboat tour of sparkling Biscayne Bay.

Scarface became a flashy habitué of Miami nightclubs, racetracks and prize fights. His houseguests included Chicago·aldermen, mobsters and crime reporters.

Big Al often hired a local seaplane pilot to fly him and his entourage to Bimini for private beach parties. Former war ace Eddie Nirmaier charged $150 for the flight, and Capone always tipped another hundred. The picnickers would eat salami sandwiches, drink beer and then return, skimming low over the brilliant blue water.

One chilly night Capone and his cohorts visited a Miami theater, eager to see the new James Cagney gangster movie. High-kicking chorus cuties performed in a stage show first. In the finale, they tugged on a long rope. The end of the rope finally appeared, tied around the neck of a small monkey. The performing monkey wore a sign: AL CAPONE.

Scarface and five companions rose quietly from their balcony seats and strolled into the lobby. Capone introduced himself to the manager, then flattened the man with an old-fashioned haymaker that smashed his nose.

Capone and his friends returned to their seats to watch the movie mobster. The bloodied manager summoned police. The officers pondered the situation, then warned him to stop making trouble or they would shut down his theater.

Scarface was conspicuously in residence at Miami Beach on February 14, 1929. He hosted a huge party that night for politicians, members of the press and local businessmen. The butler wore a shoulder holster; so did the very burly waiters. Two men armed with rifles greeted the guests, who were scrutinized closely by gunmen who even trailed them to the bathroom and waited outside the door. Machine guns were stored neatly under tarpaulins by the pool.

Seated near a table laden with food, Capone waved to arriving guests, then instructed his gunsels, "Geddem champagne."

None of the guests knew why he was celebrating—until later.

Men in police uniforms had raided a garage in wintry Chicago on that St. Valentine's Day in 1929. Police often conducted such raids, mostly for appearances' sake. Seven men who worked for Bugs Moran, Capone's archrival, were lined up against the wall, expecting at worst a night in jail. Too late they realized the uniforms were a ruse. The phony cops opened fire with machine guns. The real cops arrived later to count the bodies. The St. Valentine's Day Massacre became America's most publicized mass murder.

When a newsman who had attended Capone's party returned to ask questions about the massacre, Al looked perplexed and shook his head, saying, "The only man who kills like that is Bugs Moran."

Nobody believed him, but Capone did not let the bloody events in Chicago spoil his fun in the sun. He and his friends planned to attend the Sharkey-Stribling fight at Miami Beach on February 27. He had promised fight tickets to Eddie Nirmaier, but Big Al had other matters on his mind. The day before the fight the pilot had not received his tickets.

"I had a quantity of fireworks bombs," Nirmaier told a *Miami Herald* writer years later. "So I flew over Capone's house, triggered the fuse and tossed a bomb out of the plane. There was one hell of an explosion—in the air of course—and you've never seen so many mugs in your life. They all ran out of the house with their pistols in their hands. I thought for a moment they would start shooting at me."

He buzzed the house again, to drop a paper parachute with a note asking where his fight tickets were. "By the time I got back to the dock and got out of my plane, Capone's chauffeur was driving up with my tickets."

The prank only served to further unnerve Capone's swanky neighbors, already irate about gangsters conducting machine-gun practice off the dock in the cool of the evening.

Refreshed from his Miami stay, Big Al returned to Chicago. During a lavish dinner party, he flew into a rage, ranted that three of his guests were disloyal, picked up a baseball bat and bashed in their skulls.

Still it seemed he could never be beaten. When Capone, loud-mouthed and imperious, was finally toppled, it was not by bombs or bullets: Pencil pushers brought him down, government crime busters with adding machines, not machine guns. At first he failed to take the tax charges seriously, not even bothering to show up for court. He went to the racetrack instead.

Shortly before his 1931 trial, Capone summoned a tailor. He ordered two new lightweight suits for Miami's subtropical climate. "You don't need to be ordering fancy duds," a cohort snorted. "Why don't you have a suit made with stripes? You're going to prison."

"The hell I am," Capone replied. "I'm going to Florida for a nice long rest, and I need some new clothes before I go."

Capone was wrong. His nice long rest was for eight years—behind bars. By the time he saw Miami again, the suits no longer fit.

Expecting a slap on the wrist, Capone swaggered into court fat and smug. The judge socked him with an eleven-year sentence. His twelve-year-old son, his mother, wife, brother and sister, all saw him off to federal prison in Atlanta. He posed cheerfully for photographers and boarded the train. That was May 1932. He was thirty-three years old.

The former crime czar was soon transferred to a new island home, Alcatraz, and served seven and a half years before being released on parole.

The news swept Miami Beach: Al Capone, the city's most notorious snowbird, was coming home. His lavish island mansion was groomed and ready, newly painted and ablaze with lights that November of 1939. Reporters clustered at the barred gates and crowded sightseeing boats circled like sharks, hoping for a glimpse of the resident who made the city the least proud.

Rumors of Capone's arrival in Miami Beach proved premature. Hours after his release, he was admitted to a Baltimore hospital.

Capone's wife, Mae, pleaded with hospital personnel to "avoid publicity." His brother John blamed Big Al's illness on "his confinement in prison." Stories spread that the mobster had gone stir crazy. Gangland friends who visited called him "as crazy as a bedbug." Truth was that the mobster was undergoing treatment for paresis, a brain-destroying disease caused by syphilis. The first symptoms, confusion and slurred speech, had surfaced in prison. His Maryland doctor was the nation's foremost "syphilologist."

Years earlier, a teenage mistress had been diagnosed as syphilitic, and Capone was advised to take a blood test, but the mobster hated needles.

Capone celebrated Christmas 1939 in his hospital room, with his family and a gaily decorated tree. The patient who spent his time playing dominoes scarcely resembled the Chicago liquor king who had enjoyed a million-dollar-a-year income and ruled a mob of seven hundred.

Capone remained in Baltimore for medical treatment and did not return to Miami Beach until March 20, 1940.

Several appearances that summer fueled rumors that he was recovering. He and a party of friends strolled into a Miami Beach nightclub one evening, took a remote table, listened to the orchestra and left quietly, well before midnight. A few nights later Capone and his wife dined at a bayfront restaurant as a bodyguard watched from the bar.

The outings were a test, his doctor said later. The patient was never alone. Scarface sometimes stepped out of his car, but only to walk into a corner drugstore. "He likes to go in and buy chewing gum and Sen-Sen," his doctor said. "He likes to chew Sen-Sen." Soon even those excursions ended, and Capone was confined to his estate, where he endlessly practiced his golf swing, swam in the pool, lolled on the patio in the sun and fished from a pier. Never mentioned were the days when he was the storm center of mob wars that had cost more than one thousand lives.

"He seems to have a blank memory about that phase of his life," the doctor said. Soon Capone's only physical activity was batting a tennis ball against a wall, and that was on his good days. On the days he attempted gin rummy, family members and servants always let him win. A visitor from Chicago, unaware that he was supposed to lose, bested Al at gin. Capone flew into a rage. "Get the boys!" he shouted. "I want them to take care of this wise guy."

Other gangland friends dropped by, but Scarface barely recognized his old henchmen. His memory hazy at best, he was safe at last from mortal enemies. As far as the underworld was concerned, Al Capone had been dead a long time.

The public learned the truth when a Chicago man created a furor by accusing Capone of a plot to kill him and seize his business. With family permission, the mobster's doctors revealed to the press that Capone now had the mind of a child.

"When he first came to my attention, a large part of his brain had been destroyed," his Baltimore doctor said. "He hasn't sufficient intelligence to run his own life, much less the affairs of a vast crime syndicate."

In those days, much of Miami Beach shuttered in the summer. Even police officers were laid off during the slow season and called back to work in the fall.

Rookie cop Emery Zerick was a policemen without work that summer of 1946. He went to the Capone estate for a job. "They had lots of complaints about too many sightseeing boats and too many cars going by looking for Al Capone."

Big Al's brother Ralph paid off-duty cops good money: fifteen dollars for a twelve-hour day.

By then the world's most notorious mobster drooled and babbled unintelligibly. "During the day they would wheel him to the end of the dock and put a fishing pole in his hand," Zerick recalled. "When a sightseeing boat showed up, we had to rush him back inside. He weighed very little, he had shrunken."

Zerick guarded the front gate, equipped with a telephone. He connected visitors to Ralph, then discreetly stepped away. Ralph would give authorized visitors a signal to give the young cop at the gate. The signal was changed daily.

Zerick learned to ask no names, but recognized Meyer Lansky, a "fast walker who used to bounce when he walked," as well as Tony Accardo, Jimmy Doyle, Joe Fischetti and Joe Massei.

Capone's health worsened and a death watch began, with reporters and underworld cronies on alert. Scarface would rally, then slip away. "A bunch of black cars would show up every time he had a relapse," Zerick said. Gangland visitors always slipped twenty- and thirty-dollar tips to the young cop who admitted them. "Every time he had a relapse I would make three or four hundred dollars. There used to be a plaster statue of a saint in the yard, and as they went inside, they all used to bless themselves."

By January 1947, the end was clearly near. Scarface observed his last birthday on Friday the seventeenth. He was forty-eight. Four days later he suffered a cerebral hemorrhage. After fourteen hours in a coma, he rallied again. Capone's doctor emerged with an update at ten P.M.: The patient, though critical, would probably survive the night. The mansion remained brightly lit.

The next day, Saturday, January 25, 1947, Zerick was at the Palm Island estate, moonlighting after being recalled to the police department. Capone seemed stronger, but pneumonia had set in. "Ralph said he was having a relapse. Everybody was in an uproar. He was barely breathing." Two priests administered last rites.

Capone's heart stopped at 7:25 P.M.

"They came downstairs and said he was dead," Zerick recalled. "The wife took it hard. Ralph was blubbering. There was a leak in that place, there was a screech of cars, it seemed like a million reporters. They knew right away. I never figured out how."

A block-long line of sleek black limousines parked outside. "The hoods, all of them, showed up, making the sign of the cross and paying respects to the widow."

Tourists and curious spectators formed a promenade along the sidewalk, a regatta of rubbernecks, clustering in groups.

The Capone story did not end with his death. Hollywood has kept him alive. No hoodlum has fascinated filmmakers more. "Nobody thought this would happen," Zerick said. "Nobody ever thought the Capone story would get bigger and bigger as time goes by."

Al "Sonny" Capone, the sad little boy banished from a Miami

Beach Boy Scout troop when outraged parents learned his name, saw his children shunned and tormented when *The Untouchables* became popular on television. He and his mother sued in 1959, for invasion of privacy; they lost. Sonny, a Miami dock worker, changed his name and moved to an undisclosed address.

A Delta Airlines pilot and his wife now live in the home on Palm Island. Neighbors still wince, generations later, as guides on sightseeing boats point out the house where Scarface died.

Nothing is new under the Miami sun, only the players.

Chapter 8

CHRISTMAS IN MIAMI

A Christmas card arrived at the *Herald* a week before the holiday: Santa and a reindeer. "We liked your book," said the note inside, written in shaky ballpoint script.

> We went to the book fair and liked the panel discussion . . . Also talked with some of the authors and got some autographs! T. D. Allman was wonderful, so sincere and honest when he autographed our copy of the book *Miami*. And David Rieff mentioned that it was very tiresome writing *Going to Miami*. We stopped by the *Herald* for you to autograph our copy of your book, but you had not come in that morning, or afternoon. When the movie of your book comes out, we will see it.

The address was deep South Beach, south of Fifth Street.

I parked in front of their small condo on a Sunday afternoon, four days before Christmas. How surprised they will be, I thought, when I knock on their door and say I came to sign my book. I smiled, imagining their astonished faces.

Wrong again. They were not surprised.

It is not easy to surprise people who have seen everything.

No answer. I thought no one was home. I knocked again and was about to leave when a small blue-eyed man with graying hair and the stubble of a beard cracked open the door. He wore a T-shirt and wrinkled trousers. He regarded me thoughtfully. "You're Edna Buchanan," he announced, his voice matter-of-fact. "I'll get your book."

His wife stood behind him. Behind her I could see the small room, crowded with the possessions of a lifetime. They both stepped outside to chat.

He apologized for not shaving and explained. He had been robbed on the street, once at gunpoint. If he shaved and dressed neatly, his chances of being a target would be far greater. "When I dress like this, they leave me alone." His wife wore a San Francisco T-shirt and simple slacks. She no longer carries a purse, for the same reasons. That is also why they have not had their old Volkswagen repainted. Their last car was stolen. They have learned that the only way to keep anything is to look like you have nothing. They have lived in Miami Beach since 1955, and they have learned to be survivors. He worked in a fashionable shop on Lincoln Road Mall, but the shop is no longer there, and Lincoln Road is no longer fashionable. They saw all the changes. I signed the book and handed it back to him.

"You and this book are like part of our family," he said. They remembered stories I wrote for the Miami Beach *Daily Sun*, before joining the *Herald* twenty years ago.

I wished them a merry Christmas, and they told me about their first taste of roast suckling pig, years ago. A Cuban shopkeeper on Fourth Street had become their friend. One Christmas he brought them the delicacy and insisted they try some. Not long after, they returned home and saw police lines around a covered corpse in front of his shop. They recognized the pink sneakers and the yellow socks.

Police caught the killer. "He's probably out by now," the man with the blue eyes said. His wife always liked to sit outdoors. Last time she did, her chair was almost knocked over by a running man and the police who were chasing him. When they complained about crack cocaine dealers conducting business in the burned shell of a nearby building, an impatient cop asked, "Are you willing to be a material witness?"

Of course he was not. "I'd have to sell my condo and move," he said. How could he sell an apartment in this changed neighborhood?

When they do venture out, he said, his wife walks one way and he the other. They depart at different times and use different routes. "You can't leave at the same time every day," he explained. "You can't establish a pattern. If they know when you will be gone, they break in."

I said I was glad they liked the book, and they walked me to my car. They circled my 1984 Mercury Cougar, admiring it and asking questions about the alarm.

They are good people, survivors.

I locked the doors and drove away. Holiday carols played on the car radio. Christmas in Miami.

I work on holidays. I don't mind. Married colleagues with families deserve those special times off. Fewer of my editors and top police brass work, and a reporter can accomplish more without them. I like to write holiday stories, reporting on how the rest of Miami celebrates. There is always news: Big families get together. Some turn on each other, and the shooting starts. On the Fourth of July and New Year's Eve they play with guns and fireworks, and somebody always gets hurt. On Memorial Day and Labor Day they get drunk and careen around in high-powered speedboats. Kids race out of the house early on Christmas morning to try out new skates and bicycles. Still shaky on their new wheels, some encounter motorists hung over from the night before.

Some people never make it home from Christmas parties.

Holidays bring despair to some, rage to others.

Sometimes there are stories of hope and renewal.

Sometimes, but not often.

Even though I work on those special days, I am old-fashioned and cling to tradition. I like turkey on Thanksgiving and Christmas Eve candlelight services, but one year I missed both. The day before Thanksgiving I checked the *Herald* employee cafeteria. They were already serving turkey, cranberry sauce, pumpkin pie—the works, but I waited. They would obviously have turkey on Thanksgiving, even if it was just leftovers.

Wrong again. The *Herald* cafeteria was open, as promised, on Thanksgiving Day, but all they served was leftover macaroni and cheese, scorched in the reheating. The joke was on me. So I ate burned leftover macaroni and cheese for Thanksgiving.

That was festive compared to Christmas Eve.

John Patrick O'Neill could live with his secret no longer. Alone and jobless, O'Neill, fifty, shared his home with four stray cats, his only friends. They all lived together under the east bridge of the MacArthur Causeway. From the gloom under the bridge, as traffic rumbled by overhead, they could see the city skyline, the holiday lights and the million-dollar Star Island homes of the rich and famous. On Christmas Eve, the animals lost their friend and protector.

At dark, as motorists whizzed past, O'Neill trudged more than a mile to Miami Beach police headquarters. It was Christmas Eve, and he wanted to confess. He had killed a man, he said, and buried the corpse beneath the bridge where he lived.

O'Neill had a reason. The man he killed, who was also homeless, had hurled his beloved cats, all four of them, into Biscayne Bay to drown. The thrashing, panicky animals were unable to climb the sheer concrete embankment, but O'Neill had jumped into the water after them. He rescued them, then turned to confront the man who tried to drown them.

The man, Daniel Francis Kelly, fifty-eight, pulled a knife and lunged at him, O'Neill said. O'Neill punched and stomped Kelly until he was dead, then dug a shallow grave with his hands and a piece of board.

That was on Friday, December 19. Now, on Christmas Eve, he wanted to clear his conscience.

Police were doubtful, but detectives Nick Lluy and Robert

Hanlon listened. "He wasn't drunk," Hanlon said later. "It sounded plausible."

Everybody hoped it was not true. Everybody wanted to go home. The detectives went out to the east bridge and descended into the darkness. They scanned with flashlights, probed the ground under the bridge, and found a suspicious mound, emitting an even more suspicious odor.

A fire truck with high-intensity lights arrived to illuminate the area, directly across from the Miami Beach Coast Guard base. The detectives sent for shovels and generators and began to dig.

About to leave the *Herald* for Christmas Eve services, I heard something was afoot and called police headquarters. Detective Anthony Sabatino had just bought O'Neill a double hamburger, microwaved at a 7-Eleven. "This is a heckuva way to spend Christmas," the detective said.

He was right.

I went out to the scene to see what they would find. The underside of the bridge is a haven to street people. A number of urban bedouins had camped there from time to time. There were couches and chaise longues, even a little Christmas tree with tinsel.

Police spokesman Howard Zeifman cautioned that it might be a hoax. "People have lived under here for years," he said. "It smells of rotten food, human waste and cats."

It did.

But the story was no hoax. Cops, a prosecutor, a medical examiner and firefighters labored through the night, watched by a cautious full-grown calico and a curious, half-grown black cat with a white bib. By Christmas morning the shallow grave had yielded the remains of a dead man and O'Neill was charged with second-degree murder.

"I feel kind of sad for the guy," said Hanlon, a veteran detective. "If he didn't come in and tell us about it, there's a very good chance that we never would have found it. I guess it was bothering him."

Identified through fingerprints, the dead man had an arrest

record nineteen pages long, mostly for drunkenness, vagrancy and disorderly conduct. He was remembered by police as a "nasty drunk." Hanlon himself had arrested Kelly once. A Christmas Day autopsy confirmed that death was caused by blows to the head.

In his jail cell, O'Neill worried about his friends. He called the calico the Bandit. The black with the bib was Smokey. Satchmo was a striped gray, and the Tiger was white with golden stripes. O'Neill was served a Christmas Day dinner of roast beef, but nobody fed them.

"I'm just sorry about my cats," he told Hanlon. The detective tried to catch them, to take to the Humane Society, but they scampered away, and he had no time to spend in their pursuit.

My story appeared, and *Herald* readers who care about animals created a minor traffic jam on the causeway. One woman rescued three of the cats and took them home. She never found Satchmo. "They were well, well taken care of," she said. "These were not stray cats."

John O'Neill pleaded not guilty, and I talked to him after his arraignment. He said he was not a killer. "It was self-defense. I had five lives to protect. Four of them were my cats." The fifth, he said, was his own.

He said the cats were better friends than some people. He had found each of them on Miami Beach, lost, abandoned and hungry. He had rescued them, one by one, and taken them home, to his place under the bridge. It was home to him.

"I sure love the water," he said. "I feel free there. I like it, it's outside, no rent, no nothing. I always had cat food for them. I fed them seven o'clock in the morning. When I left in the morning, I always left a big bowl of water. I also had vitamins for them. When I came home at five or six o'clock, I would feed them again and give them fresh water."

His days were busy in Miami Beach, "picking up and recycling aluminum cans, so I could feed them and myself. I also got my beer and my smokes out of it. That was my daily routine, going to get cans and feeding my cats."

Kelly disrupted the routine the week before Christmas. Other homeless men often shared the space under the bridge, and he was one of them. He snatched up O'Neill's friends—the Bandit, the Tiger, Smokey and Satchmo—and threw them into the bay.

"They were clinging to the sea wall," O'Neill said. He saved them, then faced their attacker. "If you ever do that again, I'll break your jaw!" Kelly pulled a butcher knife, he said, and rushed him. O'Neill punched, kicked and stomped the man.

"What I did was for them. I just went on hitting him." This was the first time such a thing had ever happened to him. He did like to drink and admitted his share of trouble, "but never violence."

He had lived with the burden of his secret five days and nights, then could stand the guilt no more. A practicing Catholic, "on and off," he said, "I had to get it off my chest." Jailed without bond, he would stand trial in the spring.

I asked if he wanted me to contact anyone. His mother still lived in Port Chester, New York, where he grew up along the coast of Long Island Sound, fourteen hundred miles north of Miami. She was unaware of his trouble.

"I haven't written her," he told me. "If it was something else, it would be easy, but I don't know how to tell her this."

At the office I heard from a shocked reader, a man who had grown up with O'Neill in Port Chester, where he was known as Teedy O'Neill.

"He was a leader, the one you always chose first for a baseball team," said the boyhood friend. "He was a tough, athletic kid, but never a bully." Teedy O'Neill was a drifter and a loner even then, "an outdoorsy type guy who would just drift in and out of school. He was a hero, a good guy. He wouldn't hurt anybody. He wouldn't pick on anybody. Is he a bum? No, he is not a bum. It takes quite a man to confess when his conscience bothers him."

Stories went out on the newswire, and letters of support came from animal lovers all over the country.

A jury deliberated for an hour that spring before returning a not-guilty verdict. They believed it was self-defense. The woman who cared for Smokey, the Bandit and the Tiger found O'Neill a place to stay and work at an auto dealership.

The temperature was eighty. It was April in Miami.

But it finally felt like Christmas.

Chapter 9

BEST FRIENDS

The only way to have a friend is to be one.

—RALPH WALDO EMERSON

Fred the dog sprawls on the sofa to watch television. He chews gum until the sweet taste is gone, then spits it out. He jumps up to kiss the faces of the eight Sanders children when they come home from school.

On a Friday the thirteenth he saved their lives.

"I couldn't believe it," Metro Fire Lieutenant William Hall said. "I never heard of an animal going *back into* a burning building."

At 5:30 A.M., when fire swept their Opa-Locka home, they were all asleep: Patricia, 16; James, 15; Raquel, 14; Raymond, 13; Ali, 12; Arbury, 10; Clifford, 9; Carmen, 8; and their mother, Arbury Sanders. Smoke filled the house.

They would have been overcome in minutes, but Fred, an eighteen-month-old black-and-tan mixed breed, raced to the mother's room, pushed open the door, bounded onto the bed and pawed frantically at her chest.

The sleepy woman shooed him away. Fred dashed in and out of the room, pawed the woman again, then caught her nightclothes in his teeth and tried to drag her out of bed. Fred had never misbehaved this way before. So Arbury Sanders got up and padded to the door to see why he was so upset. Fire hit her in the face.

She choked and gasped, as she and Fred herded her dazed children through dense smoke and out of the burning house.

Then Fred turned and ran back inside, galloping through shooting flames, right to the Sanderses' bedroom.

"Fred's afraid of fire," fifteen-year-old James said, "but he went back into the house to see if anybody was there. He was trying to find my daddy."

Their father, Cornelius Sanders, had gone to work on his construction job at five A.M.

As the children screamed and a neighbor dialed 911, Fred emerged from the inferno, his head singed and the skin burned off two spots on his legs. The parakeets, Salty and Coco, perished. So did the goldfish. The house was destroyed.

But the Sanders family was saved.

"We would all be dead if it wasn't for that dog," Arbury Sanders said tearfully.

Firefighters lauded Fred's intelligence and courage but lamented the lack of smoke detectors in the house. "We do not advocate that animals take the place of smoke detectors," said fire department spokesman Stu Kaufman. "A smoke detector is the only device we can guarantee will wake you up."

I wrote the story of Fred the Dog, then watched in awe as it took on a life of its own.

Fred the Dog Day was soon observed in Opa-Locka. A brass band played, and a red carpet was rolled out. It's always a hoot to watch camera-conscious politicians maneuvering and jostling in order to stand next to a VIP, like the president, the pope or Michael Jackson, but it is a delight to watch them maneuvering and jostling when the celebrity is drooling and part Doberman.

They honored Fred with pomp and circumstance, speeches and applause. The Canine Medal of Valor was solemnly bestowed during ceremonies at a Metro-Dade fire station. The Tampa-based animal-rights group that awarded the medal also inducted Fred into its hall of fame.

Mrs. Sanders, a lovely woman, and her well-behaved children nearly burst with pride. The handsome boys, in three-piece suits and ties, escorted the girls, immaculate in party dresses. Fred yawned widely, obviously bored, as Senator Roberta Fox spoke, comparing him to Lassie, Flipper, Mister Ed, Mickey Mouse and Benji. "Dogs *are* our best friends," the senator gushed. "I envy the family who owns Fred."

Opa-Locka Mayor Helen Miller issued a proclamation. "Treat him like a king," she intoned to the Sanderses, as the honoree sprawled on the floor, eyes locked onto a box of Milk-Bones. A letter of praise was reported en route to Fred from the White House. Senator Paula Hawkins and other dignitaries unable to attend sent Fred greetings. Seated on the dais with other VIPs, Fred basked in the glow of TV lights as the bronze medal was hung ceremoniously around his neck.

Few four-footed heroes receive accolades. Most are unsung, many are without a home.

As he crossed a footbridge with his dog, Henry Hollingsworth, nearly sixty, either fell or jumped and plunged thirteen feet into the water. James White, twenty-eight, saw it happen. Paralyzed in one arm and no swimmer, he could not help, but there was one other witness who did not hesitate to try.

"The dog jumped right in behind him," James White said.

The man surfaced in the water moments later, on the far side of the bridge. "The dog paddled toward him," White said, "but the man slipped under, and the dog couldn't find him. The dog kept swimming in circles, looking for the guy."

White ran for help.

Miami police found the dog, a scrawny part-Labrador retriever, racing up and down the canal bank, barking furiously.

"He was hysterical, looking for his master," Homicide Detective Jose Fleites said. Divers searched the murky water. They could not find the victim, whose frantic dog kept running back onto the bridge to the spot where his master fell, then racing back to the canal bank, plunging through dense underbrush, searching the water's edge.

"Everywhere police went, the dog went," White said. "That man would be alive now if his dog could have got to him."

White wanted to try to find the faithful animal a home, but detectives whisked him to headquarters to give an official statement. Police gave up the search for the body and left. Only the dog remained. An animal control officer arrived soon after, caught the dog and took him away.

A boat-yard worker spotted the dead man floating in the water two days later. I was concerned about his best friend and called Animal Control. They would keep the dog for a short time, they said, in case the victim's family wanted him, but apparently Hollingsworth had lived alone. No one had reported him missing after four days, and police were not even sure where he had lived.

Since no one had claimed his body, it seemed unlikely that anyone would claim his dog. No one even knew the name of the animal, still waiting patiently at the shelter. A *Herald* photographer shot his sad face, behind bars. I quoted White, the eyewitness, in my story. "Too bad," he said, about the inevitable. "That dog had a lot of intelligence."

After dozens of *Herald* readers offered homes, the dog, henceforth to be known as Duke, went to new owners with a half-acre of fenced-in yard, a pool and a golden Labrador named Duchess.

Happy endings are as rare in real life for animals as they are for humans.

Prince, a skinny street dog, has seen more than his share of trouble. Prince has been hit by cars five times. A drunken tormentor set him on fire once—just for fun—he was shot at another time, and once he saved the life of his owner, who had been attacked by a knife-wielding man.

I heard about Prince when police blamed him for a murder.

Metro officers issued a press release after arresting a man on a homicide charge, saying that the killer had shot Curtis Gervin, thirty-six, after a long-running feud. Reason for the feud: "Gervin allowed his dog to run loose, during which time the dog attempted to attack the suspect and others, numerous times." The press release concluded that in a final showdown, Gervin was shot dead.

Another basic rule of journalism: Never believe everything you read in a police press release.

Sad, I thought, that a man's best friend caused his demise. I went to see Prince, to find out how all this happened.

Police had said the dog belonged to the dead man. Not so.

"He's my dog," Kenneth Seay, twenty, proudly told me. "He saved my life once. If he was bigger, Curtis might have had a chance."

Prince was just a puppy that nobody wanted when he came to live with the Seay family six years earlier. He grew up in a tiny house with eight children, then four grandchildren. He never bit anybody, they all said, except a man who had once tried to attack Kenneth Seay with a knife and a broken bottle.

A crazed individual, the man had beaten up his own father and then attacked Seay, a witness to the family fight. Seay tried to back away, stumbled and fell. As the crazed man lunged, swinging the knife, he was attacked by Prince, who "grabbed his leg and left a gash," according to Seay, who escaped unscathed. The man with the knife later went to jail for stabbing somebody else.

The first time Prince was hit by a car he was just a pup. Running to fetch a rubber ball for Seay, Prince scampered into the path of a car and was hurled halfway across the street. Another time a car dragged him down the block. He had three other mishaps with autos. Now, family members swear, Prince looks both ways before crossing the street.

A good watchdog, he once barked at a stranger who pulled a gun and fired. Prince ducked and kept on barking.

Nobody buys dog food for Prince, who survives on scraps and has never met a veterinarian. He is still scarred from the burns suffered when his drunken tormentor set him on fire.

Prince and the Seay family lived a block from the murder scene. Gervin, a truck driver with a baby daughter, had met Prince a few years earlier. They liked each other and became friends. Gervin fed the dog table scraps, and Prince began to divide his time and loyalties between the two households.

Gervin's neighbors saw Prince often. He never tried to bite anybody, they told me.

Now police were saying Prince had caused Gervin's murder. A bad rap, according to those who knew the dog best. His owners, the neighbors and the children who play nearby agreed that all Prince did was try to prevent the killing.

Neighbors said the long-running feud and the fatal dispute were about parking, a frequent motive for murder in Miami. The killer had a girlfriend who was Gervin's neighbor in a small quadruplex. There were only four parking spaces. Gervin owned a car and sometimes drove a truck home from work.

The killer had a gun and a long police record and had been drinking that night. Witnesses said that he muttered some complaint to Gervin, who did not want to hear it. Gervin walked back into his apartment, and the man with the gun followed.

Prince was outside. The little tan mutt heard a sudden struggle. He dashed in through the open door, bit the killer and hung on to his leg, according to witnesses.

The man, with Prince still clinging to his leg, jabbed a gun against Gervin's chest and fired. The bullet blasted a hole in his heart.

The gunman fled. Prince lay motionless outside the apartment as Gervin was rushed, dying, to the hospital.

The morning after the murder, I found Prince lying morose and sleepy-eyed in front of the Seay house. He had had a bad night. Those who know him say it was not his fault that his friend was shot.

Prince did the best he could.

Many humans return equal devotion to the pets they love.

Tony Garcia, sixty-seven, a popular news photographer, dashed back into his burning home after he and his wife escaped unharmed. He fought his way through flames to rescue his best friend, trapped inside.

He emerged with his clothes on fire, "holding the little dog like a baby," a neighbor told me.

Arrow, a bilingual dachshund who responds to commands in both English and Spanish, was singed but not seriously burned. Garcia saved the dog's life, but it cost him his own.

Burned over 50 percent of his body, he died two weeks later.

At age 103, Jose Cuello's closest friend was his dog. Every morning they walked. They were always together. The old man's wife had died fifty years earlier. Cuello now spent afternoons in the sun with Surpan, his German shepherd, at his side, telling stories of Cuba to neighborhood youngsters.

Surpan once attacked a would-be mugger who fled, leaving Jose Cuello unharmed.

One morning the old man stepped outside and found the dog dying. The veterinarian said that someone had fed him a piece of meat laced with broken glass.

Jose Cuello cried uncontrollably. He took no more walks, spent no more time sitting in the sun. One day he stepped out of the house where four generations of his family resided and wrapped one end of an electrical cord around a porch railing, the other around his throat. His horrified sixty-year-old daughter cut him down. He was hospitalized, a vertebra in his neck fractured.

I talked to the man's thirteen-year-old great-grandson. "He told us he did it because he loved his dog—and missed him," the boy said.

The loss of a pet is always painful, but to some people it is the end of the world.

A newly retired Miamian murdered his wife and killed himself. They had no children, were wealthy and in excellent health. Miami Homicide Detective Louise Vasquez investigated the puzzling murder-suicide and learned the motive: The couple had been grieving and despondent since the death of their best friend, a fluffy black poodle named Midnight.

"They had him for twelve to fifteen years," Louise said. "They were really upset about his death."

Not everybody understands how strongly some people feel about their pets. Metro's fire rescue squad responded, lights flashing, siren screaming, to a frantic 911 call for help, but the paramedics refused to treat the victim.

Candy, a four-year-old West Highland terrier, died.

"I begged them," the dog's owner, a twenty-six-year-old woman, told me. "I was crying. They were laughing."

At play on the patio at home, Candy had encountered a poisonous toad. The little dog began to foam at the mouth. The owner called her vet. He was closed and instructed her and her mother to rush Candy to an animal clinic. The address was wrong. Instead of S.W. 132nd Street, the women went to S.W. 132nd Avenue. The mother held Candy. The daughter drove as fast as she could. It was 7:30 P.M.

"I was so desperate," she told me. "I knew they could save her if I could get there in time, but I was completely lost. There were no telephones, just dark streets and houses."

They stopped a Metro police officer. He led them to an animal hospital. It was closed. He showed them another one five blocks away. It too was closed. "Drive carefully," he told them and departed. Candy was still alive.

The woman was desperate. She stopped the car and ran to the nearest house.

Gloria Rodriguez was home alone with her children. It was after eight P.M. when someone pounded on her door. "She was knocking real hard and screaming like crazy. She said, 'My husband is dying in the car!' I said, 'I cannot let you in my house, but give me the number you want to call.' She said, 'Call 911!' She was going crazy. 'Please! Please! My husband is dying!' "

The emergency operator dispatched an advanced life-support

system and a crew of three paramedics. As they rolled up to the scene, "a woman waved us down," fire rescueman Keith Tyson said. "She was crying. She wanted us to help her dog; the dog had stopped breathing. Another woman in the car had a small dog in her lap. She was giving the dog mouth-to-snout resuscitation. She admitted lying, saying it was her husband. She said they were willing to pay us any amount of money to take the dog to a veterinarian or a clinic and they would follow us."

Keith Tyson, who owns a Doberman named Magic and a poodle who answers to Tiffany, refused.

The distraught women drove away. The mother continued breathing into Candy's mouth and massaging her chest. They finally found the animal clinic, after 9:00, but it was too late. Candy was almost five years old. She had been one of the family.

"The firemen just laughed," her owner said, weeping. "They said, 'It's only a dog.' "

The paramedics were furious when I spoke to them. Tyson had run red lights and counted seconds responding to the "heart attack" call. "I don't want her to go to jail, but I'd like to see a judge explain the facts of life to her. I like dogs, but I'm not going to risk my life for one."

I saw his side. Every year firefighters, as well as innocent victims, are killed or injured en route to false alarms. False reports to 911 are against the law. What if a heart attack victim had needed the advanced life-support system miles away?

But I also understood Candy's heartbroken owner.

South Florida's poisonous *Bufo* toads often send animals into fatal convulsions. Here's what to do: Wash out the animal's mouth with a garden hose, fast, then run for the animal hospital.

But first: Be sure you know where it is.

Outright cruelty to animals is common enough to break your heart. Deranged people poison innocent neighborhood pets with cyanide and strychnine. In one neighborhood two dozen dogs and cats died in their own backyards. The killer was never caught. Some smarmy humans kill pelicans and seagulls for sport.

And then there was the man from Canada.

There were half a dozen hungry and homeless stray cats, crying for food at his door. So he began killing them.

He snared each in a noose on the end of a stick, drew it taut around their throats, then plunged them one at a time into a bucket of water, holding them down until they stopped struggling.

An outraged neighbor jumped a fence to stop him and saved the sixth cat.

"It is done all the time in Canada," Victorian Theoret, sixty-four, blandly explained to the judge, adding that he was a former priest, a Ph.D. and a university professor. He freely testified that he had even killed his own dog in the same manner. An Animal Control officer, summoned by the neighbors, testified that Theoret had handed him the five sodden bodies in a sack, saying, "This is how it's done in Canada." Autopsies confirmed that the two healthy gray-and-white tabbies, two spotted tricolors and a half-grown black cat had been drowned.

"With all the shootings and murders, you wouldn't think cats would have that much importance," defense attorney Leo Greenfield said derisively. In Canada, what his client did is "customary, to get rid of pests," he said.

Another defense lawyer insisted Theoret's method was humane. The judge responded, "Let me ask you, counselor, how you would like somebody to loop a rope around your neck, pull it tight and then drop you in the water?"

Judge James Rainwater, bless his heart, the same man who locked up errant fathers who failed to pay child support, sentenced Theoret to the max—a year behind bars—for cruelty to animals.

Sounded right to me.

Of course the man never did the time. He served two days in jail until a higher court judge ordered his release. An appeal panel later threw out the conviction.

In Miami it is always something: monkeys, elephants, pigs on the prowl. An irate retired military man, never injured in the service of his country, lost his battle with a neighbor's pet pig.

I saw Pigger myself and loved him.

Lloyd Laughlin, lying painfully in his bed, right leg bandaged, did not.

"Everybody thinks of a pig as a cuddly little thing," he muttered through clenched teeth, his injured leg elevated and packed with ice. "It was not a cute little pink pig. It was a miserable monster with black hair and yellow fangs."

It's all how you look at things.

Pigger had been the beloved pet of Suzanne Banas, twenty-five, since the porker was a day-old orphan the size of a puppy. Pigger rode in the family car, lived indoors and was housebroken.

Feed a pig and you'll have a hog, the saying goes. Pigger soon grew too large to clamber into the car or the house. Though she now lived in a pen inside a fenced-in yard, Pigger, at three hundred pounds, still thought of herself as a family pet. She still slept with a blanket and still frolicked with the nine-pound Italian greyhound. They grew up together. Once they were the same size.

"She still tries to sit in my daughter's lap," said Norma Banas, Suzanne's mother, "and rolls over with her feet in the air to have her tummy scratched."

Suzanne Banas wanted to free Pigger in the wild after she outgrew the car and the house, but no wildlife officials could guarantee her safety from hunters. "So we had to keep her," Norma Banas said.

Made sense to me.

The freedom Banas could not give her, Pigger seized for herself. She took off for the outside world while her owners were at work. Her home, a former horse pen, is electrified so she cannot break out, but a fallen tree had disconnected the wires. Pigger found a rain-weakened fence post and forced her way out of the acre-sized yard. Free at last, she trotted down Ninety-third Avenue just before one P.M.

Neighbors knew what had happened at once. Pigger is popular with their children, who love to feed her and watch her eat (like a pig). Lloyd Laughlin saw her in the street. His wife even snapped a photo of Pigger's stroll down the avenue. Then Pigger wandered into a neighbor's yard. "It was rooting a hole in their grass," Laughlin accused.

The husky retiree, six feet tall and two hundred pounds, marched out to put a stop to it. "I went to within six feet of it and yelled." He denied provoking the pig. All he did was say "Yaaaaahhhh!" trying to scare the animal off the neighbor's lawn. When he turned away, he said, Pigger charged.

"It hit me in the rear and knocked me down. I've never been hit by a car. I think this is what it feels like."

He lay still, a tactic learned in military training. The creature stood over him, staring malevolently with little piggy eyes, he said. "It was rooting around my body with its nose, a big nose." Then it sank a fang into his leg "right between the calf and the ankle."

A neighbor ran to the rescue, hurling dirt and sand into the creature's face to distract her. It worked. "She just walked off," Laughlin said. His leg bloodied, he ran to dial 911. Laughlin alerted Animal Control and wildlife officers. Metro police dispatched two cars and a helicopter.

Laughlin, fifty-nine, suffered badly bruised buttocks as well the bite. "I told the policeman at the hospital that if I had what he was wearing on his hip, I would have blown its head off."

Neighbors had called Pigger's mistress on her job at Miami Children's Hospital to report her pig on the prowl. She rushed home. So did Pigger, she said. "Two guys were following her. She couldn't wait to get back in her pen."

Pigger was a legal resident—the neighborhood is agriculturally zoned—but police cited Banas for "permitting livestock to run at large." There is no leash law for pigs, but there are livestock laws. Pigger was quarantined for ten days.

"Pigger is no attack pig," Banas insisted. Laughlin, she said, "probably scared her, or maybe Pigger was just coming over to say hello and bashed into him accidentally."

"It was not coming to say hello," Laughlin swore, swallowing a pain pill. "It's fat and it's big. It's not like having a little dog. It was walking up the middle of Ninety-third Avenue.

It deliberately wanted to knock me down; I know it wanted to bite me."

"The pig probably didn't like this guy for some reason," an Animal Control officer said. "They are very smart."

Irene was a bigger problem, by seven hundred pounds. The baby Burmese elephant ran amok through a Miami neighborhood, ramming two cars, kicking down fences and bursting through a plate-glass window during a twenty-minute, mile-long spree.

The one-thousand-pound pachyderm panicked at the sound of an ambulance siren and broke away from her trainer as she and a baby baboon were being unloaded for a benefit show at a nursing home.

Elderly patients caught only a fleeting glimpse of Irene as she lumbered into careening traffic.

"She got spooked and ran. She's really a perfect elephant," said the trainer, who worked for Hoxie Brothers Circus.

Irene, age four, stands on her head, waltzes, sits and kneels on command. This time, however, she ignored commands, knocked down her trainer half a dozen times and tried to bite him during the wild chase. A ragtag posse of police, dazed motorists who abandoned their cars, pedestrians, barking dogs and a Miami politician took up the pursuit, scattering for cover several times as Irene charged them, trumpeting angrily.

She crashed through hedges, trampled flowers and rampaged through several garages. No one was badly hurt, though several persons were knocked off their feet by Irene, who suffered a bloodied trunk.

"Here comes an elephant!" screamed a woman employee as Irene smashed through the plate-glass window at the Miami Board of Realtors.

"We heard a godawful crash," public relations director Rose Light said. "Someone in the front office yelled, 'My God, it is an elephant!' The staff was in a state of shock."

Trapped in an apartment-house trash bin by two would-be big-game hunters, the five-foot-tall creature shoved their pickup truck back ten yards, crushing the right front fender before she fled.

City Commissioner J. L. Plummer dodged the irate elephant and scaled a parked tractor screaming, "I'm a Democrat!"

The chase ended in a backyard. Irene shook off four husky men and did a fancy step out of the chains around her pudgy front legs, but she soon met her match. Miami Police Lieutenant Walter Rodak, a mounted patrol veteran, snatched her ear and talked gently until she calmed down.

"She's just a baby," Rodak said soothingly.

Hobbled by the chains now double-wrapped around her legs, Irene struggled in vain to escape, until she was finally locked inside the circus van.

Police knew where Pigger and Irene came from. Sometimes, though, you never know.

Close to midnight there was a knock at their apartment door. Gilbert Maseda, forty-three, opened it, and his wife watched.

There stood a two-foot-tall black monkey.

Startled, Maseda slammed the door. The couple scrambled to the window and peered out at the creature. That made the monkey angry, so angry that he began screaming, then jumped up and smashed the window.

Screams from the monkey and the Masedas aroused neighbors, who rushed out to chase the intruder away. He refused to go. Then he saw Estella Pena, forty-three, leave a friend's home to walk to her car. The monkey leaped onto Pena, who ran away screaming.

Three times she dashed for her car. Three times the monkey intercepted her as she shrieked and cried and neighbors ran and shouted.

"He had great big eyes," she told me. "There were lots of people there, but he kept chasing me. I never saw him before," she swore.

Finally she dove into her car and slammed the door, safe at last, or so she thought. A window was rolled down three inches.

The monkey leaped onto the car, trying to wriggle inside as she screamed and neighbors ran and shouted.

Somebody called Animal Control and the police as Estella Pena shook the monkey from her car and sped into the night. The monkey eluded the Animal Control officer and the impromptu posse of crazed neighbors.

After an hour-long chase, Miami policeman J. K. Fitzgerald and passerby Louis Moldinado, thirty, cornered the monkey under the hood of a car a block and a half away from where it had originally appeared.

The monkey, suffering from cuts and bruises, was taken to Animal Control and booked into solitary at two A.M.

The owner was never found.

And nobody knows why the monkey knocked at the Masedas' door.

Sidebar

DUCK

A bird in the hand makes a bit of a mess.

—ANONYMOUS BIRDCATCHER

He came into my life in January, along with all the other snowbirds. He was short and beady-eyed, with a waddle, and I loved him on sight.

He meandered across my front yard trailing a length of purple cloth in the dust. Thinking he was hungry, I fed him Tender Vittles and went back inside. Preoccupied, I vaguely wondered why he was there but paid no more attention until a friend arrived.

"Did you know there is a duck in your front yard?" my friend Patsy asked. Also a city girl, she was excited.

On closer inspection we could see that somebody had bound his wings with that purple cloth, apparently to keep him from flying. Even if I could hold him, I was afraid to try to remove the intricately tied binding for fear of hurting him. He was skittish anyway, but he loved those Tender Vittles.

Next morning he was still there, still hungry. There was only one thing to do: I got out the cat carrier and dropped a trail of Tender Vittles leading to a dish inside. He greedily ate his way into captivity. I slammed the door, and we were off to the vet.

A woman in the waiting room with her dog said she had seen

a duck tied just like that, with the same purple binding, near her bayfront home. She was certain it was not the same bird.

Something bizarre, as usual, was happening in Miami Beach.

Why was somebody tying up ducks? People have been arrested for sexually assaulting ducks; Santeria cultists sacrifice them along with other creatures, and some people fatten them up for Sunday dinner. I didn't want to think about it. The veterinarian had never treated a duck before. No problem—all I wanted, I said, was to set him free.

Oh, said the doctor. He picked up his scissors, severed the purple binding with a single snip and billed me ten dollars.

I will never forget the expression of relief and delight on the bird's face as he stretched out his wings and flapped them ecstatically. An impressive and beautiful sight—who knows how long they had been uncomfortably bound. He willingly stepped back into the carrier, which I took home and placed out on my little dock. I opened the door and said good-bye. He stepped out and stood for a moment, getting his bearings. I didn't wait to watch him fly away. I left home for several hours, returned and went to fetch the empty carrier.

The duck came running, webbed feet making slapping sounds on my patio, begging for some Tender Vittles.

He took up residence in the backyard. The dog was no threat, but I worried at first about the cats. No problem—the first time he was stalked he merely extended his neck and expanded his wings to full width, and the cats backed off. This bird was bigger than they were. Soon he and Sharkey the cat were eating Tender Vittles together out of the same dish.

It did occur to me that ducks should be wet. Writing at home, on leave from the *Herald*, I took breaks several times a day to go out and spray him with the garden hose. He loved it, running back and forth through the spray like a city kid at an open fire hydrant, and I observed for the first time why people say, "Like water off a duck's back."

Doubting that Tender Vittles was a balanced diet for a bird, I switched the menu to day-old bread, bagels and lettuce. My bird book said that ducks eat corn but was not more specific. This duck did not like fresh corn off the cob, canned corn or frozen niblets, but he did relish corn muffins. He probably would have liked dried corn, but none was to be found at Miami Beach supermarkets.

The bird book called ducks fresh-water fowl. The waterway behind the house branches in off the bay and is brackish, and I worried that he probably should have more access to fresh water. I had the perfect answer: a giant kitty-litter box, deeper and twice the normal size—a perfect swimming pool for a duck. Splashing furiously, he kicked his feet, flapped his wings, ducked his head and threw water into the air. I had to refill it several times a day.

Extensive remodeling was under way next door. Some of the workmen were refugees, and I was alarmed to see them gazing hungrily at my duck, busy in his bath. He had become quite corpulent on his diet of day-old bread, bagels, lettuce, corn muffins and Tender Vittles. I started to work with one eye out the window, on guard for any false moves. When the duck perched atop my chain-link fence to look at the water and caught his webbed foot on a wire, I had the fence removed. The view is better without it anyway.

He slept on a piling at the corner of the dock, head tucked under his wing. Each night before retiring I would deliver his midnight snack—a handful of Tender Vittles—stroke his glossy feathers, and we would look at the stars.

He never quacked, but he cooed while gently nibbling at my clothes and fingers. And he was intelligent. When I emerged one chilly morning wearing a long flannel nightgown instead of the usual shorts and T-shirt, he did a double-take and waddled around nibbling at the hem, looking up at me in mock surprise.

He had a roguish personality. Soon he no longer wanted me to hand feed him his bread, he wanted to play with it. He liked me to wad it up and toss it in the air so he could catch it. Better yet, after he got his little swimming pool he wanted me to toss the bread into the water from afar. He would back up, get a running start, leap into the pool and dive for it. Then he would clamber out, back away and wait for me to toss another morsel. He was hilarious.

How can anybody ever shoot a duck—or eat one? Veal was already off my menu because of the big-eyed baby calves. So was tuna, because of the murdered dolphins. Now ducks were too.

His play was so much fun that I even considered buying him a child's wading pool, but things changed the week before Palm Sunday. He grew restless, pacing up and down, staring out over the water. He flew off one day and was gone for more than an hour. I was concerned, but he returned, landing out on the water and streaming straight to the dock leaving a widening V on the mirror-bright surface behind him. Next day he flew away again and was absent longer. But still he came back. I talked to him as usual out on the dock, where he cooed and settled down on the piling for the night.

The following day he soared again into the sky, following the waterway north. When he did not return by nightfall, I almost regretted not having his wings clipped as the vet had suggested, but that wouldn't have been right.

I looked at the stars alone that night, but in the morning, there he was, running eagerly to greet me as usual. Later, the pacing began once more. He stood in the shade under the ficus tree, staring skyward for a long time. I went out and stroked his handsome head and fat little belly.

I watched later, from my Florida room, as he took to the sky.

This time he did not come back.

He left me with a fridge full of day-old bread and lettuce. The story of my life.

Part Three

THE HEROES

Chapter 10

FIRE!

Yell "Help!" or scream "Rape!" and expect to be ignored. Yell "Fire!" and a crowd comes running. Fire kindles something deep and universal in the human soul. Fires are news.

Hair and clothes smelling of smoke, sinuses clogged, head pounding, I have covered hundreds of fires and had to run to escape or to rescue my car when the flames spread or explosions began. Paint factories and lumberyards catch fire a lot—so do failing businesses and old hotels. So do homes and high-rises.

It is healthy and advisable for reporters to view with suspicion warnings from most government officials, but it pays to listen to firefighters. At one burning paint factory, I argued with a fire department chaplain who insisted I retreat from the scene. He warned that explosions might occur inside the building and we could all be showered by dangerous debris. As I pooh-poohed the hazard and refused to budge, an explosion rocked the building. Debris rocketed into the air and I ran for my life.

After that, I started wearing a hard hat at fires.

Until fire hoses were trained on me, I did not appreciate their effectiveness.

On my first newspaper job, at the Miami Beach *Daily Sun*,

where I shot my own photographs, I always wore dresses and high heels to work. That was before I knew better.

Fire erupted at a major oil facility on the MacArthur Causeway. Fuel-fed flames towered over the bay, making it a photogenic blaze. I rushed about, shooting the inferno and the firefighters at work. A tall construction crane stood abandoned nearby. Better pictures could be shot from that vantage point, I thought, and in my miniskirt and heels, I clambered awkwardly up into the cab.

The view was ideal. The fire, unfortunately, seemed to be spreading fast—in my direction. "Better wet down that crane!" the fire chief shouted. Before I could protest, they did. All I could do was try to shield the camera as, from all directions, pounding streams of water pummeled me about inside the cab. A TV camera crew caught the whole thing, much to their delight.

Fire attracts all sorts of people. Stu Kaufman was a little boy when he was chased away from a fire and told to go stand behind a rope with the media. "This is not your business," the man in charge sternly told him. Stu never forgot. He swore that someday it would be his business. He would run to fires, and they would tell him everything.

They did.

When he was a successful young businessman and reporter, he gave it all up to become public information officer for the Metro Fire Department. They gave him a beeper and the chance to do exactly what he had wanted to since childhood. He went to all the fires, disasters, plane crashes and major catastrophes and was told everything. He loved it. He went to bed at night afraid his beeper would *not* go off during the wee hours.

Relations between the press and Dade County's close-mouthed and sometimes sullen firefighters were traditionally poor. Stu taught them that they had nothing to hide. People love firemen. Stu thrived on excitement. He loved heroes and wanted to tell the world about them. When planes crashed, when a busload of migrant workers sank roof down in a deep canal, when an exploding cocaine lab shattered a quiet neighborhood, when rescue workers used the "jaws of life" to cut a dozen injured motorists out of a multi-car pile-up, Stu was always there.

Unlike many people designated to deal with the press, he had heart, compassion and sense enough to recognize a good story. He also knew that when the department was wrong it was far more effective damage control to tell the truth right up front, rather than to lie and have the scandal snowball into a far bigger story as the outraged press tracked down the truth. Stu loved firefighting and reporting, passions that made him the best at his job.

He was still a radio newsman when I first encountered him. A wealthy couple was kidnapped by a man named Thomas Otis Knight. He forced them to drive to their bank and withdraw money. The victim asked bank officials for help and they summoned the FBI. The victim took the money the kidnapper demanded and returned to his wife, held at gunpoint in the car. The kidnapper and his victims drove off with the FBI right behind them.

Everybody assumed that once the gunman got the money, the couple would go free. The agents decided a rescue attempt would risk the safety of the victims. They decided simply to trail the car until the couple was released, then swoop down on the kidnapper. Agents followed the car until they realized it was taking too long. It all went bad in a remote area, on a desolate road. Knight shot both victims in the head, executing them before the agents could make a move. The killer fled into the underbrush.

It was my day off, and I had friends in for lunch. They went hungry.

Every reporter in the world seemed to be at the crime scene. Frustrated cops, dogs and FBI agents combed the brush in an intense manhunt. Reporters, photographers, and TV news crews gathered to interview the local agent in charge of the FBI.

Suddenly a cop shouted, "I've got 'im!" He had flushed out the killer, who had literally burrowed into the ground. Everybody ran, leaving the FBI chief standing alone, his mouth still open.

Leading the stampede of running reporters was Stu, pounding after the cops and the guns and the dogs, tape-recorder mike clenched in his fist, breathlessly reporting as he ran. "They got 'im! They got 'im!" he shouted. He was not on the air live of course, but when it was broadcast later, his tape had the spell-binding urgency of news happening in your face. I loved it. Who *is* this guy? I thought.

I next saw him at a cargo-plane crash. Surly firefighters usually banned us from such scenes, but at this one, Stu seemed in charge. "Right this way," he said and led me up to the wreck. Who *IS* this guy? Still a radio reporter, he had become friendly enough to convince fire officials that what they needed was a better attitude toward the press. Next thing I knew, he was working for them, and he certainly made a reporter's life easier. Always accessible, he would put us in touch with rescuers at the scene, with the fire captains in charge, with the hero who revived a baby with mouth-to-mouth resuscitation. When he saw people in need of help, he made us aware of the story.

His energy and commitment were clear away from the fire scenes as well. He arranged funerals for fallen firefighters, friends and heroes. One fireman was driving his wife to a movie when he stopped to help a woman whose car had knocked down a power pole. He was electrocuted. A fire department paramedic drowned trying to save a girl trapped in a submerged car. A lieutenant died in a burning warehouse, another in the crash of his rescue truck while speeding to a false alarm. Stu cried every time.

When firemen told him how they hated to drive away after a house fire, leaving a burned-out family huddled on their front lawn at three A.M. with no place to go, he established a program called After the Burnout. Stu or a department chaplain would arrange to have the damaged property boarded up and coordinate with the Red Cross for shelter. Thanks to Stu, no burned-out family is left alone in the night.

After a teenage-arson epidemic, Stu set up Dade County's largest summer employment program for underprivileged youngsters. The kids wore shirts with official patches and went door to door, teaching their neighbors about smoke detectors, the importance of family escape plans and the dangers of children home alone. Stu knew that the best people to deal with neighborhood problems are neighborhood people. As important as the pay was the youngsters' sense of pride and self-worth. Many of them work for major corporations today.

Stu forgot no one. Every Sunday morning he and his children would visit headquarters to share a sack of bagels with the "unsung heroes": the fire department dispatchers.

Stu's official code designation was Staff 10. He was driving his radio-equipped county car to an airport incident one day when he heard an injury call: "A small child fell through a television set." The address that followed was his own.

He spun around on the highway median and raced toward home and family. Pedal to the floor, he heard a paramedic who had arrived at the scene. "Tell Staff 10 to slow down. It's just a small cut."

Stu even issued beepers to reporters, so Dispatch could alert us to major blazes. News agencies gave him their private frequencies so he could guide their photographers and reporters around traffic and police roadblocks to reach fires and disasters the fastest. Metro-Dade was the first fire department to set up its own photo van and shoot its own video. News photographers and TV cameramen taught firefighters how to shoot the best pictures until they arrived. A fireman shot still photos and video, then shared his pictures with the media. The van was equipped with a video recorder so footage could be copied and distributed.

Stu gave firefighters' discarded bunker gear to news photographers. He knows the best pictures are shot heading into the flames, over the shoulder of a firefighter using a hose. The resulting camaraderie sometimes saw photographers put down their cameras to help drag hoses. Stu set up a day-long news-media fire college for reporters—so we could experience what it was like to be firefighters and understand the job better when we wrote about it. We wore firefighters' gear, climbed tall ladders and ran in and out of burning buildings wearing oxygen tanks.

Nobody ever said you had to be rational to do this job.

Stu Kaufman was the best thing that ever happened to firefighting in Dade County. Too bad good things never last. After ten years, Stu had swallowed enough smoke, seen enough excitement and lost enough sleep. He felt that he owed more of his time and earning power to his wife and children and left to make big bucks in the corporate world.

I never smell smoke without missing him.

In a world full of strange people, firebugs are among the strangest.

Take June Ann Olsen, a fresh-faced blonde who once burned down an entire Miami city block.

She would lure men, including a famous TV producer, into motel rooms. After they were undressed, she would slosh lighter fluid onto the bed and torch it. "You ought to see them run," she told me. "It's pretty funny sometimes." During the afterglow, she would telephone her favorite fire captain, Frank Fitzpatrick, for long chats. She would flirt, and he would try to talk her into surrendering. Sent off to an institution, she was later released. "I'm lonesome," she said. "Maybe it's not too late to start a new life." That was the last time we talked. Next time I saw her name, it was on a police report; she was dead.

Though many amateur arsonists die trapped by their own flames, June Ann Olsen did not.

She was struck and killed by a train.

Nothing about arson is funny—or harmless.

A flaming inferno, at three A.M. on a Friday the thirteenth, killed three people and severely burned six others at a small South Beach hotel. The death toll would have climbed far higher except for the efforts of the two heroic rookie cops who arrived first. One made a perfect catch of a baby dropped out a third-floor window surrounded by flames. Several other infants and small children were dropped by adults who leaped after them. Two men hurtled horizontally out third-floor windows across a five-foot alleyway and crashed through the third-floor windows of the hotel next door. One of them, a tractor-trailer driver, said he hesitated until he saw someone else escape through the window next to his.

"He put me to shame," he told me later. "That little, skinny Latin guy flew across the alley like Superman, with flames shooting right behind him." He followed, into the next hotel, dashed down three flights to the street and darted right back into the burning building. "I had to go back," he said. "People were in there. I could hear them. They were my friends."

Three policemen stopped him on a smoky second-floor landing. "You can't go up there," they said.

"Somebody has to, you or me," he told them. He could hear Rita, a neighbor, and Bessie, a senior citizen, screaming for help. He told the officers where the women were. Firemen in oxygen masks led the women to the stairwell a short time later, and he and the officers helped them to the street.

Among the dead were a mother and her daughter, who was visiting from Cuba. They had not seen each other in thirteen years. Reunited at last, they died together, trapped in a blazing third-floor hallway. The wind-whipped blaze took a hundred firefighters hours to control. An entire block was evacuated as the flames threatened to spread. Sixty were left homeless, with nothing.

The deaths were murder. Two men ran from the hotel and sped away in a white car moments before fire erupted. Gasoline used to ignite the blaze had been siphoned from a car parked behind the building.

Some people set fires for revenge, some out of greed, some because it excites them sexually.

Others ignite the spark to cover up some other crime or sometimes to commit suicide. I have little sympathy for careless smokers, false-alarm setters, or thoughtless would-be suicides, like the man who torched the rooming house where he lived. He left his neighbors homeless and wound up in the hospital, along with three Miami firemen injured fighting the blaze.

Amateur arsonists agreed to burn a Miami Beach beauty salon

for a thousand dollars. Beginning at the front, they poured fifteen gallons of gasoline throughout the shop, working their way toward the back. Drifting gas fumes reached the back door before they did, and a pilot light in a water heater near the door ignited them. A thirteen-year-old newsboy selling papers across the street heard the salon windows explode and saw the building tremble. The million-dollar fire destroyed a block-long row of stores: a florist, a pizza restaurant, a bar, a shoe repair, a barber shop, and a pet store full of animals, all of whom perished.

The first policeman to arrive found one of the arsonists slumped against a car, moaning, his clothes burned off. "I've seen people burned before," Officer Kenneth Miller said. "But not like this. He had no ears, no nose, no fingers. He kept saying he couldn't breathe—because his nose was gone." The young man reached out his hand to Officer Chuck Hayes, pleading for help. When Hayes took it, the man's skin came off in his hand.

An accomplice escaped but was found slumped in his car miles away, critically burned over 85 percent of his body.

The last thing another inept arsonist remembered was standing on a ladder sloshing cleaning fluid around a darkened store. Next thing he knew, he was facedown on the grass behind the burning building listening to the wail of approaching sirens. He had absent-mindedly lit a cigarette while pouring the flammable liquid.

Sometimes you can spot the guilty party by checking out the would-be rescuers at the scene.

Some people actually commit mass murder because they want to be heroes.

The Avondale Hotel fire, the second worst blaze in Miami history, killed ten and injured fourteen. The first alarm came at 12:40 A.M. Flames had already engulfed the old forty-room hotel built during Miami's World War I boom.

A bus driver hit the horn and the brakes and ran to help. He placed his jacket beneath the head of a bleeding man who had just been carried from the building by two men. Then he saw the same two men urging a terrified elderly woman, screaming on a second-floor balcony, to jump. They kept shouting, promising to catch her. The flames crept closer. She arched her back as they singed her skin. Then she started screaming, "My hair! My hair!" She yanked her dress over her head and wrapped it around her burning hair to keep off the flames.

The first of seventeen fire trucks roared up to the curb. Firefighters ran with a ladder and carried her down. A number of people, hair and clothing ablaze, had already leaped from ledges and balconies, fracturing legs, spines and ankles. Others dangled from windows. Firemen used hoses to drench a seventy-seven-year-old man who was about to jump, then rescued him.

On their third or fourth inspection of the sagging second floor, four hours after they arrived, a captain heard a sound. A horribly burned woman rose from charred bedsheets, murmuring in agony, arms outstretched. Firemen swore she had not been on the bed before. She was burned over 100 percent of her body, and there was no way to save her. She died exactly a week to the hour from the moment flames and screams awoke her in the night.

The fire was arson.

Months later the two men who had played hero that hellish night were arrested. The charges: arson and ten counts of first-degree murder. Suspects from the start, each had his own motive: One wanted to be a hero, to dramatically rescue the owner, so he and his common-law wife would not be evicted as scheduled the next day. The other intended to loot his neighbors' rooms after they evacuated.

They only planned a small fire. But when one set a match to the cane bottom of a wooden chair in the lobby, the blaze escaped them. They had not considered the age and dryness of the building and the stairwell draft that caused flames to leap instantly through the old structure where innocent people were asleep in their beds.

One got twenty years; the other was sentenced to fifteen.

Sometimes you can spot the arsonist simply by scanning the crowds. You can see the look in his eyes—along with reflected flames.

A nightmare at a paint store virtually wiped out Miami Engine

Company Two eight months after they fought the Avondale blaze. Firefighters had been battling the 3:30 A.M. blaze for only fifteen minutes when disaster struck. The men of Engine Company Two had knocked down the fire and were advancing on the nearly extinguished flames. Four firemen were deep inside the building, when trapped fumes exploded with a roar.

Firemen outside were hurled ten or fifteen feet by the force of the blast and the intense heat wave accompanying it. The front of the store collapsed on a fireman, who screamed for help. Another rolled in the street in flames. Injured firemen lay scattered across the pavement, and now three businesses were ablaze, flames shooting out of the buildings.

Miami policemen manned the hoses. "There were firemen lying all over, some burned, some dazed," police officer Charles Lincoln told me later. "We didn't know if it was going to explode again. My first thought was for the firemen inside." He asked an injured fireman if everyone was out.

"Al? Where's Al?" the shocked fireman mumbled.

The young cop dashed toward the building. In the intense heat close to the flames, he found a dazed fireman, incoherent, his face cut and bleeding. "Are you Al?" he asked. The fireman said he was. Lincoln led the man to safety, then tried to help a badly burned firefighter sprawled in the street. He used a penknife to cut clothes away from burned flesh.

Fireman Louis Kickasola, thirty-one, knocked down by the blast and surrounded by flames, figured he was going to die. He crawled toward the blown-out front of the store and nearly made it, but a rush of air ignited the paint and chemicals that had spattered his gear—turning him into a ball of fire. Married, with a six-year-old son, Kickasola won a Purple Heart for Vietnam War wounds. This time all he got was months of hospitalization and a long series of skin grafts.

Injured were thirteen firemen, two police officers and an ambulance attendant, his arm seared by the red-hot air tank on a fireman he and a policeman dragged out of the inferno. "This is something you figure will never happen to you," the fire chief told me, near tears. A fireman's helmet, crushed and melted, lay in the street. Another, in worse shape, was found inside the building.

Officer Lincoln plucked the arsonist out of the crowd, spotting him right away: "He was just standing there."

Age eighteen, he had been in trouble since age ten for sniffing glue, transmission fluid and other chemicals. His arrests included attempted rape, burglary, auto theft, prowling and vandalism. Though he lived four blocks north of the fire, the officer saw him stroll up from the south and join the crowd. Green and yellow paint stained his hands. Lincoln knew the teen had been suspected two years earlier of torching his parents' home. When he approached, the youth became evasive and tried to wipe the paint off his hands. He confessed.

He had torched the store to cover up a burglary.

Cops often arrive at fires first, minus the protective gear and training. As fire ravaged a two-story auto-parts center, flames and explosions threatened nearby shops, which were evacuated. Dense smoke filled a tiny cottage on the other side of the burning building. A police sergeant ran through the choking smoke to make sure everyone was out. He was astonished to find three women in the smoke-filled living room—a sixty-year-old heart patient, her sister, fifty-four, and their mother, eighty-seven—"just sitting there . . . waiting."

The frightened women refused to move. The sergeant radioed for help, and Sergeant Doug Rice dashed in the front door, holding a wet cloth over his face.

The mother, wearing a nightgown and fuzzy pink slippers, insisted that she was not dressed to go out. The two sergeants scooped her up and stumbled to safety through the smoke. They set her down in a leather reclining chair in a furniture store across the street. Other officers brought out her daughters.

"My mother can't walk," the heart patient told me. "We couldn't get Mother out, and we couldn't leave her"—she spoke in a matter-of-fact fashion—"so we were going to stay. The smoke was very bad. The explosions were horrible. It sounded like a war." Then she began to sob.

That was Miami's fourth major blaze in a single weekend. Sixty firefighters battled it in midday eighty-plus heat to keep it from spreading. Several were injured, a number treated for smoke inhalation, and the city manager, who came by to watch, wrecked his car as he left. But the women's home was saved, and so were they.

Only twice did I ever go home from *The Miami Herald* so late and so weary that I neglected to fill my car's gas tank though it was on "E."

Never again.

Major stories broke both nights, and I had to speed off into the dark, on empty.

I hate that.

Once it was a plane crash. Next time Stu Kaufman called at nearly four A.M. I knew it was bad when I heard his voice. The toughest one of all: a house fire, in Leisure City, more than forty miles south of Miami, west of Homestead Air Force Base.

Five dead. All children.

A summer thunderstorm was raging on the island where I lived. The rain was torrential, and no service stations were open.

My mind was already racing with everything I would have to do before the *Herald*'s first-edition deadline, eleven hours away. Hopefully I would find a gas station en route, but they are never there when you need them. I literally screamed in panic all the way, one eye riveted to the gas gauge, the needle flat.

Never had I driven for so long on empty. Never had I been so lost, for so long, on roads so dark, in the middle of rural South Dade farmland.

I had no idea where I was. For all I knew, I was speeding in circles. It was almost dawn when I spotted a farmworker and asked directions. The man had no idea where *he* was, much less where I was going.

By sunrise I feared that the fire crew would change shifts and go home before I found them. I finally stumbled upon their station and burst in, totally crazed, the needle now way below empty.

They were tightly wound too, for a reason that put everything back in perspective. The tragedy had been senseless. A ten-dollar smoke detector would have saved five young lives.

Their father, a big, burly, good-natured construction superintendent who loves children, was awakened by a noise in the night. He arose, walked into the living room and saw the sofa burning. Shouting to his wife to call the fire department, he tried to splash water on the flames. The pan he used melted. He was severely burned and ran out the front door, searching in panic for a garden hose. His wife tried to dial 911, but the telephone was dead. She ran out a utility room door to the backyard for a hose.

A nineteen-year-old son was awakened by his parents' screams as they searched in the dark for the garden hose. The dazed teenager, thinking it was time to go to work, sat up and saw an "orange glow from the living room." He ran to wake his kid brother, age thirteen. When he punched out a window, oxygen collided with built-up gases from the smoldering blaze. The entire room exploded. The blast threw the older boy partially out the window, but it hurled the younger boy and his dog back into the flames.

A neighbor heard the explosion, saw the fire and tried to reach the children, but the family pets, a bird dog named Whiskers and a boxer named Kane, attacked him. The parents restrained the animals as the neighbor trained his garden hose on the children's window. The father tried to reenter the house, but the intense heat drove him back. The fire was so hot that the leaves on a hibiscus tree in the front yard withered and blackened.

The first alarm came from neighbors, logged in at 2:53 A.M. A rescue unit and a pumper roared out of the station one minute later. Firemen could see the fire a mile and a half away, an orange glow below a towering column of smoke. The rescue unit arrived first, and a medic tried to climb in a window. Heat forced him back. The lumbering pumper arrived minutes later, and the crew began to beat down the flames. They arrived four minutes after the first call, but the house was gone in ten minutes.

I talked to the firefighter who found two dead children, ages five and six, in their bed, "beautiful little blond girls in long nightgowns. One was resting her head on her hands like she was sleeping." Two baby dolls lay nearby. He carried the girls out. The body of one of them left an eerie outline on her smoke-blackened bedsheet.

The thirteen-year-old boy died trying to escape. A window screen lay atop his body, in a back bedroom. His hands were cut. His pet dog, a miniature dachshund, lay dead at his feet. The room did not burn—everything in it melted. The two three-year-old girls, two of triplets, died cringing in corners, trying to hide from the flames.

Firefighters groping in the dark missed one of the triplets at first. The fire captain had nine names, and only eight were accounted for. Himself a father of five, he hoped the missing child had escaped, was frightened and hiding safely somewhere, but they found her after forty-five minutes, covered with soot, wedged in a tiny place between a mattress and the wall.

The parents, the nineteen-year-old son and the surviving triplet, a three-year-old boy, survived. The father was airlifted to a burn center.

A worn air-conditioner wire had ignited the sofa. The fire may have smoldered for as long as two hours, investigators said, then flames raced across wall paneling and erupted into an inferno.

Had there been a smoke alarm, investigators estimated, there would have been perhaps ten or fifteen dollars damage, no more than a hundred—and no loss of life. None of the children were burned. All died of smoke inhalation.

As a result, Stu Kaufman established a smoke-alarm awareness program: Buy One, Get One Free. For each alarm sold, one was donated to a family unable to afford it. This tragedy touched Stu more than all the others. One of the dead girls, age five, had been visiting. From then on, when one of his children spent the night with friends, Stu would always make sure that the household was protected by smoke alarms.

Some time after, his ten-year-old daughter, already at a slumber party when he arrived home from work, called to say good night. Routinely, he asked about smoke alarms, and she said there were none.

Stu Kaufman spent the night outside the house in his parked car, on a fire watch.

You learn a lot covering fires—some things you wish you didn't know. Sometimes I feel like I've been on the beat too long and know too much. I avoid flying when I can, and when I can't, I wear no synthetics. Fire accompanies most air crashes, and I know that when polyester melts, skin comes off with it. So I wear cotton or wool and Reeboks. If I survive the crash, I can climb out and trudge for help.

I know that no fire department in America has a ladder that will go higher than ten floors, so neither do I.

In one city, I was booked into a twenty-seventh-floor suite. Hotel personnel could not understand why I insisted on something else, preferably on the third floor. Embarrassed, I finally confessed.

"Don't worry," the desk clerk cried, relieved that my problem was nothing more serious. "If anything happens," he promised, "the fire department helicopter will pluck you off the roof."

I don't want to be plucked off a roof. I want to be carried down a ladder by a husky fireman.

Sometimes I think I am the only person suffering from this neurotic mind-set—then I remember Stu Kaufman on his fire watch, spending that sleepless night in his car outside his daughter's slumber party.

Maybe we both have seen too much.

Chapter 11

WATER

Survival techniques can save your life, but training and knowledge are not always enough. Surviving takes something more.

Barry McCutchen, an expert on survival, will not forget the ordeal that began one Memorial Day, a perfect day for snorkeling and fishing in the calm blue-green waters off Key Largo.

He and two friends spearfished all day in the warm water off John Pennekamp Coral Reef State Park. The ocean sparkled like diamonds in the brilliant sunlight, and the afternoon was so splendid that at 4:30 they decided to dive for one more hour before returning to port. Before the snorkelers splashed again into the sun-streaked water, McCutchen, thirty-five, a popular physical education teacher and assistant football coach at Hialeah High School, repeated a litany of safety rules.

He had no dark premonition; his precautions were routine, since there were only three of them, and this was just the second diving trip for Julio Guevara, an eighteen-year-old high school athlete. The third man, Michael Melgarejo, twenty-five, owned the *Hog Wild*, their seventeen-foot open fishing boat.

Something happened to McCutchen about fifty yards from the vessel: leg cramps, for the first time in twenty years of diving, probably because he neither ate nor drank during the long day of diving. He was not alarmed; in fact, he spotted a vivid red-and-orange hogfish on the bottom and pointed it out to Julio, who speared it. Still cramped, Barry said he was returning to the boat, anchored in gentle seas five miles offshore.

He took the fish and swam toward the *Hog Wild*, but ten yards short of the vessel his legs cramped so severely that he dropped the brightly colored fish and began to float. The current carried him about ten yards behind the boat. He tried to swim toward it again, but the cramps caught him even more painfully, bunching his thigh muscles and tensing his calves. For five minutes he floated facedown, trying to massage away the pain with his fingers. A former high school football star, Barry was familiar with muscle cramps, but these were bad. Even his feet were rigid and he was unable to move his fins. He took his face out of the water and saw that the current had carried him about fifty yards from the boat. Keep floating, he thought, and wait. My friends will pick me up.

The time was 5:00 under bright skies in calm, clear waters where Barry, a muscular six feet one inch tall and 230 pounds, had felt at home all his life. Still unconcerned, he drifted for about fifteen minutes, the current taking him out. Almost imperceptibly at first, the wind began to pick up speed. He realized he was being carried away much faster than he had thought. The boat was barely visible in the distance. He checked his diving watch: nearly 5:30, their designated time of departure. His friends would return at any moment now, scan the sea and spot him.

They did return moments later. He watched them clamber aboard and saw the sudden flurry of activity when they realized he was missing. By now he was a quarter of a mile away. He tried to wave when they turned toward him, but his shoulders, arms and body cramped.

They did not see him.

Tired and hungry, he was frustrated, but still convinced he would be found quickly. He had seen a number of other diving boats and pleasure craft nearby during the day, all within a half mile of where they had snorkeled. Floating vertically, in a standing position, his face in the water, he used the drown-proofing technique he taught in water survival classes. The method takes little energy. Your lungs are like air-filled balloons and the water holds you up. Barry waited, a tiny speck in a big blue sea, as his anxious friends scanned the huge horizon.

Mike Melgarejo, captain of the *Hog Wild*, was slightly annoyed when Barry was not aboard by 5:30. Barry, he thought, must have gone off chasing a fish by himself. By 5:45 he knew something was wrong. The two were longtime friends, ever since Barry had coached Mike's 145-pound Optimist League football team in 1971. Mike hoisted anchor and made a wide sweep of the coral reef.

The lone response to their shouts came from a huge hammerhead shark that boldly circled the boat, trying to strike at the fish in the baitwell. Mike returned to their original spot to radio for help. It was 6:00. He reported a lost diver wearing only a T-shirt, shorts, dive mask and flippers. The Coast Guard instructed him to stay put so searchers could fix on the point where Barry had vanished.

A forty-one-foot search boat was dispatched out of Islamorada at 6:05 P.M. The Coast Guard from Miami to Key West was alerted by 6:15 P.M., along with the Pennekamp Park rangers.

Still adrift in a current now rapidly picking up speed, Barry realized he might be in the water longer than he first expected. He hoped his friends had notified the Coast Guard. He hoped he would not miss dinner. They had planned to stop on the way home for an all-you-can-eat buffet of prime rib and fresh shrimp.

He scouted good fishing spots and watched colorful schools of snapper in the living coral reef while awaiting rescue.

Eight private boaters and the pilot of a Cessna in the air overheard Mike's distress call and offered assistance. Barry saw the small single-engine plane fly toward the boat. When it began circling, patterning out from the *Hog Wild*, he knew they were looking for him. The searchers combed the bright green waters to the south. Barry was drifting north.

Complex cross-currents tend to sweep south inside the reef but rush north on the outside of the underwater rock formations. The wind increased. The sky faded to an overcast gray. Across the water, Barry saw mountainous dark clouds, a gathering thunderstorm. Visibility dropped rapidly, and the storm's energy kicked up the surface of the water. Daylight faded fast. Darkness was but an hour away.

Barry saw a Coast Guard helicopter out of Miami's Opa-Locka Airport whirl over Key Largo just after 7:00 P.M. and cut across open water, directly toward him. Relief and gratitude swept over him. He was not worried about dinner anymore. Having been diving since 8:30 A.M., he was weary. He wanted out of the water by dark. Before college Barry had served three years in Coast Guard search and rescue. He remembered that during those years they never found anybody in the water if they were not found by dark. He had never heard of a free diver with no flotation gear surviving a night alone at sea. He still believed he would be found, but was increasingly uncomfortable. Cramps continued to wrack his body. The waves, so gentle that afternoon, had grown choppy. When they lifted him, he could see search boats in the distance. Then he would be plunged down, surrounded by towering walls of water. All he could see was a patch of sky above, with occasional glimpses of the aircraft.

Twice, the Cessna came within a quarter of a mile. He tried to wave but pain crippled his efforts. Lack of salt and fluids reduced the reservoir of potassium in his body, and the cramps worsened as it became more and more depleted. His eyes played tricks, making him believe the plane was veering toward him, when it was actually turning away.

He watched, willing the next circle to be larger, closer. Then, he said, "he came right at me." Elated, certain he had been seen, Barry tried to wave both hands, exposing as much of his body as he could above the waves.

The small plane droned directly overhead, wheeled in a wide loop and soared toward land. The pilot had given up.

The orange-and-white Coast Guard chopper continued to beat

the darkening sky at 8:00, with thirty to forty-five minutes of light left. Whenever the search pattern brought it into view, Barry kept his eyes locked on it. In doing so, he missed the last boat of that gloomy twilight. He saw it too late, out of the corner of his eye, a sleek fifty-foot sailing schooner gliding silently across the waves, moving fast, under full sail, parallel to shore. The sails were red-and-white striped. Barry saw two people aboard, near the helm. They did not see him.

Just four hundred yards away, it shot by in a flash. Almost as quickly, it was gone.

The Coast Guard was his only hope. The circling chopper with its searchlights and red blinkers was too close to shore, and too far south. When the helicopter seemed at its closest, Barry rolled over to float on his back, knowing that otherwise only the top of his head and snorkel could be seen. The thunderstorm still rumbled twenty miles offshore, lightning and black clouds building. It was drifting his way. He could feel it in the whipping wind.

At 8:55, by the luminous dial of his diving watch, the helicopter flew directly at him. The engine throb grew louder. Jubilant, Barry peeled off his bright yellow T-shirt, tied it to his spear and waved it three times. Cramps gripped his shoulders, and the spear, with its makeshift flag, slipped out of his grasp. He dared not dive for it, fearing that the chopper crew, not quite a quarter-mile away and closing in fast, might miss him.

His shirt drifted away, slowly settling to the bottom. Tearing his eyes from it, Barry sprawled on his back in water forty feet deep, trying feebly to wave his white diving gloves. What happened next will always haunt him: The helicopter throbbed overhead—and kept going. The Coast Guard had called off the search for the night.

He was alone.

His stomach knotted, as it always did at kickoff, before a game. His chances for survival were not good. Gazing down into the black water, he asked God to take care of Susan, his best girl, his family and the kids he taught. He thought of two former students, teens on drugs. He had hoped to bring them back; now he wished he had tried harder. He felt awash in regrets. His mother had died when he was three. He had grown up close to his father, who had suffered two heart attacks. Why hadn't he called his dad more often? Why hadn't he spent more time with him? Why hadn't he showered Susan with flowers and surprises? He probably would not have the chance again.

The threatening thunderstorm passed to the south, the clouds blew by, and the moon emerged. His hopelessness passed, and something stronger took over—the spirit in every person that fights to be indestructible or immortal. Barry knew this would be a long, hard night, and he began to plan his survival.

The time was 9:30. He believed he was strong enough to stay afloat through the night, but he had to prepare for the worst: sharks. Fishing in the same area two days earlier, he had seen a fifteen-foot tiger shark feeding on the surface. The creature, large mouthed and fast moving, with formidable saw-edged teeth, was out there right now, somewhere in the dark—perhaps nearby. So were the hammerheads that frequent the warm water off Key Largo. Their fleeting shadows streaked through his mind as he scanned the moonlit surface. His spear was gone, at the bottom, but his Hawaiian-style sling, used to fire it, was still tucked in his gray athletic shorts. The sling is simply twenty-four inches of yellow surgical tubing attached to a wooden cylinder. Insert the spear, draw back the rubber tubing and let fly, like a slingshot. Now he considered another use for the unarmed sling: If attacked by a shark, he would use the tubing to fashion a tourniquet and hope to be found before he bled to death.

The *Hog Wild* remained anchored on the reef until after nightfall, when Mike radioed the Coast Guard that he would return at dawn to resume the search. He tried not to panic. Barry was a strong swimmer. Tomorrow, he told himself, the call would come that Barry swam ashore, safe somewhere. But what chance did even the strongest swimmer have of surviving the night among sharks and stinging man-of-war jellyfish?

Mike telephoned Susan to say he had bad news. "We lost Barry," he said flatly, "out in the ocean."

"That's not funny," she said. For ten minutes she refused to believe him, then burst into tears. She drove to the townhouse Barry and Mike shared. Word spread. Adults and teenagers, students and members of Barry's fellowship group began to arrive. When Mike drove up shortly before 11:00, they ran out to his van, hoping for good news. There was none. They talked and prayed. No one slept.

"Football players would walk in and break down crying," Susan says. "It was touching, how much they cared." One even promised to start going to church if only Barry was saved.

"All of Hialeah knows Barry," Mike said. "He's helped so many kids out of drugs and drinking. Kids love him. So do parents. He can take straggly, skinny, wimpy little kids with no self-confidence and no sports ability and just draw out qualities that the kid never knew he had. That's why Barry always had championship teams."

Somebody brought Cokes and sandwiches at 2:00 A.M. One high school athlete brought his favorite photo, shot when Barry took a group of youngsters white-water rafting on a wild North Carolina river. Tears, prayers and reminiscences filled the long night.

Time dragged for Barry, watching the water for shark fins slicing through the dark. He checked his watch at 10:00 P.M. After a long wait—at least thirty minutes—he checked it again. It read 10:05. He vowed not to look at it again for a long, long time. When he finally allowed himself to check it again, the time was 10:10.

To sustain himself through the long and perilous hours, he began to relive happy times: rafting down the river with kids, surfing in Hawaii, cruising the South Pacific during his Coast Guard years.

The night was beautiful. He was not alone. The moon hung directly overhead in a star-studded sky. He could make out the constellations. Occasionally he would change from his vertical, drown-proof position, roll onto his back and stare at the stars.

An unbelievably loud noise shattered the serene silence at about 1:00 A.M. Deafening engines roared across open water.

The moon was bright, but eyes straining, he saw nothing. Then it appeared, a wide, white wake in the dark. Silhouetted against it were two Cigarette boats, the fastest in the water. They streaked full throttle across the waves at fifty to sixty miles an hour. Painted dark colors, they ran without lights and rode low in the water. They came so close he was afraid of being run down, but he made no attempt to draw their attention. He knew what they were and that no drug smuggler would rescue him. The roars faded into the night, toward Elliott Key.

Another torment soon accompanied the torturous cramps that made his body ache: jellyfish stings. Tiny creatures he could not see in the dark. At 4:00 A.M. the wind began to stir, and a violent storm struck. Rain fell in such torrents that he could see nothing. Thunder seemed to crash around him and lightning lit up the entire sky. He was afraid it might strike close by and stun him into unconsciousness. The wind howled at least thirty miles an hour, with forty-mile-per-hour gusts. Battered and blinded by waves, he felt like a cork bobbing in the water. Several times great waves pushed him under. He swallowed salt water and his tongue began to swell. His throat burned, and he found it difficult to breathe. He managed to roll over in the rough sea, remove his face mask and let it fill up with fresh rainwater, which he gulped.

The storm raged for three hours, then winds began to subside. The rain stopped at 7:00 A.M. Barry watched the storm roll off the sea, across the keys, and disappear, a huge black mass, into Florida Bay. The sun was up. He felt elated. The storm he thought might kill him had propelled him toward land. Within a half-mile of North Key Largo, he was in much shallower water, just fifteen to twenty feet deep. Even more important, the waves were carrying him toward shore.

A Coast Guard helicopter whirled off the mainland about a half mile south, heading toward the search area. Barry suddenly realized that its crew was now searching for a body. He thought of all the faces, all the jaws that would drop in surprise when they saw him alive.

Mike and two friends, an elder from Barry's church and a

teenage student, had also resumed the search. Mike still harbored hope. Though haunted by thoughts of sharks, he remained certain that Barry was too calm and too strong a swimmer to drown. His companions had despaired. Their goal was to find Barry for a decent burial. A diving team from the Monroe County Sheriff's office had also been dispatched to look for a body.

By 7:30 A.M. the wind had begun to blow again and the sky was growing overcast. Today was Tuesday, the day Barry taught survival swimming to teenagers. The irony did not escape him but he was too exhausted to laugh. He wondered if anyone had called school to say he would not be there. His eyes watered, his throat was raw and his tongue so swollen he could hardly breathe.

Watching the shoreline at 11:30, he saw that he was floating a half-mile off a North Key Largo marina, the last sign of civilization for miles. He knew people were there, he could see parked cars, but his throat was too sore and his lips too cracked to cry for help. He had hoped someone would pick him up, but the weather was so nasty that no boats were out. If he drifted past the marina he could be in the water for another ten or twelve hours, perhaps another night. Fighting cramps, he began to dog-paddle toward the marina.

When the tips of his swim fins touched bottom, he said, "Thank you, God." He felt no wild elation, just gratitude for a second chance.

He put his weight on both feet and gasped as pain like knives plunged into both hips. He dog-paddled the last twenty-five yards to the beach and sat in a foot of water. It was noon, on a desolate shore of mangroves and rocks about a quarter-mile north of the marina. Every muscle in his body was tightly knotted. When he removed his swim fins and looked out at the ocean, he said, "It really struck me what a miracle it was." He looked at the sea in awe, overwhelmed.

Surrounded by mangrove swamp, he felt lightheaded and ached to lie down and rest. But if he did, he might sleep for hours. He struggled to his feet, but collapsed. Unable to move his left leg, he inched himself back into knee-deep water, just enough for buoyancy. Crawling and clawing he made his way to the mouth of the marina. It took thirty minutes. He staggered fifty yards from the surf to the office door, dragging his useless left leg.

The marina director, seated at his desk, looked startled as Barry stumbled in and slumped to the floor. "I've been out in the ocean all night," he explained.

The air-sea search for a body was canceled, and the Key Largo Volunteer Rescue Squad dispatched. Barry tried to sip a soft drink but it burned his lips and swollen tongue.

Rescuemen were incredulous. "We knew you were dead!" one told him. Red lights flashing, siren blaring, they rushed him to Homestead's James Archer Smith Hospital. Dehydrated and suffering from exposure, his feet and arms were numb and his legs and crotch raw. He was covered with painful jellyfish stings. Doctors said that after nearly thirty hours in the water, he was about three hours from possibly fatal dehydration.

Mike Melgarejo was piloting the *Hog Wild* to shore to refuel when the Coast Guard radioed the news. Engine noise drowned out part of the transmission, all he heard was that something had come ashore fifteen miles north. His passengers thought it was a corpse.

Mike cut the engine, and the Coast Guard repeated the message: Snorkeler Barry McCutchen had come ashore alive and was on the way to the hospital.

At Barry's home, Susan answered a telephone call from the Coast Guard and told the crowd, who had kept an all-night vigil.

Deafening screams and cheers filled the room. They rushed to their cars to head south, to the hospital. When Barry was transferred to a hospital closer to home, a convoy of twenty young people followed his ambulance.

He was hospitalized for four days. It took three more before he could move his left leg, but he was alive. Even the Coast Guard was impressed. Had he not kept his cool and used his survival techniques, a spokesman said, Barry would never have come home from his ordeal at sea.

Survival techniques can save your life, but training and knowledge are not always enough. It takes something more, something you don't find in the pages of handbooks.

Chapter 12

STREET COPS

Like the 10 percent of the fishermen who catch 90 percent of the fish, 10 percent of the cops catch 90 percent of the crooks.

Some call these gifted cops streetwise, but the truth is that good street cops simply use all five senses—plus a sixth. Instinct moves them to the right place at the right moment. Other cops can stand on a street corner for twenty-three hours a day, and nothing happens. Street cops are there when it counts. The secret is timing.

Gerald Green is the perfect street cop, a quick study in curiosity, dedication and brains. Events that might happen once in a lifetime to another cop occur with peculiar frequency to Jerry Green.

While waiting on a hotel balcony for a man wanted on bad-check charges, Green saw two sunny-day strollers react to the sound of a siren. The siren was nothing but a distant fire engine, but Green noted its curious effect on the men in the street below. One darted into a doorway, pressing a shopping bag to his chest. The other stepped cautiously into the street, looked both ways, then signaled the first. They began to hurry away, peering over their shoulders. When a second siren sounded, the man with the bag scrambled into a shadowy doorway and flattened himself against the wall.

Green radioed for a patrol car. As the cruiser rounded the corner, the two men stepped into a laundromat. The bag was probably full of dirty clothes, Green thought, and radioed the patrolmen to disregard his call. But as the Miami police cruiser pulled away, the two men ran out of the laundromat still carrying the sack, and leaped into a car driven by a third man. Green keyed his radio: "Disregard that disregard." The cruiser wheeled around. Officer Mike Brown jumped out in front of the car and forced it to a stop.

The men spooked by the sirens were stewards on the M.S. *Nordic Prince*, which had just docked. In the shopping bag: eight pounds of high-quality marijuana compacted into bricks.

In court on other business, Green recognized a defendant named Bobbi Jean, a slightly overweight woman with a perpetual smile. He had busted her for forgery a year earlier. Her troubles now seemed far more serious. She had confessed to the brutal slaying of a convenience-store clerk, and Metro police had charged her with first-degree murder and robbery. During her hearing, Green heard the date the crime occurred. Wait a minute, he thought. He could have sworn she was serving ninety days on his forgery case at that time. He was right. Bobbi Jean simply liked to confess. In fact, she had confessed six murders to Miami police months earlier. They did not believe her. So she tried Metro police. They did.

She pouted that Green had ruined her scheme to join her lesbian sweetheart in prison. "Sending me there," she explained to him, "would be like sending you to the Playboy Mansion."

Jerry Green seems to find crime any place, any time. It was his night off, but his honey-blond wife, Mary Jo, had a two A.M. craving for a Cuban sandwich, and he drove off to find one. Instead, he found an armed robbery taking place on a street corner. He shot one robber, chased and captured the other. Mary Jo got her sandwich—at seven A.M.

Jerry Green and Walter Clerke are the same age, joined the department at the same time and soon became a team. They were perfect partners. Clerke's father had been a police captain in Brooklyn's tough Bedford-Stuyvesant section. At nineteen, Walter followed his father into the New York City Police Department. Assigned to the notorious 41st Precinct—the area of the South Bronx known as Fort Apache—he and his pregnant wife, Susan, vacationed in Florida. They decided it was paradise, a safe place to raise their child, far from all the crime and the drugs.

It was, then.

Jerry Green and Walter Clerke are legendary. With luck, guts and a sixth sense, the pair compiled an amazing record, arresting sixty-three felons in five months. Even while attending full-time robbery seminars for two weeks, they managed to arrest four armed robbers and eight other felons.

Green was named Miami's top police officer of the year in 1973. He was first to win all three annual outstanding officer awards, presented by the Rotary, the American Legion and financier William Pawley, in the same year.

There was another first at the award luncheon, in the fancy ballroom of a posh hotel. Green made the surprise announcement that he was splitting the thousand-dollar award with his partner, who had gone unrecognized. "It was a team effort—by the three of us," he said. Team member number three was his wife, Mary Jo. "I could never give the time and the effort I do to my job without her help."

"I didn't realize that being a policeman's wife would be so lonely," Mary Jo Green, mother of Gregory, age three, told me at the luncheon. "If you have something planned, he doesn't come home. But you just put dinner back in the oven. I don't worry about him because when the situation is at its very worst, he's at his very best."

Their time together was always short. Jerry and his partner worked nights. Mary Jo sold auto insurance during the day. But he telephoned her office daily to recount his exploits of the night before. "You can hear it in his voice," she said. "He loves the work so much."

Green intended to celebrate the award with Mary Jo that night. But he did not arrive home until six A.M. the next day. Two armed bandits had been hitting a bar a day in cities north of Miami. They robbed the employees and patrons, locking them in rest rooms before fleeing in a stolen car.

Green and his partner had found a child playing with a wallet in Miami's central district and discovered that the billfold had been taken in the bar robbery that day. The robbers must live in the neighborhood, they theorized, and probably returned there quickly after stickups. They told police in Fort Lauderdale, Hallandale, Dania and Hollywood to notify them at once next time the bandits struck.

That night of the award luncheon, the robbers hit a Hollywood bar. Hollywood police radioed descriptions of the suspects and their car to Green and Clerke, who raced to the north-south expressway ramp they thought the robbers would use.

"We got there about two seconds before they came driving off the exit. They were both smiling," Green said.

They arrested the astonished robbers, recovered the gun, the loot and the stolen car.

The inseparable partners almost died together two months later.

A New Orleans man gave his clothes away that day in Miami. He no longer needed them, he said, "I'm not gonna live tonight." He later shoved a gun in the face of a homeless man and forced him to crawl in the street, weeping and begging for his life.

Shortly before midnight, the man from New Orleans stepped out of his downtown hotel, blasted on barbiturates. He called a cab for himself and a man to whom he was selling pills. The Diamond cab driver, edgy about recent robberies, refused to allow them in his taxi until they lifted their shirts to prove they were unarmed. The men angrily refused. When a hotel security man tried to intervene, the frightened cabbie stomped on the gas and drove off. The man from New Orleans pulled a gun and waved it in the air, shouting that he should have shot the driver.

From their unmarked car a block away, fifteen minutes from the end of their shift, Green spotted the disturbance as the cab sped off. "Wally," he said. "It looks like that guy in the black hat has a gun out on the street." He drove toward the man, who stuck the gun in his belt and pulled his multicolored dashiki over it.

The officers drew their guns and ordered the two men to place their hands on the car.

The New Orleans man refused. "I don't care if you're cops or not! You're going to have to kill me," he shouted. "Come on! Let's shoot it out right now. Kill me! Kill me!" He pulled his gun.

Green, frisking the other man, heard the commotion and saw the gun swing toward his partner. He ran to grab the weapon and all three grappled. Green and the gunman fell to the ground struggling. The man's gun fired.

"I knew I was shot," Jerry said later. "I had the wind knocked out of me. I was bleeding all over the place." The bullet had slammed through his left hand and into his chest.

Clerke opened fire. He shot the gunman five times in the chest, from three or four feet away. The impact of the bullets showered Jerry with the man's blood.

The man never flinched. Ignoring the five bullet holes in his chest, he fired back and shot Clerke.

"It felt like a sharp kick," Clerke said. "My leg buckled." The wounded officer stood in the middle of the street holding an empty gun; he had no place to hide, and the man who should be dead was still coming.

"Do something!" Clerke shouted to his bleeding partner. "I've got no bullets!"

Despite his wounds, Green said, the man "walked toward us, like a zombie, firing his gun. He was the living dead. I shot him, and it knocked him back to the car." Green kept shooting, and the wounded man stumbled to cover behind the police car. "He had to be dead, but he didn't know it. I shot him again. He ran down the street shooting back at us. I was shooting as fast as I could pull the trigger. None of the bullets stopped him."

A normal person would have died or lapsed into shock after

being shot, but because this man's system was loaded with barbiturates, "he was a monster," Green said, "the walking dead."

Clerke ducked behind a pillar to reload. They continued to shoot until the man went down behind the tire of an eighteen-wheeler fifty yards away. It was over, they thought. "Then he started firing again. I saw him point the gun right at me," Green said. The battle seemed neverending.

Clerke emptied his gun again, then scrambled to the car for their shotgun. Green reloaded his 9-millimeter semiautomatic Smith and Wesson. "We both opened up on him then. Wally with the shotgun, me with a handgun." All they could see was the man's legs. "Wally shot the heels off his shoes and shot holes in his legs. The man had holes in the bottoms of his feet."

The gunman finally stopped shooting and began to fumble, fishing more bullets out of his pocket, trying to reload. The cops' guns were also empty.

The gunman suddenly rolled over on his face. He had another dozen rounds of ammunition, but died before he could use them. The medical examiner counted twenty-seven entrance wounds.

During the initial struggle the gunman had dropped a bag containing several hundred pills. More were found in his room, uppers and downers, along with more bullets.

The second man had run when the shooting started. The hotel security man had chased him, but was knocked down by a ricocheting bullet.

The dead gunman was an ex-convict with a past history of rape, armed robbery, burglary, drugs and theft of a U.S. mail truck. When the death message reached his family, a half-brother in New Orleans was "indifferent." His grandmother said he was a bad man, not allowed in her home. When police notified his mother that she could claim the body, she was uninterested.

"You shot him," she said, "you bury him."

The wounded partners shared a hospital room and admitted their luck. "Instinct told us he was dangerous, but we have restrictions on our use of firearms," Green said. "We were ninety percent sure he had a gun, but we have to be a hundred percent sure. You can't start shooting when somebody reaches under his shirt. They could be hiding narcotics. Our hesitation got us shot. When we were finally sure he had a gun and was going to shoot us—we were already shot."

Clerke still carries a bullet lodged in his left thigh. In his left shirt pocket, over his heart, Jerry had a thick stack of field interrogation cards and mug shots, all fugitives he was seeking. The bullet went through his hand, plowed through the wad of pictures and slammed into his chest. Nearly spent, it penetrated no vital organs.

The wanted men may have saved his life.

Neither partner soured on police work—not then.

"This has been happening across the country," Green said. "You can't be afraid. The man wanted to take on some policemen. I'm glad he took on two who could handle him."

Wally agreed that it was all part of the job. "You have to expect it and hope that you're luckier than the next guy," he said.

Their wives were terrified. "Jerry always tells me nothing bad can happen to him," Mary Jo said fearfully. "Now I know that isn't true." The incident did have a silver lining: "He had to stay home to recover, and we were together every evening. It was great."

Susan Clerke said she never wanted Wally hurt again, "but it's been awful nice to have my man around the house."

The partners continued to solve cases, make arrests and help rehabilitate people. They considered reform a major part of their job. "We don't think in terms of punishing people who've done wrong," Green said. "When we arrest a guy we think in terms of preventing his next crime, saving his next potential victim."

"If they have any possibility of rehabilitation, we try to give it to them," Clerke said. Some were beyond saving, so they focused their efforts on those who could be helped. "You come up with about one person out of ten who really deserves to go to prison." The others responded positively to a chance.

"Junkies love their kids too," Green said.

Assigned to a federally funded robbery-control program, the

two cops worked with the courts and helped arrange probation, jobs and school enrollment for more than a hundred people. They put them in jail, then got them out and into work or college.

It worked.

Miami's robbery rate dropped by 10 percent while it climbed by 15 percent in other communities.

"Face it," Green said, "there's no way a six-man unit is going to control robbery altogether in a city this big. So we're taking another approach, trying to keep robberies down without staking out stores and shooting every hopped-up kid we see. We try to keep people from being hurt. We sit down and talk to people we know are doing robberies."

"You can sit down and convince a guy that pulling a robbery is not the way to make fifty dollars," Clerke said.

Jerry Green and Wally Clerke got exactly what they deserved: They were honored as the best cops in the country by the International Association of Chiefs of Police. *Parade* magazine published a story and pictures of them and their families.

Their bosses, displaying their usual wisdom, split up the partners.

Police brass don't understand the old adage: *If it ain't broke, don't fix it.* Green worked the bunco squad, breaking up con games, then homicide, the property bureau and back to homicide. He and Mary Jo had a second son, Jeffrey. Clerke worked patrol, riding a three-wheeler.

They hoped to work together again someday.

They never did. They never will.

The most successful partnership in Miami Police history ended forever when Officer Wally Clerke's car was firebombed in an ambush behind a looted Zayre discount store during the May 1980 riot. Clerke walked into headquarters, turned in his badge and walked out.

He never went back.

"I quit after the National Guard came in," he explained. "The situation was under control, and there was no more immediate need for me to continue helping the city." *Parade*'s writer had described them in 1973 as "such devoted policemen that neither can imagine himself ever doing any other kind of work."

True then. Not now.

Clerke said he was selling his house to move to Stuart and become a charter fishing captain. I had trouble believing it.

"He's bailing out," Green said. "I don't know what to say. He's looking for a better way of life. The firebombing didn't make him quit, but it didn't make him decide to stay either."

Disillusioned by other pressures, Clerke had been considering a career change.

For eleven years, his associates at work were the street people, the robbers, the hookers, the pimps, the punks, the drunks, the stoned-out freaks. He had found it increasingly difficult not to want to spend his off-duty hours taking baths. "I like them personally. I empathized with them, but I can't reconcile their lifestyle. I felt I was contaminating my wife and daughter." Every combat cop he knew, except Jerry Green, had been divorced, some several times. His own marriage to Susan was now shaky after thirteen years.

The riot accelerated his decision. "I'm disappointed at what happened," he said. "I'm disappointed in the black community. They were finally getting clout. The Liberty City area was being fixed up. A lot of the old buildings were being knocked down.

"And there was," he swore, "very little racial tension in the city. I could ride around and talk to people with no problem. I can't remember the last time I heard anybody yell 'Pig!' or anything like that. Now it's gone back ten years."

The career change failed to save Wally Clerke's marriage. He and Susan were divorced.

So were Jerry and Mary Jo Green, two years later, in 1982. He raised the boys alone, working midnights as a homicide investigator. Greg is in college in Tallahassee. Jeffrey is in high school. The job has not been quite the same for Green since Wally Clerke left. He lost a partner and his best friend. "When you had him around you had a hundred percent backup," he says wistfully. He and Wally remain friends, but lead differing life-styles. Wally has a new wife and a baby, and sells new cars in Broward County.

Green, now a midnight-shift sergeant, leads a homicide team in a city with one of the highest murder rates in the country. His current team maintains a better-than-85-percent clearance rate. He works weekends, investigating a growing number of street murders. Ten years ago robbers killed more innocent people: store clerks, taxi drivers, pedestrians, anybody who had a buck. Today most victims are less than innocent. Most murders are victim-related: robbers shooting dope dealers, other street people, other criminals. The use of assault rifles is on the increase. So are drive-by shootings, most by notoriously poor marksmen. At least half the time they hit someone other than the intended target.

Everything changes, and so did Jerry Green's solitary life-style. He skied on a police olympic team at Lake Tahoe, invited out to dinner a former Miamian who had moved west, and they were married in late 1989.

Jerry Green still seems to be always at the right place at the right time. At the downtown Omni Mall, where he works off-duty security, he recently witnessed a murder.

The Omni, with its multiple movie theaters, is a magnet for youngsters. This night, a group spent their movie money playing video games. When they became noisy and disruptive, Green asked them to cool it and suggested they go home. The kids spilled out onto the sidewalk in front of the J. C. Penney store at eleven P.M.

As he watched from across the street, they frolicked in youthful horseplay—nothing serious. One little boy clamped another in a headlock. Green glanced away, heard a shot, and "saw a kid holding his chest. He staggered back and fell. The boy with the gun simply watched him, then walked away. He didn't start running until he saw me."

The killer was twelve years old. The victim was eleven.

Green rushed across the street. "I looked down at him and he was dead on the sidewalk."

The boy with the gun ran a block and vanished. He eluded

police by climbing a tree. He later made his way home to Opa-Locka, where Green and other cops surrounded his house. Suddenly a shot rang out and a bullet whizzed over their heads. Startled cops scrambled. The gunfire came from next door to the house they were surrounding. The elderly neighbor who fired it stepped outside and leveled his gun at police.

It is second nature for some people to start shooting when they see the cops.

The old man's family tackled and disarmed him. Half the police present went next door to deal with him, the others flushed out the twelve-year-old killer. The murder weapon belonged to his grandmother. He had broken into her house and stolen her gun while she was in the hospital.

There was no fight, just horseplay, until the other boy squeezed his head too tight—that was why the fatal shooting took place.

The suspect faces trial as an adult, despite his age. His police record dates back for years. His mother is a drug addict—has been all her life, Green said. "He had no adult supervision, his life-style is the same as kids in El Salvador and Lebanon. The kids with guns and assault rifles—a lost generation."

Life has not changed much for Jerry Green. He is still the best street cop I ever met.

Another great street cop, Metro-Dade Sergeant Thomas Blake, is known as "Bulldog" for his relentless and dogged pursuit of professional criminals. It may take ten years and his personal vacation time, but he *will* track them down. Even his enemies call him a genius. When Bulldog Blake took the sergeant's test he ranked first among 450. His only hobby is hunting. He hunts professional criminals.

His waking hours revolve around police work. He is cunning and creative. Early one Sunday morning Bulldog tracked a jewel thief to a Hialeah home. How, he wondered, could he get the elusive fugitive, sought by the FBI for years, to open the door?

He yodeled. Yodeled. Loud and long.

"Who the hell are you?" cried the jewel thief as he threw open the door.

"Sergeant Tom Blake of the Metro Police Department. You are under arrest."

This noted tracker of thieves was the first South Florida cop to use the RICO (Racketeer Influenced and Corrupt Organizations) Act as a tool against burglars. Designed to fight organized crime, RICO allows the law to seize homes, cars and businesses purchased with profits from illegal enterprise. When he arrested longtime thieves for five burglaries, he also charged them with racketeering. "They qualify," he said. "They are career criminals, working thieves. They work with other burglars and with fences. It is their business. They have a job: stealing."

A fifty-four-year-old burglar released after nine years of a thirty-year sentence enjoyed only thirteen days of freedom. Police got a tip that the thief, once suspect in two hundred burglaries, had resumed his old and bad habits, despite his sincere lectures on home security to homeowners' associations while in prison. Bulldog decided to watch him. When the man burglarized a townhouse and carried the loot out the front door, Bulldog called for backup. To stall the culprit until they arrived, he introduced himself as a member of the homeowners' association and engaged the thief in a conversation on home security.

He met his wife, Mary, on the job, after two cars crashed onto her lawn. Mary Blake shares her husband's sense of awareness. On her way to pick up the children at school, she saw a man stroll up and down the street, studying the homes. He had the "look." She called her husband. Bulldog saw the man disappear behind a house. Minutes later, he followed. Four jalousies had been removed, and he caught the thief inside the house peering out.

When Bulldog saw a station wagon drop off a man dressed in black in front of a home in a residential neighborhood at one A.M., he assumed they were burglars. The station wagon circled the block. When the figure in black crept away from the house, Bulldog surprised him, to inquire what he was doing. The man in black claimed to be just taking a walk as the house behind him erupted in flames.

An arsonist, not a burglar, the man had been paid a thousand dollars to torch the house for the insurance. The driver who dropped him off was the homeowner.

Only once have I seen a criminal best the Bulldog. He took a captured thief, suspected of 250 burglaries, out of jail one day so the crook could point out the homes he had looted—standard procedure. At noon, Bulldog, the prisoner and another detective stopped for lunch—also standard procedure. The detectives ordered Cuban sandwiches, paying no attention as their guest placed his order in Spanish.

Then the meal arrived.

"It was a damn lobster!" cried Captain Marshall Frank, Bulldog's boss, when he got the bill. It listed $17.60—"for prisoner's lunch."

"No way!" said the captain and kicked it back.

I called the detective to ask about the thief's lobster feast. "No comment," Bulldog snarled.

Joseph Gennaro Carbone, a flashy burglar arrested in 1976, impressed Bulldog. Polite, cool, and thoroughly professional, Carbone had an associate show up to post his bond while he was still being booked. Bulldog stepped outside to catch the tag number of the man who arrived with the bond money. For eighteen months he kept a loose tail on both men. He investigated them and their activities even on his days off.

Carbone was a big-league burglar, one of the elite. A slick thief, he specialized in stealing from posh high-rise apartments, taking only cash or costly jewelry. If he found none, he simply left the apartment undisturbed. Bulldog learned that Carbone liked to flash wads of hundred-dollar bills in bars, drink Chivas Regal on the rocks and brag about wearing twenty-five thousand dollars in jewelry while pulling his burglaries. Bulldog noted where Carbone vacationed and the hotels he favored. He learned that the man summered in suburban Washington, D.C., usually at a Falls Church, Virginia, hotel.

Bulldog printed a flyer describing Carbone and five other burglars who wore cabana sets, tennis outfits or expensive suits on the job. When Tom and Mary vacationed they distributed flyers to police departments up and down the eastern seaboard, along the thief's winter route. Back in Miami, Bulldog noticed that the thief's car was unused for days. He soon found out why: Police he alerted had spotted Carbone and a confederate in Falls Church. They were tailed and caught emerging from a condominium complex, pockets stuffed with loot. Bulldog did not get the collar, but his dogged detective work had paid off.

Carbone was sentenced to eight years in prison in Virginia and Maryland, fifteen years in Florida and five years in a federal lockup in Washington, D.C.

History repeated itself eight years later. Flashy jewel thief Joseph Carbone, tanned and wearing tennis togs, met Bulldog Blake again outside a South Dade apartment complex.

"Hi, Joe," Blake said.

"Hello, Bulldog," Carbone replied.

"It's been eight years, Joe," Blake said and arrested Carbone, now thirty-seven.

"He didn't show it outwardly, but I bet he was quite chagrined," Blake said.

Carbone had been paroled to Florida a year earlier. "He likes it here, there are lots of apartments and townhouses," Bulldog said. His parole officer thought Condo Joe was working at a sports shop.

He was not.

Blake had been on vacation when fellow detectives heard Carbone was back in business. A car he had rented was spotted leaving the scene of a Kendall burglary. They called Bulldog at home.

He knew Carbone's style. Stay at a swank hotel, drive a rental car, use valet parking. Detectives found the hotel and Bulldog, still on vacation, joined the surveillance. Just like old times—

except that Blake could only stake out the suspect at night. Days he spent at home, baby-sitting his third child, a baby girl Mary had delivered three weeks earlier. So by day Bulldog Blake changed diapers and by night he stalked Carbone.

When Blake returned to work he set up a surveillance.

Spiffy in his white tennis shorts, Carbone left his hotel for work by 8:30 A.M., driving a rented blue Buick. He wore an expensive gold watch, a gold ring with a diamond, thick gold chains and a gold bracelet. Detectives watched him stroll through a complex. "Casing apartments," Bulldog said.

They trailed him to a building where only residents have keys, and watched him slip inside with a resident who was arriving home. "A common ruse to get into those buildings," Blake said.

Detectives were unable to follow without a key. They waited until he emerged. Carbone, ever friendly, smiled, "Hi, how are you?"

Then he saw Bulldog Blake.

At their surprise reunion Bulldog charged Carbone with violating parole, attempted burglary and possession of burglary tools—lock picks found in the pocket of his tennis shorts.

"He's put on some weight," Blake observed later. "But so have I, I'm thirty-seven too, so I'm sympathetic."

After eight years, Bulldog Blake finally made the collar.

Pete Corso was a spit-and-polish fresh-faced rookie when we met—not yet the seasoned street cop he soon became. A member of the elite Miami Beach Police task force, he was smart, eager and not afraid to talk to a reporter. One night Corso and crew busted a sleazy but influential bail bondsman with friends powerful enough to get him unarrested, which was what he boasted would happen. I didn't know the task force even knew where I lived, but they pounded on my door, shotguns and all, at two A.M. Neighbors must have thought it was a raid. Awakened from a sound sleep, I found a notebook and took down the information from Pete while the others waited outside in an unmarked car.

Arrest reports are public record, unless they disappear. Corso was smart enough to know that if a reporter knew all about an arrest it could not be surreptitiously undone.

Next time we talked he wanted advice. A budding Joseph Wambaugh, he was working on a novel about the job he loved. He had a good start but never finished it. His career got in the way.

He loved police work and took it so seriously that he suffered an ulcer. At one point, he even quit the force to sell insurance. The pay was better and the job easier on his ulcer, but he missed police work. The department welcomed him back. One of his assignments on the way up was public information officer, the spokesman designated to talk to the press. He jokingly posted a one-word sign above his desk: OMERTA, the Italian code of silence.

Pete Corso's most endearing quality was his affection for his wife—his high school sweetheart—and his two little daughters. They had adopted one, then had one of their own. Both girls were beautiful, their pictures on his desk. "One's adopted," he would say, "but I can't remember which one."

He played tennis and stayed in shape, despite feeding his ulcer with milk shakes and ice cream. At age thirty-eight, Pete Corso was named Miami Beach police chief—evidence that sometimes there is justice, after all.

Good news is so rare on the police beat.

Pete seemed born to be chief. He tackled the job with the same vigor with which he tackled burglars and robbers fifteen years earlier as a rookie.

Still spit-and-polish, gregarious and glib, with a quirky grin and a ready laugh, the chief was apt to answer his own telephone, hours after his office staff quit for the day. He pursued a grueling schedule, instituting major changes in the 250-person department. Pete had advocated a strong "police presence" for years and now practiced it. He ordered detectives back into uniform, yanked officers out from behind desks, traded unmarked cars for police cruisers and sent them out to patrol the streets.

Appointed in April 1980, the popular young chief was on a speaking binge that summer, talking to as many as three major civic groups a day. In May, the Mariel boatlift delivered thousands of Cuban refugees, and by the end of July and early August, the city faced a sudden, dramatic increase in violent crime.

The chief reported the skyrocketing crime rate to the City Commission, attributing the rampage to criminals among the new Cuban refugees. It was the first time anyone had dared suggest such a thing in public. Cubans took offense. An editorial slamming the chief for his insensitivity to them was written for the "Miami Beach Neighbors" section of the *Herald*, an insert printed on Friday and distributed with the Sunday newspaper.

A Miami Beach publicist, a friend of Corso's, called me in the newsroom late Saturday afternoon. "What do you think about Pete Corso?" he said grimly. From my vantage point on the police beat, I said, I was convinced that the chief was right and would safely ride out the storm. I thought the caller was talking about the controversy. He was not. He thought I knew.

Pete Corso was dead.

The police chief had spent the afternoon relaxing around his backyard pool. Three other families, all longtime friends, were guests. Corso barbecued hot dogs and hamburgers. Shortly after five P.M., he splashed into the pool. North Miami Deputy Police Chief Thomas Flom, a friend of eighteen years, was with him. Five children and three adults frolicked in the water, playing a fast-paced game of Keep Away with a rubber ball. Flom saw Pete gasping, his face down, in the shallow end of the pool. He thought Corso was joking. Then Pete's wife screamed.

Flom dragged him from the pool and began CPR. A Pembroke Pines firefighter who lives nearby hurdled backyard fences racing to help. A city rescue unit arrived in three minutes. Medics suspected a heart attack. The CPR was excellent but it failed. He was pronounced dead at the hospital.

Pete was thirty-eight and seemed in splendid health. But it is not uncommon for someone under fifty to fail to respond after a coronary. Older people build up collateral circulation that helps to save them. Pembroke Pines Police Chief Jack Tighe, a former Beach police captain, once Corso's boss, hurried to the hospital.

"It's a nightmare," Flom said. "We tried. We tried everything to revive him."

The official finding was drowning, during a heart attack. Corso's blood pressure had been normal. He had no history of heart trouble. Yet he had "hardening of the artery disease, similar to that of a seventy-year-old man," said Broward medical examiner Dr. Ronald Wright. "For thirty to fifty percent of the people with this kind of disease, the first symptom is sudden death."

An autopsy found no trace of the ulcer that had plagued him as a young cop fighting the world.

My story about the untimely death of the popular young chief appeared in the newspaper the same day as the already-published critical editorial, an awkward situation to say the least. Particularly since Pete Corso was absolutely right—perhaps the first public official to realize that Castro had flushed his toilets on us, sending the mentally deranged, the criminally insane and some of the most ruthless killers ever seen in this country.

Pete Corso was police chief for only four months.

Sometimes there is no justice, after all.

Chapter 13

SHOT COPS

Policemen are soldiers who act alone; soldiers are policemen who act in unison.

—Herbert Spencer

Work the police beat long enough and the moment you dread will come: A cop you know will be gunned down. The moment you hear there has been a shooting, that a cop is down, you grab a notebook and dash for your car, mind racing, scanning a mental roster of men and women you know who work this shift, in that neighborhood. Could it be one of them? Sometimes it is.

Miami Beach cop Donald Kramer seemed an unlikely target. He worked no dangerous drug details, patrolled no seething ghetto, and was not a member of SWAT. He rounded up vagrants, drunks and derelicts and drove the paddy wagon to transport his prisoners.

Kramer came late to police work, and he sacrificed to do it. At the height of the Mariel boatlift, the city issued an appeal for more officers. Kramer, a dollar-a-year volunteer auxiliary officer for ten years, responded. At age thirty-nine, he sold his successful TV-repair shop to pursue a lifelong dream: He joined the department full time. An exuberant, fun-loving, laughing man, he loved attention and the job. The biggest joy for this pudgy middle-aged Jewish cop was to distribute Thanksgiving baskets to the needy and wear a Santa suit, with a silver badge, while rounding up drunks at Christmastime. The self-appointed guardian of South Beach winos and street people, he distributed cigarettes and a buck or two out of his own pocket. He often arrested the homeless so they could have a hot meal and a shower in jail.

One of them, a scrawny derelict known as "El Loco," shot Kramer in the back.

It happened at dawn, before Kramer was even officially on duty. It was not unusual for him to be out at daybreak, sweeping South Beach streets for vagrants. On this morning, he parked his paddy wagon and walked alone down an alley behind a crumbling Washington Avenue apartment house. He was not wearing his bulletproof vest.

At the rear of the building, he encountered Andres Garcia Marrero, twenty-seven. The Mariel refugee known as El Loco had a history of arrests for weapons, rape, trespassing and resisting police. Kramer felt in no immediate danger. He did not radio for a backup. His rapport with transients and South Beach residents was excellent.

Georgi Caboerte, twenty-four, was in the bakery across the street, preparing the day's deliveries of fresh bagels, corn muffins and pastries. He heard five shots. An old man, a neighbor, came running across the street yelling, "Call the police! Call the police! A cop is shot!"

Berta McArthur, fifty-four, lived next door to the shooting scene. She heard shots, threw open her window and saw the crumpled officer facedown, blood gushing from head wounds, his service revolver still holstered.

Neighbor Maria Mercedes, fifteen, told me she heard footsteps. Then "Pow! Pow! Pow! Pow! I thought it was firecrackers. Then somebody was yelling. 'He's dead! He's dead!' And I saw cops running."

Two rescue units, both with doctors aboard, arrived in minutes. The medics all knew Kramer. They tore open his uniform and began frantic attempts to revive him, radioing ahead to Mount Sinai Medical Center. The hospital alerted a trauma team and notified Dr. Mario Nanes, a neurosurgeon, at his nearby home. He sped to the emergency room, arriving only three minutes behind the wounded officer. "Time counts in these cases," the doctor told me later.

Shot twice in the back of the head at close range and once in the back, Kramer had no pulse or blood pressure. Ten doctors joined a heroic attempt to save him and within fifteen minutes had restored his blood pressure.

A police escort rushed the officer's mother, Gladys, a small, bewildered woman, into the emergency room. His ailing father, Nathan, a patient undergoing kidney dialysis, checked out of another hospital and hurried to Mount Sinai.

As the doctors labored, police swarmed into the low-rent neighborhood where the shooting took place. SWAT conducted a building-to-building search. A police helicopter swooped low over rooftops.

El Loco was known to sleep on the roof of a block-long pastel building that housed the bakery, an Italian restaurant, a vegetable market, a clinic and a shuttered restaurant. Police had found his mattress and a makeshift lean-to after a small fire a week earlier. K-9 dogs were mustered in the hope they could pick up a scent. Seventy searchers closed off Washington Avenue.

The fugitive, disheveled and dirty, was spotted on a sandy strip of beach at 12:32 P.M., five and a half hours after the shooting. He tried to run but never drew the murder weapon, a rusted Smith and Wesson .38-caliber revolver, or the knife he carried. Eyes vacant and bloodshot, he was whisked away in a patrol car.

El Loco was a bizarre and familiar figure to South Beach residents. Some thought him mute because he rarely spoke. Others said he continually paced Washington Avenue mumbling to himself in high-pitched Spanish.

"He has the IQ of someone you would find in an alley. I don't know why the hell he did it," Lieutenant Alan Solowitz said.

Garcia, Officer Thomas Hoolahan said, was simply "tired of

being hassled, tired of being arrested, tired of people telling him he would have to go. He apparently felt he had the right to do it."

Kramer remained on life support, his brain damaged by bullets and bone fragments.

More than one hundred calls jammed the hospital switchboard, many from South Beach derelicts. Some had obviously been drinking. Many were crying. A man who slurred his words left a message. "Tell him all his buddies on South Beach are praying for him."

I found Roy Howard, eighty-four, at a nearby bar, hoisting his first brandy of the day. "He's a good cop, everybody knows him," he told me. The barmaid had once waitressed at a restaurant where Kramer would come in for "soup and matzoh balls." He loved to eat, she said. "He was friendly, not mean like some officers."

"He arrested me once for fighting in the street," Robert Amor, twenty, offered. "He's a fair man. He's cool. The guy who shot him had to be insane or something."

The mayor, the city manager, city commissioners and brother officers joined the grim hospital vigil. "We're hoping and we're praying," Miami Beach Police Chief Kenneth Glassman said.

Kramer died two days later, four minutes after doctors disconnected his life-support system. He was forty-two.

Fellow cops, black mourning tape across their badges, remained at his side in death. Lieutenant Solowitz and several detectives accompanied the body to the Dade medical examiner's office for the autopsy and then to the funeral home.

"We just didn't want him alone there in the morgue. It wouldn't be right," Solowitz said.

Repose was between seven and nine P.M. at the funeral home. The first mourner, a weeping elderly woman, arrived at eight A.M. Hundreds of people from all walks of life filed past the coffin, where Kramer lay in uniform, flanked by a police honor guard at attention.

Two rabbis presided, but the loss was ecumenical. At Miami

Beach Community Church, the city's oldest place of worship, the Reverend Garth Thompson described Kramer as a "loving person who looked out for South Beach derelicts. He loved these people, and by one of them he was killed."

Kramer made his usual rounds of South Beach one last time, in a hearse.

The fastest way to find out something is not true is to put it in the newspaper. City officials and cops all announced without hesitation that Donald Kramer was the first Miami Beach policeman killed on the job.

They were wrong.

One of my frequent correspondents among Florida pioneers clearly recalled a Miami Beach policeman killed in a gun battle during the late 1920s. No one at police headquarters or City Hall knew about any such thing. But there it was, in newspaper archives, on hard-to-read microfiche.

The old-timer was right. The first Miami Beach police officer killed in the line of duty fought a blazing predawn gun duel with desperados. He died a hero.

Thieves broke into a Fort Lauderdale auto dealership after midnight on Monday, March 19, 1928. The brazen bandits stole cash and a shotgun, then drove a brand new Hupmobile sedan out the showroom window.

Police set up roadblocks. At 3:45 A.M., three Miami Beach police officers spotted the stolen motorcar traveling south on Washington Avenue toward Fifth Street. They ordered the driver to stop. The passenger in the big, boxy sedan opened fire. The police shot back, in a running gun battle. They lost the faster, more powerful car after a wild chase. The abandoned Hupmobile was found minutes later, its windows shattered by police gunshots.

The occupants had vanished.

Just before dawn, Officer David C. Bearden, husky and handsome, spotted two men walking along Ocean Drive near Twenty-second Street.

He asked what they were doing. They said they had been at the beach.

As Officer Bearden stepped from his car, one of the bandits fired a gun concealed behind a cap he held in front of him. The bullet caught Bearden just above his heart and exited his back, knocking him down.

No bulletproof vests in those days.

The fallen officer drew his own gun and returned the bandits' fire as they closed in on him. He shot both men, who scrambled into the officer's patrol car and drove off. Bearden crawled in pain to a police alarm box at Twenty-third Street and the ocean, a block away.

No hand-held walkie-talkies in those days.

Hotel employee Roy Widden, on his way to work, found Bearden slumped at the base of the pole, too weak from blood loss to stand. Following the officer's gasped instructions, he took the call-box key from his pocket and sounded the alarm.

Bearden was taken to the hospital. At 7:10 A.M., Miami police found the two wounded men sprawled unconscious in a vacant lot.

One died soon after. In his pocket he carried a small metal disc. On it was inscribed: THE WAGES OF SIN ARE DEATH.

The other man, shot in the head, would survive.

Bearden lingered for a day or so. He told his chief on his deathbed that his last wish was to be buried in his native Alabama. He was twenty-four.

On March 21, 1928, a news story reported that Chief R. H. Wood had escorted Bearden's body to Maplesville, Alabama.

My pioneer correspondent, John Bledsoe, nearly seventy-seven and retired to Okeechobee, was a Miami Beach milkman at the time. "Chief Wood," he told me, "was a caring man, a good chief who thought a lot of his men, and they thought a lot of him."

In the musty archives of the old City Hall on Washington Avenue was long-forgotten Resolution 1744, passed on that March 21, over sixty years ago.

Signed by then council president John Levi, it calls Bearden a "gallant officer," and in flowery odes to his bravery, lauds his "supreme sacrifice . . . the shining example of his heroism and a quality of courage that would bring glory to any community."

Officer Bearden had left "his name on the hearts of the citizenry of this city. . . . We shall remember what David Bearden did here. . . . His memory will be as inspiring as the light upon the mountains, or as the sunshine on the sea."

Sounds like politicians.

They hailed his courage, and swore never to forget his "unselfish devotion."

Then they did.

There was no other official trace, no record, no memorial.

Intrigued, I looked to Maplesville, Alabama, for more about the forgotten hero. Beardens still lived there, but none remembered the fallen policeman or where he was buried.

How sad, I thought, after calling what seemed like everyone in that small town.

But then I found David Bearden still alive in one heart.

"Everybody loved David," Ora Carter Davis told me. "It was sorrowful when he was killed. He was a nice boy, he wasn't rough like a lot of people, and he was nice-looking."

They were childhood sweethearts.

David lived in Pleasant Grove and came down to Maplesville where they "courted" at Saturday night square dances.

"We thought a lot of each other," she said wistfully. "But we were kinfolk." They were first cousins.

In 1919 she met a soldier named Joe Davis, and they got married. She was fifteen. "I married young," she said, "and David, he just left."

The girl David Bearden loved moved to a cabin on a creek bank and raised seven children. Her husband had died five years before my call.

Ora Carter Davis said David Bearden is buried in a churchyard at Pleasant Grove. At eighty, she now lived alone, with her memories. "My life has been sad," she confided.

The deaths of Bearden and Kramer, fifty-six years and nineteen blocks apart, were similar: both caught by surprise, both shot at dawn without warning, both in a leap year, both lingering briefly in local hospitals before dying.

"He was a true hero," Chief Glassman said on reading the old newspaper story, "and it's only right that we remember him."

City manager Rob Parkins, a former cop himself, said, "It would be tragic to be killed like that and forgotten."

David Bearden, dead at age twenty-four in 1928, was remembered officially for the first time in more than half a century.

When I visit Miami Beach police headquarters now I always reread the shiny plaque in the lobby, honoring both David Bearden and Donald Kramer.

Neither is forgotten.

Shot cops are overlooked in many ways. The system slighted Donald Kramer. El Loco never went to trial for his murder.

He never will.

Experts concluded that El Loco was crazy. That should have been no surprise, given his nickname. In 1989, after five years of testing and legal arguments, a judge threw out the murder case against him. El Loco was considered too incompetent to be tried.

El Loco's public defender said his client was mentally deficient and dyslexic, had only a fourth-grade education in Cuba, was born partially deaf and then further damaged his hearing with a hand grenade. He speaks no English, and syphilis has caused more damage to his brain.

"He's a mess," agreed the prosecutor.

Prosecutors translated twenty pages of testimony from an old murder trial into Spanish, had El Loco read it aloud and then asked questions. Their conclusion: He did not understand a thing. Both sides agreed there was no way El Loco could comprehend his own trial.

"He's as sane as he can be," insisted the dead cop's still-bewildered mother. "Our son was our best friend, one of the nicest guys who ever lived. It's hard to believe that someone like this man can get away with killing him."

The judge ordered El Loco confined in a maximum-security

state hospital, but lawyers for the state objected, arguing that it is unconstitutional to jail someone who is no longer charged with a crime. Maximum-security state hospitals are for defendants tried and found not guilty by reason of insanity. Insanity, however, was why El Loco could not be tried. State officials offered to place him in a "campuslike" facility from which he would be released when considered no longer a threat.

The Miami Herald reported the Catch-22 situation. Public outrage persuaded the state to relent and lock El Loco in a hospital for the criminally insane. No one knows if or when he will be released.

In the final analysis, nobody is paying for Donald Kramer's death—except us.

Nearly all cop killers have prior criminal records. They are usually on parole or probation or free on bond. Most often the distance between cop and killer is zero to five feet, nose-to-nose confrontations, not drawn-out firefights. The officer stands little chance.

That was the case with three Metro auto-theft detectives who possessed an uncanny sixth sense about stolen cars.

Frank Dazevedo and Thomas Hodges, both thirty-two, and Clark Curlette, twenty-eight, were never off duty, even when away from their office and out of their jurisdiction.

Miami Beach was not their turf, but a tip they had passed to the Florida Highway Patrol had panned out, and three employees were about to be arrested for selling fake licenses right out of the Miami Beach motor vehicle bureau. It was a big deal; the FHP state commander had flown in from Tallahassee to wrap up the investigation. As a courtesy, the FHP invited the detectives to attend the bust.

Dazevedo had recently cracked a stolen car ring that specialized in Lincoln Continental Mark IVs. As they stood outside the motor vehicle bureau that afternoon, a light-color Mark IV cruised by in traffic. The three detectives exchanged glances. Their sixth sense said it was stolen. They watched the driver park the Lincoln behind a motel a block away. Two decided to go have a look, while Dazevedo remained with the FHP officials.

Hodges and Curlette clipped their badges to their clothing, drove over to the motel and stopped their unmarked car next to the Mark IV. From inside his room, the driver was watching.

As Hodges walked toward the room, window glass shattered and shotgun blast caught him in the face and shoulder. The detective, the father of three small children, stumbled back thirty feet and fell, dying.

The man burst from the motel room, firing his twelve-gauge shotgun as he ran. He also carried a .38-caliber revolver. Curlette, still standing next to the Mark IV, was shotgunned in the chest. He died on the parking-lot pavement.

A Miami Beach policeman passing on routine patrol had noticed the detectives with clipped-on badges. Now he heard the gunfire and radioed for help. A block away, at the motor vehicle bureau, Dazevedo also heard the shooting and saw his partners down. He asked the troopers if they were armed. Only one was.

Dazevedo sprinted after the man with the shotgun. Fellow detectives agonized later over why he did not wait for help, why he never took cover. Instead he charged in pursuit of the man who had shot his partners. He fired his service revolver, no match for a shotgun. The gunman wheeled and blasted Dazevedo in the face and shoulder with the twelve-gauge. The detective was already dying when the killer shot him again, in the stomach.

An editor shouted across the newsroom to me that a cop had been shot, on the Beach. I snatched up a notebook and started to ask the location. He put down his telephone and said, "That's two cops shot."

As I headed for the elevator, somebody called after me, "Three cops shot."

I sped across the causeway, tuning the police scanner in my car to the Miami Beach frequency. In the confusion, a policeman had left his microphone open. The enraged, almost hysterical shouts of cops in pursuit of the killer were chilling. The fear, the fury and the stress in their voices were terrifying. Beach task force officers were sweeping across a stretch of ocean beach. They had the killer cornered, surrounded in a dense clump of vegetation, palms and sea grapes. Screaming obscenities, they ordered him to surrender. I heard the shot that killed him and nearly drove off the road.

He had shot himself in the head as cops closed in. They half-carried, half-dragged him out of the undergrowth as I pulled up.

"Somebody call an ambulance for this piece of shit!" somebody shouted, but it was too late. They were all dead: three cops and their killer.

As their three children played nearby, Hodges's wife, Karen, saw TV news bulletins reporting the shotgun murders of three Metro detectives in Miami Beach. She knew that her husband and his two partners had gone to Miami Beach that day. The knock at the door found her gripped by a growing fear.

"I thought it could be them," she quietly told me later.

The partners who shared a sixth sense about stolen cars were right. The Lincoln was stolen, from Palm Beach, the license plates from Fort Lauderdale.

Cops are human. You know that, but sometimes it slips your mind. That is why it is devastating to see a cop cry.

As a rookie reporter covering demonstrators at the 1972 Republican National Convention in Miami Beach, I met undercover officers Harrison Crenshaw, Jr., and Gerald Rudoff. A salt-and-pepper team—Rudoff white, Crenshaw black—with the Metro Organized Crime Bureau, they wore beards, beads and hippie hats and infiltrated protest groups. Crenshaw and Rudoff were responsible for the firebombing convictions of Black Afro Militant Movement (BAMM) members and the indictment of the Gainesville Eight on charges of planning to disrupt the convention.

They were as close as brothers. When Crenshaw married a legal secretary named Margaret she half-jokingly asked if Rudoff was joining them on the honeymoon. Promoted to sergeants and no longer partners, they still spent time together. Until late one night, in an unmarked car on his way home from a fruitless stake-out, Crenshaw stopped a Buick. The driver had a gun. They scuffled, and five shots were fired. One dented the gold badge in Crenshaw's pocket. The fatal bullet struck him in the chest.

The shooting happened in front of the home of Metro Officer Simmons Arrington, thirty-one. He heard the shots, ran outside and found Crenshaw in the street. He cradled the dying policeman in his arms.

A petty criminal named Charles Vassar, twenty-two, was arrested the same night.

Rudoff broke down in unashamed sobs. "Harry didn't make mistakes," he told me. "We were involved in many, many explosive situations that we managed to walk away from without anybody getting hurt. Somebody caught him off guard."

Rudoff rushed to his partner's neatly fenced, sunshine-yellow and white house and took Margaret to her parents. Later that night somebody broke in and ransacked the dead cop's home.

What occurred between Crenshaw and his killer was never clearly established. We will never know for sure. After a court hearing, at which he was ordered to stand trial, Vassar hanged himself in his cell.

Three days after Harrison Crenshaw's death, Officer Simmons Arrington, in uniform, on patrol, was dispatched to a routine neighborhood dispute. A resident complained that a man named Sam Smith threatened him. Smith was seated in a car when Officer Arrington arrived.

"I'm the man you're looking for," he called out. As the officer walked toward him, Smith fired a shotgun at point-blank range.

Seventy-two hours earlier, Arrington had cradled a fellow policeman who died in his arms. Now he too was dead.

Cops who survive shootings sometimes lose heart and want out of police work. Who could blame them? Few are like Everett Titus, determined to come back, against all odds. A Metro cop, he risked his own life to save one.

A young man, troubled at nineteen and bent on suicide, braced a rifle against his own stomach. He had seen his father shotgunned seven years earlier by a neighbor. Now he wanted to die.

"He was definitely going to shoot himself," Titus said later. "He'd taken up the slack on the trigger. The only way to stop him was to take the gun away." As they scuffled, the rifle barrel swung toward the doorway. "My partner was coming in. I knew it would have shot him. I pushed the gun down."

It fired. The shot shattered Titus's thigh, blasting away three inches of bone. Doctors wanted to amputate, but he fought them. Three doctors said he would never use the leg again, so he found a fourth doctor. The new plan was to let the fragmented stubs of bone heal and then perform a bone graft with metal plates.

The bone graft never took place. There are no metal plates in his leg. Titus returned to work, despite the doctors who said he would never walk or be a policeman again, despite the wheelchair, despite the brace, despite the cane, despite the doctors' orders.

His comeback was excruciating. He lay in traction, forty-pound weights attached to either side of a pin through his leg. Amazingly, the shattered stumps, three inches apart, began to shoot calcium, like a cobweb building. It took half a year, but the bone regenerated. Muscles written off as destroyed began to rebuild. His secret may have been the daily swimming in a therapeutic pool.

Titus is the father of five. His wife discovered she was pregnant with their youngest while he was hospitalized, still uncertain if he would ever walk again. "She came running into my room all smiles," he said. Soon after his release from the hospital, he discarded his wheelchair. They strapped his brawny six-foot four-inch frame into an ankle-to-waist brace, but it made him feel handicapped, and he swore not to wear it anymore. He took it off, stood up and walked. He could have retired, but this was a man who left a junior executive position with Minnesota Mining and Manufacturing Co., and took a six-thousand-dollar-a-year pay cut to be a cop.

One year after the shooting, Everett Titus went back to work.

And the man who shot him? Just before the case was to go to a jury, the defendant won a dismissal on a legal technicality and walked free.

"Too bad," Titus said, "because the boy really needs psychiatric help. I don't feel bad for myself. I did what I thought was right. I'd do it again. I get paid for that. I only feel bad for my family.

"I'd been shot at at least four times before I got hit. Every police officer and his family realizes he can be shot. It's just something that happens."

Patrol is the most dangerous job for a cop. Men and women in uniform are easy targets. Other police officers may encounter hazards—but not with the same frequency as patrolmen. Growing numbers of police shootings are drug related, but most shot cops are gunned down during routine traffic stops or while handling domestic disturbances.

The day after Police Memorial Day on May 15, a nationwide observance of officers fallen in the line of duty, three more Metro cops were gunned down—patrolmen. This time it was at a Liberty City intersection. The shooter was a lovesick husband stalking his estranged wife.

They had married young—too young. The bride was fourteen, the groom seventeen. Now, three and a half years later, she wanted out. He was AWOL from the army, wearing a red warm-up suit, carrying a satchel, and lurking in the pine trees near the house where she lived with her mother, her 79-year-old grandmother and her 101-year-old great-grandmother.

When his wife arrived in her best friend's car at two P.M., he opened fire. The wounded driver stumbled out and fled. Another teenage girl also ran. The terrified wife scrambled from the backseat to the front and tried to drive away. He overtook her at the corner, caught her by the throat, jammed his pistol to her head and forced his way into the car. The couple struggled as the car bucked and lurched down the street. Neighbors called police.

Officers Keith DiGenova, twenty-seven, his best friend, William Cook, twenty-five, and Robert Edgerton, thirty-nine, arrived first.

Another officer had been dispatched but the call was a "shooting in progress," and they were closer. The time was 2:10 P.M., forty minutes before shift change, five minutes before they would have begun to clear out of Liberty City to start back to the station. Each was in his own patrol car.

A pharmacist who lived nearby heard the fracas and approached the car, now stalled in the intersection. The terrified wife begged him to call police. The husband waved his gun and ordered him away. The pharmacist saw DiGenova's approaching patrol car and flagged it down.

"That's the car, the one in the intersection," he said. "He's got a gun. The man inside has got a gun." Cook and Edgerton arrived moments after. A reserve officer was riding with Cook.

While police distracted her husband, the wounded wife fled the car. Officer DiGenova, his service revolver in his hand, reached in the open passenger window to disarm the driver. The reserve officer, on the driver's side, tried to hold on to the man, who was struggling and screaming threats.

DiGenova's upper body was completely inside the passenger window when the driver suddenly broke free and shot him point-blank in the face. DiGenova's service revolver dropped onto the car seat as he crumpled to the pavement.

In the seconds that followed, Officer Edgerton shot the gunman through a vent window, holstered his gun and rushed to help DiGenova. The wounded man was out of ammunition, but he found the fallen policeman's revolver on the seat beside him and used it to shoot both Edgerton and William Cook.

Robbery Detective Dan Blocker had also responded to the shooting call. He took cover as the gunman stepped away from his car, firing at him.

Blocker took careful aim and killed him.

Officer Cook was dead, hit under the arm, a quarter-inch above his bulletproof vest. Edgerton had not been wearing a vest. Shot in the chest and right arm, he survived his serious wounds and returned to work. DiGenova suffered permanent brain damage and will never wear a badge again.

The shooting provoked angry controversy among cops.

Maron Hayes, fifty-nine, a painter and plasterer, had seen the whole thing. "I don't see how the policemen let him shoot them," he said. "The police were standing outside his car with their guns on him. There was one officer at each door, one pointing his gun at the windshield and one at the back. They said, 'Freeze, drop your gun!' He shot one more time at the woman. Then he shot him three policemen. None of them policemen should have been shot—not one. I don't know why they didn't shoot him first."

Police thought they knew why, and were mad as hell. With a chance to shoot the gunman, DiGenova had tried instead to disarm him. "He should have shot the son of a bitch," Homicide Sergeant James Duckworth told me. "The logical policeman of a few years ago would have shot him through that open window. It's just a shame that policemen nowadays can't be policemen."

He claimed the officers lost life-saving seconds because recent brutality charges had made them hesitate to use force. The charges stemmed from a wrong-house raid. White Metro cops were accused of beating a black schoolteacher and his family, whom they mistook for drug suspects.

Duckworth, now investigating the case of three white cops shot by a black man, believed that the officers all felt, "I don't want to be the next one sued."

There is no way to know what the officers were thinking.

A number of other Metro cops had not hesitated or held their fire since the wrong-house raid: One had shot a pistol-waving man outside a bar. An off-duty officer had killed an unarmed college football star in a bar brawl, and a third, also off duty, did not hesitate to shoot dead a neighbor's pet pony that had wandered into his yard.

But Dade cops, angry and in mourning, charged that the tragedy illustrated a grim truth: "Shoot and you're brutal; don't shoot and you die."

Nobody ever said police work was easy.

The only people not bitter were the bereaved family of William Cook. As a teenager he had come home from college classes and announced, "Mom, I'm gonna be a police officer." He was so proud of the uniform, family members said, that you could slide down the crease in his pants. He had been a Boy Scout and a trumpet-playing member of a state-champion high school band. An avid amateur photographer, he had hoped to someday work in the crime lab. He was on a waiting list for the transfer when he died.

He had just switched to days from the night shift, eager for Saturdays and Sundays off. The upcoming weekend was to have been his first. He had planned to shoot nature photos in the Everglades. He and his young wife, Karen, had no children, but he played Santa Claus at Christmas for his little niece and nephew.

"When they needed somebody to handle a domestic disturbance, they would call Billy," his mother told me. "He had such a wonderful way of talking and smoothing things over."

Cook stopped by to see his widowed mother every day. When he did not that day, she was uneasy. She telephoned his wife at four P.M. Karen assured her that Billy was fine and must have had a late call. The worried mother put down the telephone and stepped out onto her front porch. Two policemen stood there.

"Is it my son Billy?" she asked. They nodded.

She had pinned on his silver badge at the police academy graduation six years earlier. He promised that day, "Mom, I'll always make you proud of me."

He did.

And Billy would have been proud of his family. Through tears, Julia Cook, sixty-three, encouraged others to follow her only son's footsteps into the profession he loved.

"We're not bitter against police work," his sister, Nancy Colamatteo, told me. Neither was the family bitter toward the man who killed her brother. "He had to be crazy," she said. "If he had known Billy, he wouldn't have shot him."

"If the man who shot him could have spent a day with him, he would have loved him," said her husband, Jim Colamatteo.

The most gigantic manhunt in Miami history was launched for the tollgate killer of young Florida Highway Patrolman Bradley

Glascock. Again my telephone rang in the middle of the night. A trooper had been cut down at 2:50 A.M. by a motorist stopped for failing to pay a ten-cent expressway toll.

I knew Glascock. He had studied for the ministry before joining the highway patrol. He was twenty-four.

The killer was at the wheel of a borrowed car, a faded 1969 Cadillac Eldorado, when the well-built six-foot four-inch, 214-pound trooper stopped him just past the toll plaza. The motorist was armed with a stolen gun. He was wanted on a bench warrant for driving without a valid license, and he was also a mule—a low-level courier for narcotics traffickers.

To the trooper, the roadside stop seemed routine, but when he asked for a driver's license, the motorist opened fire. The trooper reached for his own gun, too late.

A .38-caliber slug shattered the trooper's heart. Another severed his spinal cord. Either would have been fatal.

A young man eager to learn about law enforcement was riding with the trooper that night, as an observer. He snatched the shotgun from its rack in the patrol car and fired four times, blasting out the back window of the Cadillac and slightly wounding the fleeing killer.

The bloodstained car was found abandoned a short time later. The killer was quickly identified as Felix Ramon Cardenas Casanova.

A short, muscular twenty-nine-year-old fisherman known for carrying guns and fighting in bars, Cardenas had a tough-guy reputation at Miami riverfront hangouts. An old enemy, wounded by him in a 1973 bar fight, evened the score by supplying his name to detectives.

Only five feet five inches tall and 146 pounds, Cardenas was a man with a past: drug charges in Tampa, a murder arrest in Nassau and the Miami barroom shooting.

Miami Homicide Sergeant Mike Gonzalez, Miami's SWAT team, motorcycle crews, a Metro helicopter, detectives, and police dogs searched for the wounded cop killer. Hospitals were on alert. So was every Florida fishing port. Boats along the Miami

River and a twenty-one-block area near the airport were searched door to door by more than a hundred police officers.

Scores of cops volunteered free time to join the manhunt. One brother officer gave even more: Rookie Trooper John Rambach volunteered for twelve hours, then went home to his modest apartment, discussed it with his wife, Debbie—and wrote a check for most of the trooper's monthly take-home pay. The parents of two little girls, Debbie and John Rambach posted five hundred dollars as a reward for information leading to the killer's arrest. If the money went unclaimed, they said, they wanted it used to buy bulletproof vests for other troopers.

The Florida Legislature had twice considered and rejected the purchase of protective vests for troopers. At that time the vests cost $82 to $110 each.

"There are so many out there who don't have vests—and have wives and kids," Debbie Rambach said softly.

Her husband religiously wore his, a gift from his father, a Jacksonville police officer.

Their gesture touched readers. Money began to pour in from the public, to buy bulletproof vests and to increase the bounty on the killer's head.

Most manhunts wind down as the trail grows cold, but this one accelerated, leapfrogging all over the state. Roadblocks were set up in Naples, on Florida's west coast, after a hotel employee reported a guest who resembled Cardenas; a lookalike was snatched off a Little Havana street; Southern Bell employees chased a suspicious car; residents willingly permitted SWAT teams to search their homes. Three days after the killing, police seemed no closer to an arrest despite more than a thousand tips. Many had not slept since the shooting.

"You feel so helpless," said one trooper, wearing the black-striped badge of mourning. "Everybody's on edge because of lack of sleep—and anticipation."

"He's hiding," a Miami detective sergeant said flatly, "and he won't come out of his hole until the heat's off."

The detective who spotted the Little Havana lookalike was stunned by the resemblance. The man, carrying a newspaper under his arm, denied he was Cardenas. Told to look at the fugitive's picture in the paper, he paled. "It looks like me," he acknowledged. He was photographed, fingerprinted and warned he would probably be stopped again. Trooper Glascock went to his grave, with the reward fund growing, vest donations mounting and the killer still running.

The public defender's office opened a hotline for Cardenas to arrange a safe surrender. "We're hoping the police will allow us to get to him first," said assistant public defender Michael Von Zamft. "We don't want anybody hurt. We're trying to help the police."

Minutes after the hotline number was broadcast on Spanish-language radio, somebody used it.

"Come get me. Come get me. The McAllister Hotel," the caller said and hung up. Two assistant public defenders and one of their investigators raced to the downtown hotel. They ran up and down corridors and hollered down stairwells: "We're here, Felix! We're here to help you!" No one answered, much less Felix Ramon Cardenas Casanova, simultaneously sought in Palm Beach by police who believed they were hot on his trail and detectives in Miami who had surrounded a motel.

The manhunt became hell for the Felix Ramon Cardenas Casanova lookalike, who was afraid to be seen in public. Raul Llerena, a mild-mannered carpet installer with a wife and child, suffered nightmares, waking up screaming, "I'm not him! I'm not him!" He drove down back streets, stayed out of crowds and tried to avoid police. A dead ringer, he was "captured" repeatedly, fingerprinted, photographed, and questioned, fingerprinted and photographed again—"front, side, with a shirt and without a shirt"—and questioned some more. He feared being shot the most.

We met in a shadowy Little Havana parking lot. I brought a photographer. Nervously glancing over his shoulder, Llerena said urgently, "I want everybody to know it's not me." He stared bleakly at a news photo of Felix. "It's my face," he said, "but it's not me."

Three years earlier, he said, people began telling him he had a double. The two frequented some of the same Little Havana establishments but had never met. Now his double was the most-wanted fugitive in the country, a man with a price on his head.

"He's in a spot," said Eduardo Perez, a friend with him. "If I was a policeman I'd shoot him right in the head and collect the reward." Llerena did not laugh.

Police had issued him a card stating that he was not Cardenas. But the Highway Patrol never gave him a chance to whip it out when they "captured" him again that night.

When police showed the fugitive's photo in Llerena's neighborhood, helpful residents sent them to his mother-in-law's home. They flashed the fugitive's picture. "It's looks like my brother-in-law," his wife's brother said truthfully.

"I can't afford plastic surgery," he said desperately. "I'm afraid I'll get shot."

"I guess you'll be relieved when Felix is captured," I said.

"I don't want bad things to happen to anybody," he quickly insisted, unwilling to offend even the fugitive. "All I want is for my life to be like before—quiet." He had canceled two carpet-laying jobs that week, afraid to go out on the street. Wherever he went now, he said, people stared, acted strange and headed for telephones. Many tips to police had obviously been sightings of the terrified Llerena.

I told him not to worry, our story would make it clear he was not the wanted man.

"Look at him," said his cheerful friend, Perez, who also knew Felix Cardenas. "The same nose, the same hair, the eyes . . ."

Sirens wailed in the distance, growing louder. "Please, tell them it isn't me," Raul pleaded, then darted into the shadows.

Shortly after ten A.M. the next day, the fugitive called Miami homicide and offered to surrender quietly "with no uniformed police, no sirens, no publicity and no lawyers."

Trooper Anthony Valdes and Miami Homicide Detective Luis Albuerne asked the caller for Cardenas's birth date. His answer was correct: November 11. "I'm the one who shot the trooper," he announced and promised to surrender shirtless, to show he was unarmed.

Cardenas had wandered into the tiny meter room at the rear of a friend's marine shop at three A.M. He slept on dirty newspapers until the man opened for business. Cardenas said he had expected the heat to fade, but it had not, and he realized he was going to be caught. They decided he should surrender and called homicide. Cheers rang out at headquarters when Albuerne radioed that he had Felix in his car.

He freely admitted shooting the trooper but said, "I don't know why I did it."

During his eight days on the run, he had been sneaking around in the night, hiding in palmetto bushes and sleeping in cars and utility rooms. On the second or third night he had rented a Little Havana motel room and paid a man twenty-five dollars to buy bandages for his wounded trigger finger. He hid in the motel bathroom so the maid could not see his face. Fearing she was suspicious, he had fled. He had asked many people for help but got none.

"We want to thank the public," Sergeant Mike Gonzalez said. "They helped us by not helping him."

Tired, nervous and disheveled, his wounded left index finger swollen and infected, Cardenas appeared relieved that the manhunt was over. "I know what I did was wrong, and I'm willing to accept the consequence," he said.

The consequence was a life sentence.

A week after the arrest, Highway Patrolman Don Boniface, a colleague of the murdered trooper, answered his door. There stood five neighborhood youngsters he had known for years. "Here's the money," one said. "Go get yourself a bulletproof vest." They handed him a bulky sack containing seventy dollars in nickels, dimes and quarters and fifty dollars in one-dollar bills they had painstakingly collected.

These were kids he had spanked, taken home and lectured. He had coached some of them in Little League and, when they grew up, had issued traffic tickets to a few. The youngest contributor, age three, had donated her candy money.

The six-foot, two-hundred-pound trooper had to duck back inside for a moment in order to maintain his tough-guy composure. The kids wanted Boniface to buy his vest at once and said that any money left should help buy vests for other troopers. They warned that if they ever caught him not wearing his, he would be fined five dollars.

Sounded right to me.

Bulletproof vests work. A lot of cops don't like to wear them, especially in the summer—but there are police officers in Dade County and a growing legion throughout the nation who would be dead today without them.

Metro-Dade Officer Michael Cain stopped at one A.M. to check a suspicious man in the shadows behind a convenience store. When he stepped out of his cruiser, the man walked quickly around the building. Cain followed. The man was waiting. "I heard a pop and saw the muzzle flash," Cain told me. The bullet slammed into his midsection. I've been shot, he thought, but I'm still standing.

The vest held.

The impact, however, nearly knocked him off his feet. Staggering back, he fired at the fleeing man, who got away.

"I've been hit," Cain radioed. "But I'm okay." He asked everybody speeding to his aid to slow down. No sense in anybody being hurt.

This was the third time he had been shot at, the first time he was hit. The bullet had ripped through five layers of the twelve-layer Point Blank bulletproof vest. The flattened slug left a small, neat hole in his brown uniform shirt and a painful red bruise over his liver, but the skin was not broken.

The $242 vest was Cain's second in six years. He wore out the first one. He had almost stopped wearing it after suffering heat stroke while chasing a suspect four years earlier. But now, from a wheelchair in the hospital where he had been taken for observation, he said: "The vest is cumbersome. It's heavy. It's hot in the summer and it's warm in the winter. But I wish all my friends would wear them."

When Miami Officer Nathaniel Broom was shot, his bulletproof vest was hanging in his locker at headquarters blocks away. Had he worn it, it might have saved his life.

A steel-jacketed, hollow-point bullet fired from a .38-caliber Smith and Wesson pierced his heart. The fatal impact hurled him back, off his feet, and a second slug slammed through the sole of his shoe.

He was twenty-three. He had stopped a green Volkswagen Beetle headed the wrong way on a one-way street in Overtown. He had been a Police Explorer and served as a military policeman, but Broom was still only eight months out of the police academy. His partner was also a rookie, two months out of the academy. They had no way of knowing the Volkswagen was stolen—or that the driver who jumped out and ran was armed.

Broom bailed out of his patrol car and darted after him, across a busy intersection. Two months earlier, Broom had stopped a stolen motorcycle several blocks from where he had stopped the Bug. That driver also ran. Broom won a commendation for chasing him down, which may explain, in part, the young officer's zeal this day.

By the time his rookie partner wheeled their patrol car around, Broom was out of sight, pounding down an alleyway after the suspect. The alley stretches between an aging church and a two-story structure with businesses at street level and apartments above. It is a dead end. The fleeing man tried to escape through an adjacent shop. An employee saw him and shouted to a fellow worker.

"I looked in his face, and he looked in mine," one of them said later. The cornered man turned and drew a black revolver. "He fell back behind the building for cover. He had the gun in his right hand, balanced it with his left, took his time, aimed and fired. I was astonished. I haven't seen anything like it since Vietnam. Then he jumped the fence and ran."

From his vantage point, the man I spoke to could not see the gunman's target but was sure from his reaction that the victim had fallen. He ran into the street and heard a shout, "Somebody just shot a black policeman!"

It took several minutes for his partner to find Broom, sprawled in a clump of weeds behind the building.

It was too late. They tried anyway. In the emergency room they opened his heart to try to clamp the aorta and saw that nothing could be done.

His brief career had been so outstanding that Broom had been scheduled to be a training officer for the next academy class.

More than 150 Miami police, joined by more than fifty Metro officers, searched buildings and fields with helicopters and dogs, stopping dozens of suspects. They found guns everywhere, in a dumpster, near an expressway embankment, in a patch of weeds. Guns are not unusual in that neighborhood.

Miami's crime rate was the nation's highest at the time.

It was not a cop, a chopper or a dog that cornered the killer —it was a machine, a half-million-dollar Rockwell computer system put online by police six months earlier. Forty-eight minutes after the shooting, fingerprints lifted from the Beetle were fed into the computer. It instantly compares a print with hundreds of thousands on file. Within minutes, the computer spit out the name of car thief Robert Patten, age twenty-seven. Such an accomplishment would be a lifetime task for technicians comparing fingerprints by hand.

Witnesses identified photos of the rail-thin six-foot, 120-pound suspect as the cop killer. The murder weapon was found hidden at his grandmother's home. Cops staked out a motel where Patten's girlfriend and infant daughter were staying. Police hoped he would appear, and he did. He tried to run, but they tackled him.

His girlfriend told me it might have been all her fault. They'd had a jealous spat before dawn, "I kicked him out," she said, "and told him he couldn't see his baby no more." Now more forgiving, she called him a "gentle man who goes to the park and plays John Denver songs on his guitar for the children."

Police called him something else: a career criminal. His mother washed her hands of him, saying he had been nothing but trouble all his life. Nathaniel Broom worked a paper route, bagged groceries, graduated from high school and enlisted in the army while Robert Patten was stealing, using drugs, dropping out and building a police record. The gun was stolen, and he was on his way to sell it when he drove the wrong way down a one-way street.

This cop killer was convicted in 1982 and sentenced to die in the electric chair. That's not the end of his story.

To wile away his hours behind bars, Robert Patten ran a personal ad in a supermarket tabloid. He and a Rhode Island woman exchanged photos and letters and fell in love. She moved to Florida, and they were married—presumably, to live happily ever after, or at least until his appeals run out. A color photo was published of Robert Patten and his new bride, grinning and cuddling in front of a gaily decorated Christmas tree: Merry Christmas from Death Row.

Too bad Nathaniel Broom, the young black cop killed by a white car thief, will never marry or see another Christmas.

Chapter 14

HEROES

Courage is "being scared to death—and saddling up anyway."

—JOHN WAYNE

The stories I most love to write chronicle the daring and the noble deeds of Miami's real-life heroes. The best and the bravest among us are not necessarily cops or firefighters; they are often ordinary people who do the extraordinary when they must.

Take bus driver George P. Brown, who was tooling along the airport expressway, following another empty bus back to the barn after an uneventful day. An inner tire on the other bus blew out, and fire began to fall from the wheels. Brown leaned on his horn, drove up alongside and shouted to the other driver, who pulled over where the expressway curves above a low-income residential neighborhood, where dozens of children play on streets that dead-end at the highway. Brown maneuvered his lumbering vehicle through traffic and parked it across the expressway to create a barricade. A security guard stopped to help as the two bus drivers scrambled down the embankment to call the fire department.

What Brown feared happened as they returned: Flames ate through the brake linings, and the burning bus began to roll backward, rapidly picking up speed. A Miami policeman came charging up the side of the hill carrying a fire extinguisher—too late. The flaming bus careened off the security guard's car and crashed into Brown's bus, setting both afire, but no one was hurt. No one knows where the burning, driverless bus would have gone had it not been for Brown, but in its path were houses, traffic and children.

George P. Brown never read about the technique he used in any driver's manual. He improvised.

Take the Miami banker faced by a man brandishing a gun and what appeared to be a bomb. The man demanded fifty thousand dollars. The banker coolly reached into his desk drawer for a revolver. "If you blow us up, we go together," he announced. "Put the gun down, put the bomb down, and raise your hands." The robber folded first. By the time police and the FBI burst into the bank, he was spread-eagled against the wall. His .357 Magnum was loaded, but his bomb was only a cardboard Kotex box rigged with wires and a light switch.

For years I have tried to figure out what makes a real hero and what they share in common. Real heroes think about the safety of others first, not what might happen to themselves. Unlike Hollywood heroes, real heroes are usually unimpressive in appearance and diminutive in stature. None looks like Rambo.

Take Manuel Rodriguez. He was in a nearby Burger King when a van struck a light pole and overturned. The driver, who delivered fruit and vegetables to Miami Beach hotels and restaurants, was pinned underneath. His two small stepchildren were hurled through the windshield.

Rodriguez, twenty, heard the crash and came running. So did Dan Jacobson, forty, a photographer, from his studio across the street.

The driver's feet protruded from under the truck. There seemed little hope he could still be alive. Rodriguez prayed in Spanish as he tried to pull the truck off the man. Jacobson screamed for jacks.

Rodriguez, five feet seven inches tall and an insulin-dependent diabetic, yelled for help. Motorists came running, with sticks and jacks from their cars. When Miami Beach Police Officer Rick Trado arrived, a dozen people were straining to lift the truck.

They managed to hoist it high enough for Trado to scramble beneath. The truck gushed gasoline, and Trado cut his hands on broken glass crawling to the unconscious driver. Then the truck started to slip and the would-be rescuers struggled to hold on to it. Trado wanted out of there. He looked back in alarm and saw "this guy put his shoulder under it." It was Rodriguez, praying aloud, "Lord, give me the strength! Give us the strength!"

Rodriguez put his back under the truck and groaned, shouldering the weight until Trado dragged the driver to safety. Shaken and trembling afterward, all Rodriguez could remember was praying.

The truck driver died later, but not because no one tried to save him.

Some people resist rescue, and an unpredictable public often refuses to help.

Taxi driver James Pearl, slightly built at 130 pounds, fought for fifteen minutes to save a stranger as people ignored his pleas and slammed doors in his face. A station wagon weaved all over the street in front of Pearl and another cabbie just after dark. Drivers slammed on brakes and leaned on horns as the drunk rammed a parked car head on. The man was a menace. Pearl stayed to help, as the other cabbie left to report the accident. The intoxicated driver climbed out of his damaged station wagon and fell down, staggered to his feet and fell again. A car almost hit him. Pearl dragged the man out of traffic and asked a truck driver to help him put the drunk back into his car. The trucker refused. Pearl asked other motorists to help him get the man out of the street because another car had just missed him. They drove away. Pearl tried to lead the man to safety, but "he lurched away so hard he nearly fell in front of another car."

The driver stumbled up one street and down another. Pearl followed, seeking help from six or seven passersby, all of whom ignored him. He knocked at a house and asked a woman to call police. She slammed the door. He shouted to a security guard at a nearby office building. The guard called the police, but the drunk wandered behind an apartment house three blocks from the accident, staggered out onto a boat dock and plunged into the water before they arrived. Pearl lay on the ground in the dark, reaching out to the thrashing man who did not even seem aware he was in danger. Pearl found a pole and shoved it into the water. The man did not take it. Pearl told me later that he was screaming louder than the police sirens—people *had* to hear him—but no one came until after the officers arrived. He knew it was too late. Police and firemen fished the dead man from the water.

"People don't care," Pearl told me in despair. "Next time I'll know better."

People are unpredictable. You never know when you can count on them. Sometimes, when least expected, they perform like champs. Other times, when they are needed the most, they slam doors or walk away. Sometimes you are forced to go it alone.

A hapless fellow taken hostage in the lobby of a run-down South Beach hotel was held at rifle point for ten hours by a troubled Vietnam veteran who demanded to talk to the Secret Service. For more than six hours, his plight was ignored. "Call the police," he pleaded with a young woman passing by. "I'm being held hostage."

"That's your problem. Call them yourself," she said and flounced off.

The rifleman slid a threatening note out under the door of the room where he and his hostage were barricaded. A tenant read it, shrugged it off and failed to report the crime. When they were finally notified, police set up a perimeter, sent in two SWAT teams, diverted traffic, evacuated neighbors and rushed in negotiators. They were disappointed. Before they could mount a rescue effort, the hostage, who had despaired of rescue, saved himself. He talked his captor into boiling eggs for lunch, hurled the pot of scalding water on him and ran for his life.

At the other extreme are citizens who seize the initiative and become involved, sometimes in packs, eager to right wrongs and pursue justice. Thomas Hill, twenty-five, a salesman and former high school track star, heard screams and ran after the two robbers who had mugged a woman in front of a downtown Sears store. The victim ran after them too. So did another Sears employee. A passerby came running and joined the pursuit.

Everybody pounded down the pavement, the woman screaming, the men shouting, the robbers sprinting. The chase streaked by a rooming house, where thirty residents lounged on the porch. One leaped to his feet and shouted that the fleeing suspects were the same men who had robbed him earlier. Pursuers poured off the porch and the impromptu posse grew to thirty irate citizens, who cornered and captured the pair at a dead end under the expressway.

The robbers were delighted to see Major Philip Doherty, the first policeman to arrive. "Several citizens were sitting on them to hold them down. It was heartwarming," Doherty said, pleased. "Young, old, black, white—everybody in the neighborhood joined in."

Some tragic heroes sacrifice everything for someone else. On the way home after a Saturday night date, Susan Schnitzer and her fiancé saw an accident on the rainswept expressway. He wanted to drive on, to notify police, but Susan, a slim blond nursing student, insisted they stop. He trotted toward oncoming traffic to wave motorists away from the wreck. She ran to help the severely injured driver.

The accident victim lived, but Susan Schnitzer died moments later, hit and carried 140 feet on the hood of a car occupied by two teenagers returning from a high school prom.

Most heroes give no thought to their own safety, especially when the person in danger is someone they love. Take the fifty-nine-year-old man, a poor swimmer at best, who charged fully clothed into an Opa-Locka lake to save his drowning son, age eighteen. They died together.

"He could have used his fishing pole to reach for the kid," a perplexed cop told me later. But people panic.

That father-son drowning was the second in two weeks. A forty-five-year-old man and his son, eight, fished at a remote rock pit. Scuff marks on the bank indicated that the boy, who could not swim, fell in first. His father plunged into water thirty-five feet deep to try to save him.

The world is full of courage of all kinds. You see it in stout-hearted children, as well as in the frail and elderly. Most behave heroically because their character does not allow them to do anything less. Few expect thanks.

A short, stocky truck driver was there for Metro Police Officer Milan Pilat the day his worst nightmare came true.

When Pilat approached an illegally parked car, the driver hastily stuffed several tinfoil packets into a cigarette pack, leaped from his car, punched the cop in the face and ran. The officer tackled him after a fifty-yard chase, and the two grappled on the ground. A crowd formed, and people in it tried to free the suspect, kicking and striking the officer, who clung stubbornly to his prisoner and the incriminating cigarette pack. The mob grew to 150 unruly people. Far from the safety of his patrol car and its radio life-link to help, knocked to the ground, battered and kicked, this cop was in trouble. He shouted in vain to passing traffic. As the crowd surged in, there was the piercing sound of air brakes. A huge dump truck stopped on a dime, and the driver jumped out.

"He was just a little guy, really—but everybody backed off," Pilat said. Shoving people away, the trucker asked the cop if he was all right. Pilat staggered to his feet, still clinging to his prisoner. Backup officers arrived fast, summoned by the trucker on his CB. Cut and bruised, his face battered, Pilat handcuffed his prisoner, turned to thank the trucker, and found him gone.

He had driven away without leaving his name.

You never know when you might be called upon—or if you will rise to the occasion should it occur. One moment you can be taking a nap and the next one of America's most wanted fugitives may be in your living room. How would *you* handle it?

Linda Major had a pounding headache that day. Though it is impossible to rest in a house full of children, she kept trying. But Major was disturbed again, this time by five-year-old Thomas, who bustled breathless to her side. "Mama, I just saw the police running after a man!" Trying to ignore him, she told him to hush.

"But," he persisted, "the man is in our house."

He was.

Through the back door that one of the children forgot to lock had barged a stranger, a fugitive charged with gunning down a New York City policeman. Object of a nationwide manhunt, he too was breathless. Cops with shotguns were right behind him.

The stranger strode through the house as the family watchdog, a poodle named Monique, dove behind the kitchen stove. Major's kid sister, thirteen, hit the floor. Her children, ages four, five and six, and their cousins, ten and twelve, were speechless. "Be cool," the stranger warned. "Be cool."

Major did not wait to find out what that meant. She looked out a window and saw police shotguns. Shouting, "My children are coming out!" she herded the youngsters toward the door. "Run to your grandfather's house. Now!" she told them.

"For the first time," she said later, "they did just what I asked them to do."

Six sets of skinny legs churned in all directions. Major saw the children all pounding to safety down the street, then dashed out her back door, shouting, "He's in the house!"

The fugitive had apparently planned to hold hostages, but Linda Major was too quick. When he refused to come out, police sent in a German shepherd named Thunder, one of their K-9 officers. Monique the poodle continued to cringe behind the stove as Thunder padded purposefully through the house, found the fugitive and sank his teeth into him.

The children later chattered nonstop about the big guns brandished by police. Monique, still cringing, had to be dragged from behind the stove to join in a family portrait shot by a *Herald* photographer. Major told me the excitement had cured her headache and promised to listen the next time five-year-old Thomas had something urgent to say.

Bravery comes in all colors and descriptions, and physical heroics are not always required. Sometimes just doing the right thing, even making a simple telephone call, takes courage.

Soon after the Miami riots, a young woman lost her way, took the wrong expressway exit, tried to turn around and found herself in a strange, riot-torn neighborhood late at night. At a red light, two men with guns ran up beside her Volkswagen. One reached through the window, jammed his gun to her head and cocked it. They forced their way into her car, took her money and ordered the terrified woman to drive them to an apartment complex parking lot. They took her jewelry, raped her and decided to kill her by locking her in the trunk of her car and shooting through the metal. She pleaded for her life as they forced her, naked, into the tiny trunk. When the lid would not close, they tied it to the bumper with one of her garments.

A middle-aged couple in a nearby apartment saw and heard what was happening. The man kept watch as the woman ran for the telephone. "Get here now!" she told police. They did, just in time. The witnesses who saved the woman were black. So were the rapists. She was white.

Proof again, as Homicide Sergeant Mike Gonzalez said that night, that "there are still some good people in the world."

Age is no barrier to bravery; quite the contrary, the simple act of aging often takes valor. Ethel Lottman, a no-nonsense Miami Beach widow, seventy-two, handled her heart condition, her arthritis and a homicidal maniac with the same aplomb.

A young bank teller was the innocent victim. Hunting an apartment near the bank where she worked, the woman had arranged a 10:30 A.M. appointment with a landlord. As she walked briskly toward the building, a strange woman rushed up behind her. "Do you think you are going to bury me?" she shouted, and plunged a stiletto into the young teller's back.

The bleeding victim ran screaming toward Ethel Lottman, who had just emerged from her nearby condo, on her way to a doctor's appointment. "Put that knife away. Don't be so temperamental," chided the widow, and stepped to block the pursuing attacker. "You'll get in trouble if a policeman sees you."

The woman with the knife was momentarily distracted and her victim escaped. "I ought to give it to you!" the attacker snarled at Lottman. Stared down, the attacker fled.

Ethel Lottman, in her red-and-white saddle shoes, limped slowly after the woman, ignoring the painful arthritis in her toe. She "walked slow and laid low," she told me later, trailing at a distance. The woman she was following was a thirty-nine-year-old mental patient who had won acquittals, by reason of insanity, after five prior knife attacks. When she ducked into a hotel several blocks away, Ethel Lottman stepped into an adjacent hotel. She told the desk clerk about the stabbing and asked him to call police. He refused.

Lottman's toe ached. Frustrated and late for her appointment, she went on to the doctor. On the way home she spotted a policeman. He was knocking on doors, seeking information. The stabbing victim was in intensive care.

"You're never around when you're needed," Lottman complained to the startled officer. She took him to the attacker, psychotic, unpredictable and still lurking in the hotel lobby, knife in hand. The attacker was arrested and locked in an isolation cell until doctors decide once again that she is well enough to unleash on an unsuspecting public.

The system may not always look out for the other guy, but luckily some people do.

Like good cops, heroes are somehow at the right place at the right time. Timing is everything.

When the year's worst sudden storm slammed into Miami and ruined their fishing trip, all Joyce and Richard Chicvara thought about was towing their boat safely home through hazardous high winds.

The couple strained to see through the rain that hammered the windshield. A stalled truck and two Florida Highway Patrol cars blocked an expressway exit ramp ahead. A bolt of lightning crashed so close that the two troopers felt the tingle and ran to the nearest patrol car for cover. As Trooper James Benton grasped the metal door handle, a blinding bolt of lightning flashed.

"I saw the trooper fly through the air, do a back flip, hit the ground and roll down the ramp," said Chicvara, a fire department paramedic. His wife is a cardiovascular hospital technician. Both scrambled out into the drenching downpour and turned the trooper over. Chicvara began mouth-to-mouth resuscitation as his wife searched for a pulse. When the trooper began to breathe, they rushed him into the other patrolman's car for the race to a hospital. During the trip, the trooper went into cardiac arrest. Chicvara pounded his chest over and over until the fifth blow restored a heartbeat. He continued mouth-to-mouth breathing.

The trooper survived because, of all the motorists who could have passed by at that fateful moment, the ones who did were the two best trained to save him.

Who can explain the forces that place a person in the right place at the right time?

When Hilde Madorsky moved to Miami, she found that her new apartment was not ready. Exhausted by the long car trip, she had nowhere else to go, so management provided a waterfront substitute for the night, high on the twenty-second floor.

Transplanted from Manhattan, "where nothing ever happened," she relaxed and stepped out onto the terrace for her first glimpse of Miami's star-studded skyline. As she drank it all in, she heard the screams.

Her first thought was of *Miami Vice*.

The cries came from out in the water, carried inland and up by a strong easterly wind. "I heard one of them yell, 'Holy shit, Michael! Hold on! Help! Help!' " She did not waste a heartbeat. She dashed inside, fumbled for the card a security guard had given her and dialed the number. As police were dispatched, at 10:26 P.M., two security men from the apartment complex ran to the marina. Now they too heard the screams and swiftly lowered a twenty-foot open fisherman into the water.

The tide was sweeping out; waves were rough. With only running lights, they would have to try to follow the sound of the screams. Then they spotted police arriving at the seawall and wheeled to pick them up. It was 10:28 P.M.

"You could hear people yelling out in the bay, screaming for help," Officer Steven Sadowski said. Had it not been for the wind blowing out of the east, no one would have heard them. Twenty-two stories up, Madorsky was screaming back at the panicky voices. "Hold on, hold on! Help is coming!"

"I never yelled so loud in my life," she said later. "I felt like I could dive off the terrace to help them."

Police switched on their high-beam headlights and powerful spotlights. Sadowski and another officer took flashlights and jumped aboard the boat, along with paramedics. In the light from their cruisers, they could now see arms flailing, two hundred yards offshore. When they reached the two boys clinging to their capsized fifteen-foot aluminum canoe, the frightened teenagers' first words were "Thank God."

The boys, ages seventeen and nineteen, had paddled their canoe out a canal and into the bay. When they tried to turn back, rough water capsized the canoe. They had no life jackets. If not for the wind out of the east, Hilde Madorsky never would have heard them.

"It's strange," she told me. "I'll never know them. They'll never know who I am." But, she said, they made her first night in Miami unforgettable.

Wilfred Yunque was driving to pick up his elderly mother at church. Traveling westbound across the MacArthur Causeway, between Miami and Miami Beach, he stopped at a red light. A young woman's red Corvair roared past, through the light, at about sixty-five miles an hour. A minute later, as he continued west, he saw the red car again—sinking in Biscayne Bay. Other motorists slowed and stared but did not stop. Yunque pulled his Vega to the roadside, jumped out and dived into the water fully dressed. He never even removed his watch. Water pressure prevented him from opening the red car's door, but the window was open. He grasped the driver's shoulder and tried to drag her out but could not. She was limp, unconscious, slumped across the seat. He crawled in through the window unable to do more until the car sank, equalizing the pressure inside and out. Crouched on the front seat beside the twenty-three-year-old woman, he waited as water filled the car. When it submerged completely, settling onto the bay bottom, he floated her out the window to the surface, holding his breath and keeping his hand over her nose and mouth.

Miami and Miami Beach police, coast guard and police boats, a flotilla of pleasure boats, several fire department units and a city commissioner all rushed to the scene, but Yunque, forty-nine, had everything under control.

I was impressed. How, I asked him, could he do what he had just done?

"I'm an old sailor," he said modestly, retired from the Merchant Marine. His seventy-nine-year-old mother was waiting patiently outside her church. He had never been late before.

"I had to stop and pull a girl from the bay," he explained.

"I knew God had a reason," she said.

One Father's Day, Lawrence B. Eaton, fifty-two, was driving to his part-time job as a security guard when he saw a wrecked Pinto in the median strip. The car had knocked down a palm tree. He stopped, turned around, walked toward the smoking car and heard a sound that chilled his heart: a baby's wail. Dashing into the roadway, he flagged down cars, telling drivers to call the police, "There's a baby in the car!"

He ran back to the Pinto and peered inside. The driver was pinned behind the steering wheel, gasping, his neck obviously broken. The baby, an injured toddler, lay pinned to the floor on the passenger's side, part of the engine on top of him. Crying and covered with blood, he reached out his little arms. Eaton pulled the wreckage off him and tossed it aside. A tree blocked half the window, and he could not quite grasp the baby. Another motorist stopped to help, reached down and held the baby's feet. Eaton slid his hand under the child's back. They lifted him from the car, slowly and carefully. It took about five minutes. The wreck was full of food wrappers, beer cans and junk. The windshield was blown out. There was no baby seat.

Larry Eaton carried the baby in his arms and gently put him down in a grassy area. He was scared, afraid the child would die. He thought of his own son, now grown. "All I could see was a young life, wasted. I kind of cried a little bit."

It took medics half an hour to free the driver, who was pronounced dead. Larry Eaton, his uniform covered with blood, went on to work. The seriously injured baby went to the hospital. Officials later told Eaton that he had saved the child's life. The good news made an otherwise lonely Father's Day special—he had not heard from his own two children.

The identity of the injured baby was a mystery. The dead driver was Kenneth Wayne Thrift, forty-five. Through fingerprints, the Florida Highway Patrol learned that he had a long criminal record. He carried a California driver's license, but the car's ID number checked back to Lakeland, Florida. That lead dead-ended, they said, grimly announcing that the child might be a kidnap victim. The injured baby's fingerprints went to the Missing Children's Network in Washington, and the FHP appealed to the media to help launch a major nationwide search for the baby's parents.

Before writing the "mystery baby" story, I asked the Lakeland information operator if anybody named Thrift was listed. Soon I was speaking to relatives of the injured baby, who was no missing mystery child after all. Kenneth Wayne Thrift, baby-sitting for his two-year-old nephew, Robert, agreed to drive a friend to Miami. He took little Robert along for the ride. They must have been about to return when the accident took place.

Unlike most people I write about, Larry Eaton stays in touch, drops a line now and then, the first time to say that the story about the baby's rescue had resulted in a happy reunion with his own son.

Putting it in the newspaper works.

■

So many people owe their survival to strangers who are there for them when it counts. Sometimes it takes courage just to hang on a little bit longer.

A young girl, wearing a denim skirt and platform shoes, sat poised at the edge of eternity, her feet dangling over the edge of the seven-story parking garage at Jackson Memorial Hospital.

Somewhere below, nurse Janet Gilliam had arrived on her day off to help move the hospital's crisis intervention unit into new quarters. Two detectives were also arriving, to show mug shots to an assault victim, and at that moment somebody in the high-rise Cedars of Lebanon Hospital nearby glanced out a window and ran to a telephone. The girl on the ledge was no longer alone with her secrets.

As the detectives stepped from their car, their radio reported a possible jumper on the parking garage roof. They dashed across the street. Detective Ray Vaught ran up six flights. Detective Ozzie Austin radioed for fire rescue and police. Then he too sprinted up the stairs. It was raining. "Go away!" she screamed at them. "No men!"

Nurse Gilliam volunteered and ran up the six flights. The girl on the ledge and the nurse stared at each other. Sergeant Mike Gonzalez joined the rooftop rescuers and asked the girl, "What do you want us to do?"

"You all get back. I want to talk to her," she said, pointing to the nurse.

Police left them alone, and Nurse Gilliam sat down on the roof twenty feet from the girl. She knew she could not stop the girl if she tried to jump. She had to rely on talk and trust.

For a time, the girl seemed to respond. She even swung her legs back inside. But an hour after she was first seen, she suddenly threw one leg over the side again. We all gasped.

"Oh my God!" a policeman cried aloud.

She did not jump. Thirteen minutes later, she slid off the ledge onto the rooftop and walked toward Gilliam.

"I wanted to grab her and hold her—to assure her and just

know she was in my arms, safe." Instead the nurse gently took the girl's arm, and they walked down the stairwell together.

"My hands are still shaking," said Detective Austin, soaked by rain and perspiration. "The butterflies in my stomach were so bad, I thought I would be sick."

Heroism in high places does not always succeed, but people of conscience always try. One hero risked his life so close to the *Herald* building that I did not have to drive to the scene. I ran.

Humberto Alfau, twenty-nine, a carpenter, was weary, on his way down from the sixth-floor level of the huge Omni project at quitting time, when he heard a worker at the fourth level shout. He saw a pretty young woman in white.

"I couldn't believe what I was seeing. If you do see a woman on a construction site, she's usually in a hard hat." This girl was a nursing student, the daughter of a veteran police officer. She stood precariously on narrow, unfinished beams extending several feet off the edge of the building. "I knew it was a suicide. I wanted to sneak up behind her and grab her, but she turned and saw me."

The woman never said a word.

"Take it easy," he told her. "I want to talk to you. Think it over. Don't do this. Let me talk to you. Wait." He wanted to talk until he could grab her with both hands. The woman paid no attention and squatted into a diving position. There was no time. She began to lower herself between the two-by-fours, like someone descending into a pool. Alfau, the father of four small children, scrambled out onto the two narrow beams.

He hated going out there. He teetered, balanced, catlike, with each foot on a four-by-four-inch beam jutting several feet off the sheer side of the complex. "I had to either let her do it or make my try. If I didn't try I would have felt guilty the rest of my life." She was suspended in the air, holding on to the beams with both hands. He lunged for her wrist and caught it as she let go. For heart-stopping moments she swung back and forth in space, four floors above the street, as he clutched her left wrist with one hand. Then she wrenched away in a half-twist and was gone.

Alfau closed his eyes and yelled for an ambulance. "She twisted out of my hand," he said. "It was terrible, having her slip away like that. She didn't want to be saved. The look on her face . . ."

Sometimes just surviving is heroic.

No one can tell me that Rose Bennett is not a hero. In her prime, she and her handsome husband, Navy Lieutenant Commander Daniel J. Bennett, traveled the globe in the service of their country. "I loved the Navy life," she told me the first time we met.

He retired in 1957, and they settled in Miami. His retirement pay ended with his life when he died of cancer in 1974. I met Rose Bennett in February 1984, after she had been brutalized, beaten, threatened with death, bound and robbed in her own home, for the third time in three weeks.

Intruders had forced their way into her rented frame cottage in downtown Miami nine times in six months. A sympathetic cop called me to report the latest outrage.

Caught in a nightmare of terror and violence, the frail, eighty-year-old, ninety-four-pound widow was living her twilight years in fear, fighting a daily battle to survive.

She lived on $175 a month from Social Security and had dwelled in the same house for twenty-five years. The building was scheduled for demolition in a few months. Her rent was $185 a month, and when I asked how she got by, she shyly explained that she was "thrifty." She was still a proud woman, a Navy wife.

She was too embarrassed to tell me what I learned later: that she foraged for food among the discarded cartons behind a nearby supermarket, that she dined on salads from overripe, bruised and spoiled fruit and vegetables, that she carefully collected damaged and outdated canned goods dumped behind the failing store, scheduled soon to close its doors.

She survived by doing odd baby-sitting or housework jobs,

returning deposit bottles and checking pay phones for forgotten change. She had no phone herself, thanks to intruders who broke into the house repeatedly. "The first thing they do is cut or rip out the wires," she said, matter-of-factly.

"I had some nice friends before the riot and the crime wave," she said, "but they all picked up and moved away." Her best friend, a retired nutritionist, was killed by muggers.

She was lucky herself to be alive. Burglars who invaded her home in the past had not been as violent. "When they broke in when I was home," she said, "they were meek and apologetic" —until recently.

She had heard a noise during the night of January 30, walked into her living room and encountered two strangers who had ripped out a screen and climbed in a window. The one with the fishing knife punched her in the face and forced her to remove her clothes. "If you're naked, you can't chase us," he told her. They ransacked the entire house, tearing apart her possessions.

Two weeks later, at five A.M., a window shattered. One of the robbers had come back. He hurled her to the floor, cut her eye, bloodied her face, bruised her forehead, tied her hands and legs and stuffed a shirt in her mouth. He threatened to kill her, then ransacked the house. She gave police a detailed description, down to his missing front tooth. Officers were touched by the plight of this alert and bright woman. They asked why she did not seek welfare, food stamps, subsidized housing or other benefits.

"I don't want to bother the welfare people," she said. "It weakens people to give them too much help. I like to work and be resourceful."

Crime-lab expert Ralph Garcia called the Veterans Administration and other agencies seeking help. Feminist Roxcy Bolton called Senator Paula Hawkins's office, and aides promised to investigate. Three days later, neighbors heard Rose screaming—the robber had returned. He threw her to the floor, tied her with an extension cord and began rummaging through her belongings. A neighbor, herself six times a burglary victim, ran to a service station to call police.

They arrived in time. The robber was filling his bicycle basket with the loot: Rose Bennett's dishes. Her face and eyes still bruised and swollen from the earlier assault, she had been battered again. She sought no medical treatment. "They'd make a federal case out of it and bill me for a couple of thousand dollars," she said. She treated her eye injuries herself, with witch hazel. "I knew he was dangerous and ruthless," she said. "He is a vicious and cruel man. I sure hope they won't let him out again."

Rose Bennett cleaned up the mess and the breakage—again. Gone to thieves were her radio, her costume jewelry, her wristwatch and a cuckoo clock she and her husband had bought abroad. "You cherish those things and hate to lose them," she said wistfully, without a trace of self-pity. She proudly showed me photos of her dashing husband in his white uniform. "He was so handsome," she said. "He looked a lot like Gary Cooper." His ashes sat on a shelf in a box covered by a small American flag. They met in Norfolk, Virginia, and married in 1932. He had joined the Navy in 1928 and retired after twenty-nine years. They had no children. If he had retired today, she would be eligible for 55 percent of his retirement salary. But no survivors' benefit plan was in effect when Lieutenant Commander Daniel J. Bennett retired.

"It's amazing how she's survived on so little food," Roxcy Bolton said. "She is a classic example of a military wife who has served her country and served her husband and this is how she lives out her last days on earth. This is the way it all ends."

Roxcy said she would seek to have an ID card issued entitling Rose to care at Homestead Air Force Hospital. Medical care "would be wonderful," Bennett said hesitantly. "Are you sure they don't mind old people there?"

Her refrigerator was empty that day, except for a chunk of moldy cheese. "It's fun to do housework," she said. "As long as I'm busy, I'm happy. There isn't a thing I need. All I want is protection from burglars." Asked if she had advice for other military widows in similar circumstances, Rose did not hesitate: "Get a job," she said. "They would be happiest if they got a job and worked instead of worrying about a pension. People are always happiest when they are active and working. People shouldn't have their hands out. We can be self-supporting up to a hundred years old. You can sit in a wheelchair and sell newspapers." Her father, a Philadelphia businessman, she said, "left all his money to the needy, not the greedy. He knew I was the type who didn't need money, a chip off the old block. I can make it."

After her story in the *Herald*, volunteers hammered boards over the windows of her rented cottage to keep out intruders. Strangers stocked her empty pantry with food, others sent prayers, letters and money. Two women brought dishes and a warm nightgown. A retired major sent a hundred-dollar check.

I was delighted. Rose was not. "I'm okay now," she complained, "and I don't need any more help. It isn't fair for me to take things from people who need them for themselves."

Senator Paula Hawkins's aide said bills that would have helped all the Rose Bennetts "were filed at least four times since 1972" but never made it out of committee.

Some time later, after not seeing Rose for months, I called the police officer who had helped find her a new place to live. I asked how Rose Bennett was. Dead, she said, brusquely. She had returned from a long vacation, gone by to see Rose and was told by a neighbor that she had died.

Shocked and saddened, I wanted to know what happened. I could find no record, no death certificate, so I knocked on doors in the neighborhood where she had lived last. No one knew anything. One woman said she thought Rose had moved to an apartment near Twelfth Street.

I drove through the neighborhood, looking for people to ask and trying to figure out what to do next. The weather was hot and steamy, and few people were out on the street. I saw a pedestrian a block away, a neatly dressed woman pushing a supermarket shopping cart. Tired and ready to give up, I noticed how the woman resembled Rose. As I drove closer, it looked even more like her. I stopped alongside. It was Rose Bennett!

We hugged and sat on a bus bench to talk. She could not stay long, she said, because she was very busy. She had an appointment somewhere. No, she said, she did not need a thing. Everything was fine.

Rose Bennett does not rescue people from burning buildings, or swim the rapids to save someone or perform any other daring feats—but no one can tell me that Rose Bennett is not a hero.

Sometimes just surviving is heroic.

Sidebar

NO HERO

Heroism is the shortest-lived profession on earth.

—WILL ROGERS

Some people do not believe in heroes.

Despite all that happened, Ann Siegel believes.

Thieves smashed the plate-glass window and stole the displays from her small handbag-and-jewelry shop in Surfside. Another time they hacked a hole in the roof and looted the place. Then a man with a gun invaded the shop one Tuesday night at eight and demanded her money. She fled, screaming, into the street.

Jeff Miller, twenty-one, was walking by. "I thought she was being beat up or hurt. I ran to see what I could do."

The gunman cleaned out the cash register, took Ann Siegel's purse and sprinted down an alley. Miller chased him. A foot apart, in the dark, the robber spun around and shot Miller in the neck at point-blank range. The slug left powder burns on his throat, missed his carotid artery by a fraction of an inch and exited his back. The gunman got away.

Miller staggered from the alley, collapsed on the sidewalk and was taken to a Miami Beach hospital. Ann Siegel, sixty-one, followed. "I'm glad it was me instead of you," he told her.

"He is an absolutely lovely, darling boy," she said. "I feel so bad. Here is a man who could have minded his own business like all the others who didn't get involved." She remained at the hospital emergency room for hours.

Before he was shot, Jeff Miller had been looking for a job to earn traveling money back to Chicago. In town only three days, he was alone and broke in a strange city, with no place to stay, stranded by friends who left without him. Now pain and medical expenses joined his other troubles.

Ann Siegel brought him concern, gratitude and home-baked cookies.

"She is one of the best people I ever met," he said. Hurting, with no feeling in his right shoulder, he displayed no bitterness. "Miami is wonderful," he said, "but it's an odd city. It's sad. Say hello to somebody, and they grab their purse and hang on. People shouldn't have to live in constant fear."

The *Herald* story ran alongside a touching photo of Ann Siegel hugging the boyish young man as he sat smiling in his hospital bed, wearing a hospital gown and the look of a homeless puppy being cuddled, eyes half-closed in contentment.

He cried the day the story appeared, because he suddenly had more friends than he ever knew. "It's incredible," he whispered, still groggy from medication, "that people care."

The Fontainebleau Hilton in Miami Beach invited him to recuperate for a few days after his release from the hospital. "They invited me to stay at the hotel. They're gonna pick me up in a limousine," he told me disbelievingly. "I never rode in one before. I'll be the poorest person there." Hotel officials offered to arrange transportation back to Chicago or help find him a job in Miami. "I like to work. I don't like to sit around. I want to start life over," he said eagerly, "get a good job and a nice place to stay and maybe go to school."

His mother was dead, he said, and he had grown up in foster homes. Jeff Miller's future promised to be brighter than his past.

Readers offered rooms, plane tickets and money to help pay his medical bills. Words of praise and encouragement came from politicians and show-business personalities.

The lead singer of the legendary Ink Spots sent a hundred dollars and invited Miller and Siegel to be his guests at the group's dinner show at a local hotel. Surfside merchants collected $450. "What he did was nothing short of committed," wrote a member of the Dade County Citizens Advisory Committee, enclosing a check.

The Fontainebleau limo whisked him in style from the hospital to his luxury suite, a three-hundred-dollar-a-day penthouse with an ocean view.

That was when things began to go awry, Siegel recalled later. "The Fontainebleau was the biggest mistake. It went to his head." Miller lolled about his celebrity suite, wondering, she said, "if the president is going to call me." Flashing his newfound fortune, he bought rounds of drinks for total strangers and ran up a ninety-dollar tab for a single room-service meal. Hotel officials soon tired of their guest.

Siegel talked a woman friend into taking Miller into her home. The young hero soon vanished, along with the woman's television set. Siegel told no one, fearing that people would not help the next person in need.

Fame and fortune faded fast. Next time Jeff Miller hit the headlines he was back in Illinois and on his way to prison. Arrested for a candy-store burglary, he had been released on bond. Two days later, police caught him red-handed, inside a closed stereo store. A judge told him he was going to do time.

Back in Miami where he had won the hearts of a crime-weary public, where he was wined and dined and bathed in the fickle spotlight of publicity, police began to doubt aloud if he ever had been a hero.

"He was a floater, a bum," Surfside Police Officer Warren Corbin said. "The whole thing smelled." He said he had always had the suspicion, never voiced, that Miller himself might have been involved in the robbery of Ann Siegel's store, shot by mistake by an accomplice.

Sentenced to five years, Miller reminisced with Illinois reporters about his short-lived celebrity. "I was on all the major television stations in Miami. The big newspapers—I was in all of them. I was getting money from everywhere. It was beautiful. It was too much."

Maybe it was.

Nevertheless, Ann Siegel remained steadfast. "I will remember his birthday and Christmas. I will let him know that there is someone who still really cares." She refused to believe the speculation that Miller was involved in the robbery. He was a true hero, she said. "I swear by it. Nobody else would come to my aid, and he did."

The doubts reminded me of something Miller had said to me in Miami, at the height of his glory. "To me, a hero is like Superman," he said. "It doesn't exist. It's only in Hollywood."

I would not agree.

Neither would Ann Siegel.

Part Four

THE STORIES

Chapter 15

LORRI

Some people *are* characters; others *have* character.

Lorri Kellogg has character. She is a nurturer, full of laughter, boundless energy and good common sense. A fearless woman, she does not take no for an answer, and would have been a great reporter. We met when militant feminists torched a stack of mattresses at the Playboy Plaza Hotel during a national political convention. We had nothing to do with the arson.

Lorri was divorced with no children. In fact, that is why she was divorced: Unable to bear a child, she was eager to adopt, but her husband wanted biological offspring and, therefore, a divorce.

Lorri moved to Miami and a job as a real estate executive. Hers was the good life: an apartment overlooking the bay, sailing, scuba diving, swimming with dolphins, playing tennis, and channeling her free time and vitality into the POW-MIA movement. A volunteer, Lorri founded a Florida organization to distribute petitions, leaflets and bracelets. Those who wore them pledged not to remove the wristbands until the man whose name was on it was free or accounted for. I wore my bracelet, with the name of Lieutenant Colonel Brendan Foley, for more than ten years.

Lorri's life seemed full, yet something was missing: We briefly lost touch after the convention, and the next time I saw her she had a new goal: to become a mother.

Like many other Americans, she had seen Art Linkletter on a TV show about Korean orphans in need of food and clothing, and like many other Americans, she agreed to sponsor a child with a monthly pledge. Weeks later a small snapshot arrived from the orphanage, a tiny face with sad eyes. Her name was Myung Sook.

Lorri devoured everything in the library on Korea and its children. Myung Sook, an infant abandoned in a cardboard box at a post office, faced bleakness at best. Lorri decided to adopt the child she sponsored. It seemed so simple. But nothing worthwhile ever is. The would-be mother was unmarried and the child was foreign; the bureaucracy was double-barreled and the international red tape an unintelligible maze that led to roadblock after roadblock.

Lorri never doubted she would succeed. She gave up her career to open a daycare center, so Myung, to be renamed Jaime, would have playmates when she arrived. She enlisted the aid of politicians, senators, representatives, reporters and the bureaucrats themselves.

Eventually she did the impossible: Jaime Myung was the first foreign child adopted by a single parent in this country under a new law passed at Lorri's behest. It took three years.

Jaime arrived in New York on an April night, rumpled and exhausted after a twenty-seven-hour flight and a twelve-hour time change. She spoke no English and wore shoes that did not fit and winter leggings. The long-awaited moment came when the Traveler's Aid guardian placed the child's small hand in Lorri's. The terrified four-year-old took one look at her new mother and exploded in a three-hour tantrum of sobs, kicks and hysterical screams.

For this, I thought, Lorri gave up the good life.

She rocked the child in her arms, repeating "uhm-ma, uhm-ma," the Korean word for mother. After three hours, the child stopped crying, hugged Lorri and smiled.

Jaime flushed her first toilet in New York and saw her first TV. The movie was *Brigadoon*, and Jaime tried to feed Gene Kelly her banana. She and Lorri sat on the floor and ate bowls of rice.

Jaime finally dozed off at three A.M., but the new mother stared at her all night. "I wanted to be awake if she needed me."

By the time they arrived in Miami, twelve hours later, they were getting along famously. Jaime wore a dress and a matching bonnet in red, white and blue, symbolic of her new home.

"How unfair that she couldn't be here when she was seventeen months old," Lorri said.

Jaime was a playful and lovable child. She still is.

That spring day in 1976, Lorri announced the order of business: "Disney World, sailing, lots of love and just a good happy, normal, busy home life." The future, she said, might bring Jaime a sister.

The future arrived on Mother's Day, a year later: Hee Jin Jung, age twenty-two months, known forever more as Tarabeth JJ Kellogg. Her homecoming climaxed a roller-coaster week of visa snafus and missed airline flights. "Giving birth would be easier," Lorri swore. "Emotional labor pains are much more difficult."

Her new daughter arrived snuggled in the arms of an Eastern flight attendant who had volunteered to escort the baby. "No better way to spend Mother's Day," the flight attendant said.

Everybody cried except Tarabeth. The pint-sized traveler clung dry-eyed to her new mom and curiously studied her new sister.

"I'm going to help take care of my sister," Jaime, now five, announced in perfect English.

Tarabeth was petite and pretty. She still is.

A year later Tarabeth became the littlest American naturalized as citizenship was administered en masse to 927 people. For weeks she had announced, "I'm gonna be an American." Her age exempted her from taking the oath, but she raised her right hand and took it anyway.

"I do," she sang out loudly, flashing a victory sign to her mom.

The ceremony was unique for more than one reason: Jaime had not been eligible for citizenship until two years after her adoption. Lorri's reaction: "Ridiculous." Tarabeth, patriotic in a navy-blue sailor frock with an American eagle on the sleeve, did not have to wait like her sister.

Lorri had done it again. This time, she had changed the law—with a little help from Senator Edward Kennedy and Florida Representative William Lehman.

The federal judge conducting the swearing-in ceremony solemnly explained that Tarabeth now enjoyed all but one of the rights and privileges of any native-born American: She could never be president.

Uh-oh, I thought, as Lorri bristled.

By then, Lorri realized that more children and other would-be parents needed help. She founded Universal Aid for Children, Inc., a private, nonprofit adoption agency specializing in placing foreign-born youngsters with American families and providing relief and medical assistance to needy children all over the world.

Daughter number three spoke her first English words only hours after she arrived. "Coca-Cola," said Jillian Catharine Kellogg, the former Hee Jung Lee, age five.

"I feel like she's always been here," Lorri said. Jillian and her sisters played, romped and giggled through their first day together. Like the others, Jillian had never seen a telephone or a television, a modern bathroom, an ice cube or ice cream.

She caught on fast.

Lorri happily described them as "very typical 'give me, get me, buy me, take me' American kids."

A *Herald* photographer shot Lorri's children at play for the Sunday magazine section. The assignment changed his life—forever.

Months later we were all waiting at the airport again, to meet his new daughter, Hae Jung Kang, age two.

Lorri has brought many children to this country for medical treatment. One little girl named Sara, age eight, from El Salvador, was horribly burned in a bombing that obliterated her village in 1983. Sara has undergone ten operations for reconstructive surgery since 1985. She faces twelve more. Since Sara has little family left and would live in a refugee camp, her grandmother's wish was that she stay in America. That is how Sara became Kellogg daughter number four.

Now thirteen, Sara has visited her grandmother several times. Lorri makes frequent trips to El Salvador, to deliver wheelchairs and crutches. For a decade, throughout the war, she has worked with the ravaged nation's first ladies and their volunteer committees. Lorri visits refugee camps and, through her agency, gathers urgent supplies for orphanages. One of her daughters usually accompanies her. Jaime and Tarabeth, at ages eight and five, worked with her in the mountains of Honduras. Even the littlest child can fold diapers.

I worry, but Lorri must have a guardian angel. She missed a devastating earthquake by a day and a half, a deadly raid on the capital of El Salvador by hours.

She recently returned home from Rumania and is placing orphans from that country too.

Tarabeth, my goddaughter, seems to harbor no political aspirations—as yet. At sixteen, she is far more interested in the New Kids on the Block and riding her bike. She is a part-time bag girl at Publix Supermarket and as American as apple pie. So is Jaime, now eighteen, and sisters Jillian, sixteen, and Sara.

When Jaime called recently with the news that Tarabeth had been hit by a truck while riding her bike, I thought I would have a heart attack. Her collarbone was broken, but she mended quickly. Kids are resilient, but it took me days to recover. This, I thought, must be Lorri's life, every day. How does she do it?

Asking her that question is like asking me how I can do my job year after year. The answer, I am sure, is the same.

How can you *not* do it?

Chapter 16

LAWYERS AND JUDGES

There are 9,276 lawyers in Miami. It only seems like more.

They are all here: the best, the worst, the flamboyant and scheming, the treacherous, the conniving, the good, the bad and the ugly. All help to make Miami one of the most litigious cities in America, a place with more lawyers per man, woman and child than most cities in the world.

All are out to make a buck.

On my first newspaper job, I met a lawyer representing a notorious jewel thief. He agreed to discuss the case and suggested we meet in the bar at the club where he lived. I had skipped lunch, and it was eight P.M. I scarcely touched my drink and declined another, while he kept hailing the bartender. Soon five sweating drinks stood lined up like soldiers on the bar in front of me.

He downed his and invited me to dinner, in his apartment. When I declined and left, he tagged along, suggesting we sit in my car and talk about the case. He slid into the tiny Triumph I drove then. For a moment, we talked. Then suddenly he hurtled through the air toward me—and impaled himself on the gear shift. His screams were pitiful.

That was my first encounter with one of Miami's vast army of lawyers.

During my second year at the *Herald* I was assigned to the criminal-court beat. I worked long hours, hard-pressed to cover the cases before all five criminal-court judges (today there are twenty-four). Most striking to me was the joy young public defenders took in beating the prosecution and winning their cases and how their office seemed to attract the very best young lawyers.

Their charismatic boss, public defender Phillip Hubbart, thirty-four, recruited many of his underpaid and aggressively loyal staff from the criminal-court workshop he taught at the University of Miami.

Hubbart called them a new breed, and they were, back in the early 1970s. They wore their hair longer and their clothes more mod than most lawyers. They were under thirty, believed marijuana should be legal and spent a great deal of time in jail conferring with clients. The days of their lives revolved around violence, victory and disaster.

They were never boring. Impeccable Christian Dior suit hanging elegantly from his lean frame, Stephen Mechanic exuded the style of a matinee idol and the aroma of expensive after-shave. Soft leather boots gleaming, blond hair curling at his collar, he battled for his clients with the zeal of an alley fighter who did not hesitate to slug below the belt. He did not earn enough to support his wife, but luckily his father owned Miami Beach hotels and had set up a trust fund.

Roy Black, the son of a daredevil racecar driver, went to college on an athletic scholarship. Seven hundred took the bar exam with him; he ranked number one. Formerly of the University of Miami championship swim team, he now spent weekends in the smelly, sweltering Dade County Jail and pounding ghetto pavements in search of witnesses. When Dennis Holober was a senior law student, he so successfully impugned the victim's character in a rape case that he won freedom for the defendant and a tooth-rattling punch in the mouth from the victim's enraged father.

Arthur Rothenberg sported a neatly trimmed mustache, rimless glasses and the well-tailored demeanor of an English nobleman. A health-food aficionado who lunched on homemade yogurt, he talked his way through college on a debate scholarship.

"I found myself terribly involved with making money. It was depressing," Rothenberg told me, explaining why he dropped out of private practice and took a major pay cut to work for Hubbart. "Money isn't worth getting out of bed for every morning. A man's life is his work. I wanted to make mine as meaningful as possible—I struck gold. This is worth my day. It's worth my time. It fulfills me. I have to draw on every ounce of energy and talent I have, every day. There's pressure from all sides: defendants, families, police, the prosecution. You've got somebody's life at stake.

"I realize the weakness and foibles of man—the ignorant and the uneducated. If you gave a man a choice, he wouldn't consciously choose to be a criminal. Individuals are trapped by their surroundings, their heritage of genes. That could be me in jail. I think it's pretty much out of a person's hands what they will be."

Ray Windsor, boyish and curly-haired, agreed: "At some point in life money is not necessary. I don't need it right now. I can't think of anything more fascinating to do. You rap with some of these guys for fifteen minutes, and it's difficult to believe they committed the crimes you know they have. Once you've pierced their subculture a little, you realize why they are here. They're truly victims—they're as much a victim as the victim of the crime they committed. The state is supposed to be the plaintiff, but our repressive society can very often be the defendant and all those people in jail the victims of our crimes."

They were serious—dead serious. Where did they learn this stuff?

No wonder State Attorney Richard Gerstein, a World War II hero who lost an eye in combat, usually looked grim.

At that time, his office was more than three times the size of the public defender's. Prosecutors had larger support staffs and were paid twice as much. Yet morale seemed higher in Hubbart's office. Defender Tom Morgan, twenty-five, explained. "Their office is far more bureaucratic than ours." Married, with a child, he said that he joined Hubbart's staff because "there wasn't anybody smarter to work for."

The daily pace was hectic, the responsibility harrowing. When Roy Black joined the staff, the backlog was so great that on one of his first days on the job he had thirty trials. He defended a steady stream of clients whom he had never seen before, until ten P.M. He went home and swore he would never come back, but he did go back. So did the others, every day—to the chilly, crowded fourth-floor criminal courtrooms where every minute counted. In a system awash in thousands of cases, constant frenzied plea-bargaining took place in corridors, judges' chambers and in whispers during trials in progress. They tried more than half their cases.

There was something more appealing and romantic about defending, rather than prosecuting. "It's the revolution in the criminal law field itself," Black explained. "The Warren Supreme Court has revolutionized the field, making it a popular arm of the profession instead of the stepchild it used to be."

Policemen freely offered less positive impressions of the Warren court.

His first day on the job, Holober was tossed the defense of a man accused of second-degree murder. He pleaded his client not guilty and began cross-examining witnesses with deliberate lack of speed, awaiting the return of his investigator dispatched in a frenzy to view and photograph the murder scene.

The defendant and his wife had fought. He wrestled a knife away from her and stepped outside to cool off—the knife still in his hand. Her brother lunged at him with a shovel and was stabbed to death, in what Holober creatively described to the jury as a "combination of self-defense and accident"—though the victim was stabbed six times. Holober eloquently talked himself to tears in his emotional closing argument. The jury said not guilty. In one week, Holober took five indigents to jury trials—and won acquittals for all five.

The defenders seemed even more zestfully exuberant when

winning cases for defendants who were obviously guilty. If only the prosecution could recruit lawyers with such passion and zeal.

I always knew when a case, somehow bumbled and about to embarrass the state attorney's office, was to be called—and lost. Some persuasive young prosecutor would seek me out, urgently suggesting that we go somewhere quiet to chat over coffee, a decoy sent in an attempt to divert me from the courtroom where the debacle was about to occur.

The ploy never worked. There were always too many people eager to spill the beans: court clerks, bailiffs, corrections officers, angry witnesses, opposing lawyers, irate cops and civilian-court watchers, usually senior citizens who enjoyed watching real-life drama more than TV soap opera.

There was never a dull moment on the beat. It was always chaos in the courts—frequent escape attempts, suicides and hysterics. Defendants collapsed, killed themselves or ran. One prisoner bolted out of a courtroom, pursued by a stampede of police, witnesses, jailers and his screaming family and friends, who had come to root for him at his trial. The escapee charged up a down escalator, then vaulted over the side. He knocked down several secretaries from the public defender's office, who were then trampled by pursuing police. Miami Police Officer Robert Weatherholt finally dropped him with a flying tackle off the escalator. They landed in a heap at the feet of State Attorney Gerstein, who called the cop's tackle "worthy of the NFL." The escape attempt was the third that week. A prosecutor had drop-kicked another escaping defendant off the escalator, and a third had leaped out a third-floor window.

Crisis was the rule, not the exception. It was always something: the speedy-trial-rule crisis, the probation-department crisis, the jury-selection crisis, the ever-simmering jail crisis and the visiting-judge crisis. Backlogged calendars created a state of emergency and visiting and interim judges were appointed to help reduce the case load. One of them was the courtly, Tennessee-born Judge George Holt, a controversial former state representative. Years earlier he had been the target of Florida's first impeachment proceedings against a judge and had barely weathered the storm. A senate vote necessary to remove him from office came up two ballots short. Now, age sixty-eight and frisky, he was summoned from his South Carolina retirement to help ease the crisis in Miami's courts—out of the frying pan and into the fire.

Holt was good-humored, plain-talking, and colorful to say the least. Assigned to speed things up in the court system, he did so, to the horror of the prosecution. He tossed out charges against an embezzlement suspect, saying, "I'm not going to hear any three-dollar case." In a fit of pique, he dismissed a day's entire calendar of armed robbers and drug suspects, throwing out their cases, after clashing with a prosecutor.

A SWAT team could not have pried me from his courtroom.

The judge was about to conduct the jury trial of a notorious defendant facing two counts of robbery when a set of briefs caught his eye. They were not of the legal variety—they were suede and looked hot. An attractive woman wearing short pants and boots was among prospective jurors thronged in the corridor when he arrived to pursue justice and impanel a jury. Judge Holt did a double take.

"What's her number?"—her juror number, he asked the clerk, in front of the entire courtroom. The clerk had no idea.

"Find out," His Honor ordered.

A dutiful deputy marched out and pretended to be checking subpoenas. He returned and reported in a stage whisper, "She's number nineteen."

"Call number nineteen," the judge ordered.

The dark-haired woman, in her fringed boots, stepped to the jury box, unaware of the conspiracy. Public defender Tom Morgan and prosecutor Sky Smith promptly accepted her. Both young lawyers were eager to keep the judge happy.

"I knew she was being called out of order," Smith would say later, "but she was acceptable. Even if she hadn't been, I would have been hesitant to excuse her in view of the judge's preference."

During routine questioning, the woman was asked if she would follow Holt's instructions during the trial. "I'll do anything the judge tells me," she cooed.

The judge beamed. "Hear that?" He nudged a bailiff. "I think she likes me."

The trial got under way as the victims, a Coconut Grove couple, testified to a night of terror, awakened in the dark by a figure at the foot of their bed. The intruder's face was grotesquely distorted by a stocking mask. He held a flickering candle high in one hand, a sawed-off shotgun in the other. He fired a blast into their mattress. The husband leaped up and grappled with the gunman, who battered them both with the weapon before he dropped it and fled. The intruder also left his jacket behind.

Police said the jacket belonged to the defendant. A shell matching those in the shotgun was found in his closet. Scratches on his leg were consistent with the struggle. The public defender was morose. The prosecution had an air-tight case.

The judge enlivened the proceedings with country-boy jokes and wisecracks and ordered miniskirted women to sit where he could see their legs. Leaving the other jurors locked up, he summoned number nineteen from the jury room to request her telephone number. She flirted back as they discussed the best-selling book *The Sensuous Woman*.

"You won't need any book, honey, when you're out with me," the judge told her from the bench.

The prosecutor finally protested, "Judge, I'm shocked."

He seemed to be the only one. Peals of laughter rang out from the jury room, where members were playing *Concentration*.

On his way back from lunch, Judge Holt confided to me that he intended to hand the defendant two ninety-nine-year terms.

Sounded right to me.

The jury did not deliberate long at all.

Not guilty.

The stunned prosecutor and I pursued the jurors outside. "I'm sorry," one apologized, "but we were just having too much fun to send anybody to jail."

I wrote about the case, then had occasion to write about it again two months later, after the wife of an ice-cream vendor was shot to death, the latest victim in a series of Coconut Grove robbery-murders.

They arrested the killer, the same man acquitted in Judge George Holt's courtroom.

Some things are worse than a clogged calendar.

Take Judge Murray Goodman, insecure and fearful of criticism from the press, who would refuse to call any newsworthy or controversial case if a reporter was present. I took to lurking outside his courtroom, peeping in from time to time. When an interesting case was called, I would slip inside and take a seat. The judge would look up in horror, call a recess and flee the bench.

In a muddled attempt to keep track of what calendar page he was on, Judge Goodman had devised his own method, using a child's numbered building blocks.

Daniel Fritchie, a defendant in Goodman's court, was penniless on the street when a Miamian offered him a place to stay. During the night, Fritchie slammed his sleeping benefactor over the head with a heavy frying pan and slit his throat. The killer called police. His confession was detailed. "I am mentally unstable and need to be confined," he said. Judge Goodman found Fritchie not guilty of murder by reason of insanity and ordered him committed. Released as no longer dangerous less than three months later, Fritchie traveled to Los Angeles. He was penniless on the street when a man offered him a place to stay. During the night he slammed his benefactor over the head with a statue of St. Francis and slit his throat. He explained to Los Angeles police: "I'm a danger to myself and others. I tried to tell them that in Miami, but they let me go."

When I sought his comment for my story, Judge Goodman said he could not recall the case. I believed him.

Then there was defendant Sherry Ann Gray, eighteen, one of Dade County's busiest burglars. "She's been in more houses than Santa Claus," an investigator told me. Police attributed more than 400 burglaries to this blue-eyed teenager, a heroin addict since age sixteen. She led detectives to the scenes of 150 crimes that she recalled.

I interviewed her in a cell. Slim and pretty, she smiled a lot and wore the word LOVE on her left arm—burned into the flesh with matches. She told me about the burglaries. "I did three to five a day. I had a hundred-and-fifty-dollar habit. I was high most of the time. I lost all fear. I didn't care if the people were home and shot me when I broke in."

Cellmates insisted she should have been a con artist, not a burglar. Officials agreed that she was 90 percent con. A trace of the little girl remained, however. She had been jailed since March—this was May. "I've never been away from my mother so long."

Sherry the junkie-thief stole a $26,000 diamond ring and sold it for four $10 bags of heroin. Stronger than she looked, she once outran pursuing cops while carrying a stolen nineteen-inch color portable. She stole a gun and sold it to a man in a bar. He used it to commit murder twenty-four hours later. She had been questioned in the killing of a Miami police officer, and federal agents wanted her before a grand jury. They were looking for the counterfeiting plates she had stolen in a burglary.

Sherry the little girl said she was twelve when her father's death and her rape by a family friend took place three months apart. When her stepfather was killed in a brawl with a cousin, the family moved from South Carolina to Florida.

"I tried sniffing Carbona when I was fifteen. It was on a rag in a bag. It blew my mind. I started looking for myself in the bag. The first day of ninth grade I skipped school. My girlfriend told me she smoked pot and saw peanut butter and jelly sandwiches hanging on a tree. I said, 'Man, I have to try that!' I didn't see any peanut butter and jelly sandwiches. I just kept laughing. Next day my jaws were sore from laughing so much. We all started smoking pot. We could get it anytime."

Then she met some boys at a carnival. "They had these tabs, like sugar, and said it was LSD. I had the worst trip. It lasted twenty-seven hours; I thought I would never be normal again.

The boy I was with was chewing gum. I felt like I was the piece of gum. I could feel him chewing me. I thought he was killing me. I was screaming. Everybody was so ugly. They took me home. The cat was lying near the door; I thought it was a lion. They had to hold it, so I could walk by."

Her bad trip did not deter Sherry and her friends. LSD was available at one of Miami's first psychedelic shops. "We tripped every Wednesday, Friday and Saturday," she said.

Soon she was using hard drugs and associating with two boys who broke into houses. A Miami doctor wrote them prescriptions in exchange for new television sets. One boy later went to prison, the other died of an overdose.

"When you need a bag of dope you've got to think fast," Sherry explained. A man "used to give me five bags of heroin to sell for fifty dollars. He'd give me two bags for selling it. I'd sell them milk sugar. I'd beat the bags I sold to people and do their dope too. I used to make up aluminum-foil dummy bags that looked like his. I'd tell him people out in the car wanted to buy but had to see the dope first. I'd give him back the dummy bags of milk sugar, go home and get off. He never caught me."

A friend fronted her four hundred dollars to buy some dope and go into business for herself. She planned to cut it, three to one, and deal, but she got ripped off. "The contact I went to sold me milk sugar and quinine mixed with a little Tuinal. It would gum up in the cooker. It was awful! I got so mad I just cried." She went back to demand a refund, but he kept putting her off. One day she went back and he wasn't home. "I just took the jalousies out. I took his two color TVs, stereo tape player, and his .45-caliber gun. I was just trying to get my four hundred dollars back."

That was her first burglary. "I'd ride down the street. If there was no car in the driveway and it was a nice house, I'd go knock on the door. If somebody answered, I asked for a phony name. I can get in any jalousie door. Roll-up windows are easy too. I used to cut myself a lot. One time I cut myself pretty bad, bled all over the place. Later, when the detectives took me back to the house, the woman just stood there and cried because I was so young.

"I took mainly cash, coins and guns. I found out all about guns. I know every model. My connections gave me three or four bags for them. I had an old man who gave me three dollars apiece for silver dollars. A guy who runs a gas station used to buy any jewelry I got. I broke into one house when it was raining. My mascara was running so I went in the bathroom and was using the woman's cold cream to take it off when I felt something in the cold cream jar. A hundred-dollar bill wrapped in aluminum foil. Another time I found twenty-four tabs of LSD, nineteen tabs of THC, three of mescaline and eight ounces of grass in a refrigerator. I took the stereo and some out-of-sight tapes too. I bet they were surprised."

She never wore gloves. Metro Detective Robert Rossman thought he knew why: that she wanted to be caught, that she was begging for help.

A Boy Scout copied the tag number of a car she used in a burglary, and she became Miami's most wanted woman. Sergeant Rossman, a father of five, tracked her, missing her many times by minutes. "We kept finding her fingerprints," he said. Because of her wholesome appearance, the pretty teenager could blend right into residential neighborhoods.

His search ended in a staked-out trailer park, when Sherry arrived with a full day's loot. A judge agreed to release her in her mother's custody if she would help close burglary cases, recover stolen property and lead police to one of her friends who was wanted for shooting a policeman. She never did the latter.

"She was in withdrawal and ran us in circles," Rossman said. "She did help us though. She took us to pushers."

Sherry grew to trust the veteran detective. "She called me every day," Rossman said. "That was one of the rules. She kept her word and I kept mine. We had a mutual understanding." Working with him, she divulged information and helped track down stolen valuables. But after a routine meeting one night, she was stopped by a waiting Opa-Locka detective, who handcuffed and arrested her on a months-old case.

She swore Rossman had betrayed her.

He said he did not. "I treated Sherry like I'd want one of my children treated," he told me. "The third time we arrested her she was barefoot. My wife gave her a pair of slippers and a sweater"—but the bond was broken.

"I dropped a tab of acid. All I saw was jail, and every man looked like a cop." She fled to New Mexico, a trip financed by stolen credit cards, and was arrested in Arizona. Rossman drew fire from his superiors and Sherry's victims.

"She let me down," he said. "I don't think she's got enough moral character to stay off the junk. If she can't, there's only one way she can support it."

"Sherry is a classic case," said her matinee-idol lawyer, Steve Mechanic. "Take a basically nice girl with looks, intelligence and a parent who cares—string her out on drugs and the next fix is her only reality."

Mechanic negotiated guilty pleas on twenty-two burglary counts. Judge Murray Goodman sentenced her to six months to five years, then said he might give her a break.

Everybody involved advised against it—strongly.

The judge talked to Sherry the con artist alone in his chambers and decided they were all wrong. He sent her to a drug rehabilitation program at Concept House. This was her last chance, he told her. She promised not to let him down. Sherry went to Concept House, announced she was stepping out to do her laundry and disappeared. The program's director suggested she might experience a change of heart and come back.

"I wouldn't put money on it," said her parole and probation investigator.

"I wish I had been wrong," said Detective Rossman. "Without will power you can't make it. I'm sorry. I was rooting for her."

"Sherry must have a reason for this," insisted Steve Mechanic, her staunch public defender. "It may not be a good reason, but she must have one."

Judge Goodman expressed his keen disappointment—and embarrassment.

Sherry traded her last chance for eight days of freedom. Police spotted her in a Cadillac with an ex-convict. She saw them, slammed her foot over the driver's on the gas pedal, and tried to outrun them. She had a gun in the waistband of her red slacks. The three policemen it took to subdue her said she tried to pull the weapon on them.

This time Sherry Ann Gray went to prison.

When a 315-pound woman was hauled before him, accused of assaulting a police officer with a knife, Murray Goodman sentenced her to a diet: Lose three pounds a week or go to jail. He ordered her to weigh in weekly and bring proof of her weight until she reached a svelte 250 pounds, which she claimed to be her normal weight.

Sounded right to Goodman, who was overweight himself.

Another time Judge Goodman kept a robbery suspect who kept pleading for a hearing and protesting his innocence in jail for five weeks. When Goodman went on vacation, Judge Alfonso C. Sepe scheduled a hearing and instructed the state to have the victim present. The victim appeared and identified the defendant—as the wrong man.

Judge Sepe seemed at the opposite end of the spectrum from these other judges. He had innovative ideas and gave unforgettable sentencing speeches. He used both his heart and his brain to create meaningful sentencing.

He gave two-year prison terms to two young robbers who terrorized three old ladies, then reduced the sentences to ten years of tightly structured probation. Both defendants were to start college and earn four-year degrees, with their grades regularly submitted to the court. They were to observe a curfew, attend regular religious services and abstain from alcoholic beverages and association with anyone using drugs or weapons. Each was to write letters of apology to the victims. Since the defendants' attorneys and emotional parents had called the crime a childish prank, and they had admittedly behaved like children, the judge ordered each to write *I shall not disobey the law* ten thousand times and deliver it to him within thirty days.

One defendant decided those probation terms were too tough. He preferred to do the time. The other met the challenge, lived up to the terms, won a degree in hotel and restaurant management and operates a successful Miami Beach restaurant.

Sepe sentenced a University of Miami art student, charged with cocaine possession, to volunteer work at a school for retarded children. His sentence became a career. The principal hired the defendant full time as his school's art director.

Long before the environment became the major concern it is today, Judge Sepe organized the Miami River cleanup project. Establishing work crews of probationers, he assigned one as foreman and sent them to clean up the river, the beach and the county parks.

With logic, common sense and eloquence, he reached defendants; most were receptive. Sepe sentenced some men to death and others to life—appearing before him may well be the best thing that ever happened to them.

Take the defendant who could neither speak nor hear. The judge agonized over how a young man who could not communicate could comprehend the proceedings.

"I'm not going to bring this boy to trial until he can understand what we're saying," Judge Sepe told lawyers. Classes were arranged at a university center for the handicapped. Nearly a year later, the defendant, now adept at sign language, appeared in court, his mother at his side.

"This is the first time I've ever heard my son call me Momma," she said, weeping, along with almost everybody else present.

Unfortunately, something happened. As of this writing Sepe himself faces indictment: corruption, taking bribes. Federal agents swooped down with search warrants on his office and home and came away with wads of hundred-dollar bills. A tragedy for everyone concerned—especially the taxpayers who trusted him.

Marvin Emory was a busy young defense attorney whose career I covered during my year on the criminal-court beat. Fair-haired and fine-featured, he was well spoken, well prepared and concise. Low-key, with a quiet wit, unlike his more flamboyant colleagues, he was no desk pounder. He hardly ever raised his voice and never became ruffled. He was instrumental in changing Florida's abortion law. Despite his success he was quiet, a loner. I was at the Miami Homicide Bureau one weekend, talking to Sergeant Arthur Beck, when we got a call: Somebody had taken a fatal dive fourteen floors from Marvin Emory's penthouse apartment.

There had been quite a mêlée. The place was a shambles, lamps and furniture smashed, pictures knocked off the walls. Emory was alive, his pale face flushed. He wore a cabana set, shorts and an open shirt. The young man who had plunged from his balcony was a former client with a history of mental problems. He had arrived unexpectedly and attacked another young man he found visiting. To escape, the original visitor managed to barricade himself in a bedroom.

The attacker was resolute. He propped a chair on the balcony so he could reach the bedroom window. The chair gave way, and he plummeted fourteen floors to his death. The incident appeared suspicious at first. The man barricaded in the bedroom did not see his attacker fall. Still frightened, he had hurled a lamp out a window to attract attention and help. The dead man's family later questioned when the lamp was thrown. Some suspected it might have been thrown during a struggle, that the victim was pushed. But witnesses on the ground insisted that the body had landed first, that a short time later, moments before we arrived, a window shattered and the lamp came down, amid a shower of glass.

Emory survived the messy scandal, becoming even more quiet

and low-key. You never knew what he was thinking. He approached me one day at the Justice Building, with an announcement of sorts. "I'm sure you'll be relieved," he said, "to hear that I've moved, bought a house. It's just one story." That said, he walked away.

Miami's most colorful judge, Ellen Morphonios, achieved success on her own. She did it the hard way: no silver spoons or silver platter. She worked her way through law school at night, carrying her baby son in a basket to classes with her. Crack rifle shot, ex–beauty queen and tireless worker, she rose through the ranks of the state attorney's office—strictly a man's world at the time—to become chief prosecutor of major crimes.

When I first covered the court, almost two decades ago, she wore stiletto heels and tight skirts. She still does. Her hair is still long and blond and wavy. They call her the Hanging Judge, the Time Machine, Maximum Morphonios and Lady Ellen. She is especially tough on criminals who harm animals or children. She sentenced one brutal robber to 1,698 years, saying, "He deserves to do each and every day of it." She keeps a small replica of the electric chair in her office and will not hesitate to sentence those who deserve it to the real thing.

She has done so nine times.

Common-sense, down-home justice is her trademark, along with a gutsy sense of humor. One of the most persistent stories about her is that after sentencing a rapist to a long stretch, she hiked up her black robe, exposed her terrific legs, and said, "Take a good look at these, pal. They're the last ones you'll be seeing for a long, long time."

She likes men, always had a flock of them around her, including three husbands, two sons and her dad, until he was ninety. Domestic difficulties never interfered with her work—even when she was assigned armed guards for several days after reported threats from her estranged first husband, a junior college professor. When the professor invaded the Justice Building and her chambers one day, she rejected his pleas for reconciliation. He retaliated, by banging his head on her desk until he drew blood.

Led away, down a back staircase into a parking lot, nose bleeding, he cried, "Take your hands off me! I'm no criminal."

That day was especially hectic for Judge Ellen Morphonios. The press, present in force because of an important trial, jumped on the story with gusto. Ellen had brought her baby chimpanzee, Toto, to work with her. Anne Cates, her secretary, baby-sat Toto while the judge was on the bench. Perhaps due to all the excitement, Toto's disposable diaper was soon in dire need of a change. Anne attempted to do so, laying him down like a baby and removing the dirty diaper, but Toto resisted and threw a tantrum. He pinched Anne, hard, then chased her around the office, bouncing off furniture and swinging from the purple drapes.

Ellen loves purple, so everything in her office was purple—including the ink she used to sign official decrees.

Toto chased Anne right out of the purple office. She headed for the courtroom, to inform Ellen of the new emergency, but Toto tried to follow. She scuffled with the creature, who had one hairy arm and leg outside the door, as she tried to force him back inside and close it quietly, without attracting the attention of salacious news crews stampeding through the building seeking footage of the judge's bloodied husband.

Ellen took a recess and changed Toto, who cooed like a baby, letting her diaper him and powder his hairy bottom.

Is it any wonder I loved that beat?

An awkward situation arose the day the back zipper on my dress split apart. Judge Morphonios was on the bench, and I ducked into her purple chambers. Anne recalled there was a sewing kit up in the clerk's office. "Take it off," she said, "I'll take it up there and fix it." She said she'd lock the door and that I should wait until she got back. Only she and Ellen had keys, she reassured me, and the judge was in trial and not expected back in chambers soon.

Anne left with my dress. I felt a bit uncomfortable, lounging around the judge's purple office at midday in my underwear.

Hearing voices and a key in the lock, I ducked into the judge's large walk-in closet. She had called a recess for a private conference with several lawyers. There seemed to be five or six of them. If I announced my presence, someone would no doubt throw open the closet door. Too embarrassing, I thought. If I kept silent, they would probably return to the courtroom soon, none the wiser—and, in the interim, with my ear to the closet door, I might happen to overhear inside information on important cases.

I was still undecided about the proper course to take when Anne returned with the repaired dress. Startled, she spilled the beans. There was only one way out, and she feared I might be sprinting down a crowded corridor.

"Where's Edna Buchanan?" she blurted, waving my dress at the judge and assembled lawyers.

Silence.

The time seemed right to speak up. "Here I am," I cried.

What impressed me most is that no one ever asked for an explanation.

Judge Morphonios takes everything in stride.

Her second husband, a greyhound trainer, was soon out of the running. Her third marriage was made in heaven, or so I thought. Maximum Morphonios eloped to Reno on a Friday the thirteenth with a handsome, young gung-ho police lieutenant assigned to narcotics and vice. They seemed meant for each other.

When Cindy, Judge Sepe's red-haired secretary, married a foot doctor and got pregnant, the baby shower was at Ellen's house. Her lieutenant was on the job that night. The all-female baby shower festivities were at their height when he made an appearance. He and his squad were conducting a narcotics raid in the neighborhood. He charged in, wearing camouflage gear and carrying a shotgun, gave her a little smooch, then charged back out into the night.

Nobody lifted an eyebrow—domestic bliss, Ozzie and Harriet, Miami style.

Ellen, I thought, had made the perfect match.

It was, for a while. Then he did the unthinkable, as men so

often do. He fell in love—with her son's young wife. Both divorces were painful. The young couple had children. The lieutenant, who had since gone to law school and passed the bar, went from being Ellen's husband to being her grandchildren's stepfather.

Nobody ever said life was simple.

AFTERMATH

Arthur Rothenberg, the assistant public defender, who once told me, "If a man serves only himself, he can never be satisfied," left Miami for Yap, a thirty-nine-mile-square island where women wore nothing from the waist up and ancient stone money is still in use. He signed on for two years, to defend the natives of Micronesia, twenty-two hundred tropical islands strung out across the Pacific. His title was public defender for the District of Yap, which encompassed slightly more than seven thousand people on twenty inhabited islands scattered over seven hundred miles of sea. The entire district had reported only twenty-two violent crimes the year before.

Rothenberg had defended more than that on one bad day in Miami.

"I'm going so I'll gain perspective," he told me. "What happens in Dade County is not the end of the world."

But he did come back to Miami, where he is now a circuit judge.

One night not long after our last conversation, Marvin Emory's new Cadillac Seville slammed into a fire hydrant, rupturing the gas tank. The car then crashed into a light pole. Hot wires fell and sparked, and the car caught fire. Emory had been drinking. Witnesses say he simply sat there making no effort to escape. The flames were so intense they melted the tires and the door handles, scorched all the paint off the car and the name off his Rolex. He was thirty-nine.

Former assistant public defender Roy Black, now one of Miami's richest and most successful defense attorneys, recently won an acquittal for William Kennedy Smith on rape charges.

Steve Mechanic, the matinee-idol lawyer, Ray Windsor and Tom Morgan all have successful private practices. Charismatic public defender Phillip Hubbart is now an appeals court judge.

And Toto resides in a zoo in Sanford, Florida, far from the commotion of the criminal court.

Chapter 17

MRS. Z

The photographs of two sturdy little blond boys and their baby sister, Amanda, arrive regularly at my desk. At two and a half, Amanda is silky-haired, wearing ruffles on her dress and little white shoes.

She does not remember of course, but we took her first airplane trip together when she was three weeks old. We journeyed from Miami to Chicago in the dead of winter, at the height of a snowstorm. She was the better traveler, by far. I hate to fly, but we were on a mission: Amanda, her parents and me.

We wanted to solve a murder.

This story differed from the others in many ways, some of them personal. "Careful," my editor warned. "Don't get too involved with the people you write about."

One lesson I have learned on the police beat is that life is cheap and editors are treacherous, but this one was right. I have no big, extended family, and never yearn for one—solo is my style—but if I could choose a family to belong to, this might be the one.

I was not sure that such family ties existed, except on television. One reason this murder is so unforgivable is because the very woman who instilled the warmth and values in these people was the victim.

To the state of Florida, the murder of Mrs. Z remains an "unsolved" crime. Yet everyone involved believes they know who did it, and why.

Z stands for Zinsmeister, Evelyn Louise Zinsmeister. A doting grandmother, age forty-seven, she painted landscapes, wore a gold *Mrs. Z* necklace and drove a Honda with a MRS. Z vanity plate.

Someone slipped into her suburban four-bedroom home in Perrine, south of Miami, on the afternoon of January 21, 1985, pursued her from room to room, and shot her again and again and again. Bullets blew away parts of her face and right hand. The murderer did not break into the house or steal anything from it —except a life.

Police have no witnesses.

The night before she died, Evelyn Louise Zinsmeister saw the Dolphins lose Super Bowl XIX on television. Her husband, Charles Frederick Zinsmeister, did not watch with her. His beeper chirped shortly after the kickoff. He said it was Dade Correctional Institution, the prison where he worked. He was a major. "Can't you get anybody else?" his family heard him say.

He hung up the telephone and said Broward County police had captured an escaped convict. Z, as he is known, said he had to go bring back the prisoner.

But there was no escaped prisoner.

Instead, Z would later admit, he went to see Jane Mathis. She too worked at the prison. She was twenty-six; he was fifty-one. They had been lovers.

This story of murder, a doomed marriage and illicit love that flowered in a state prison began twenty-eight years earlier in the Alabama town of Cullman.

Louise and Frederick Zinsmeister grew up there. Their mothers knew each other. They married on March 4, 1957, he twenty-three, a sailor on leave, she nineteen, a girl with a bell-clear soprano voice. They had four children.

Louise, the dutiful military wife, was once awarded a plaque for sewing curtains for an admiral's barge. Z loved his life aboard Navy tankers. "I was an E-9," he told me, "as high as you can go in enlisted status."

Life changed after he retired in 1977. Z began using Grecian Formula and had an affair with a nineteen-year-old.

"It was the only vindictive thing I ever did to my wife in my life," Z acknowledged. Z, who often refers to himself in the third person, later told me, "If there was ever a time that Charles F. Zinsmeister was going to do anything criminal against his wife, that would have been the time, in 1977."

Z went to work at the prison, an institution surrounded by farmland and barbed wire, on August 22, 1978.

Jane Susan Mathis went to work there on June 26, 1981. She had worked at a McDonald's, a W. T. Grant and at Cook's Gas Co., in Homestead. She left Cook's after a shortage of nearly ten thousand dollars was discovered. "Her husband came down and paid back the money in a lump sum," says company president Tim Kent. The prison, he said, never called for a reference.

Z and Jane Mathis became lovers. They exchanged messages. "We may have to move with more caution," Z once wrote, "and at times just plain use of restraint—but if it means getting you after this is all over . . . then the waiting is worth it. . . . I can't even think of my world without you."

She wrote: "I enjoyed every aspect of playing house with you. . . . My entire body melts at your gentle touch." She signed it, "Your Hairy Kitten."

In September 1982, Jane Mathis divorced her husband of five years. She got the house. He got the 1923 Roadster.

In February 1983, Z filed for divorce. Louise was served with the papers on St. Valentine's Day.

Z and Jane Mathis lived together for a while. Z describes her as "very soft-hearted, the type who cries if somebody shoots a dog," though he did suffer minor injuries twice during the romance. "I hit my own damn elbow, all in playing," he said. "We were scuffling around on the bed, and I smacked my elbow. Can you imagine Jane Mathis, a hundred and ten pounds, slamming my elbow into something?"

Then came a "damn freak accident . . . I stuck a stick in my eye at the institution. A day or so later I was lying on the bed, and I asked her to toss my glasses to me. They hit my hand, glanced off and hit my sore eye. She didn't violently slam the glasses into my eye."

Z went back to his wife in July 1984, the same month he insured both himself and Louise for $100,000. She welcomed him home. They even renewed their marriage vows at the church wedding of their daughter Lisa on August 18.

Louise sewed for weeks making the bride's gown, the bridesmaids' dresses, and her own elegant blue-voile formal.

The reunited couple paid Z's ex-lover about two thousand dollars. "It was a personal debt," Z said later. "I was doing the right thing."

That autumn, Z decided to teach his wife to fish. On the cold night of November 10 they drove to a dark and remote Homestead rock pit.

Something happened.

"The grass was slippery, and the rear end slipped off and drug the front end right into the rock quarry," Z said. His 1978 Alfa Romeo sports car sank in twenty-five to thirty feet of water.

"Blub, blub, blub," he recalled. "It was strange. I yelled at her to get the window down and get out, but I came to the surface and didn't see her. I was wearing heavy boots that were full of water, heavy jeans and a heavy jacket. I said, 'Oh, hell,' and dove back down." The water was black as ink. A "higher power" must have been his guide, Z said. "I went in through my window. She was still sitting there with the damn tackle box on her lap." Z shoved her out the passenger window. "I pushed her butt through there like a marshmallow. When I came up she was about ten feet from the bank, yelling 'Help! Help!' She had lost her glasses."

Z helped her up onto the bank. "We lay there and laughed for a while, freezing our butts off. Then she got hysterical."

He joked about the hundred-thousand-dollar life insurance policy. She joked about changing her will. She told her sister, Joyce Shafer: "He saved my life. I know he loves me."

Privately, however, she quizzed her daughter Tia: "Do you think your father could have done it for the insurance? The hundred thousand dollars?" Louise and her husband gave up fishing.

That month Z selected Sergeant Mathis as the prison's custodial employee of the month. "Keep up the good work," he wrote.

On January 21, the day after the Super Bowl, Louise called in sick to her job at a Coral Gables architectural firm. She planned to apply for another job that day.

Z said he last saw his wife about 11:00 A.M., then drove to the prison to meet co-worker Franklin Tousley for a trip to a three-day seminar in St. Petersburg.

Louise's oldest daughter, Tia, twenty-four, telephoned her mother about 12:45 P.M. She knew her mother had told the office she was "sick."

"Are you sick?" she asked.

"I am now."

Tia says her mother told her that Jane Mathis had telephoned that morning to ask if Z was home yet, revealing that he had been with her the night before.

"Mom was very upset. It was like everything was drained out of her," says Tia. "Like the end of the world."

Joy, twenty, the youngest daughter, arrived home for lunch with her fiancé a moment later. Louise was on the telephone with her father. "I knew something was wrong," Joy said. "Mom told him she was going to have a computer readout done of calls coming in and out of the house. She said, 'Then, we'll know.' She sat on a couch and didn't say anything, kind of staring off, like she was in her own little world." Joy and her fiancé, Bobby Twisdale, left at 1:10 P.M. to return to work, she at a Fayva shoe store, he at Zayre.

Lisa, twenty-three, the middle daughter, saw her father about 1:30 P.M., at a Carvel ice-cream shop where she worked, about a mile from her parents' home. Lisa saw her dad nervously pat down his pockets. She thought he had lost his keys. "Just my cigarettes," he said.

Lisa called her mother at 1:50 P.M. No answer. She tried all afternoon. Lisa went to the house just before 5:00 P.M. She heard the TV inside—loud. The door was not locked. She opened it and saw her mother lying in the foyer.

"My first thought was, what are you doing on the floor?" She did not see the blood; the floor is brick-red tile. She felt for a pulse. "She was so clammy and cold." She saw a streak of blood on the wall, recoiled and rushed to the telephone to call her husband, Jason Peterson. As she waited for him to answer, she switched off the blaring TV.

In the sudden silence, she realized the telephone was dead, the cord ripped out of the wall.

Lisa fled weeping, her hands bloody. She pounded on a neighbor's door. Someone called 911. Police arrived. When the paramedics came, a policewoman said, "Never mind," and waved them away.

Lisa saw her sister Joy's car come down the street. "I was crying and calling her name, 'Joy! Joy!' When she saw me, she was already crying. She was saying, 'No, no.' I saw her mouthing the words."

"Tell me everything's all right," Joy pleaded.

Tia arrived about an hour later and collapsed in the arms of her sisters.

It was the coldest night of the year, 28 degrees. At Miami International, forgiving fans braved a windchill factor of 12 degrees to welcome home the Dolphins.

Metro-Dade Detective John King had the sisters taken downtown to headquarters, a thirty-minute drive.

"We were sitting on hard benches, waiting and waiting," Tia says. "My youngest sister was throwing up. The officers were all joking that it was such a cold night that the bodies out in the ocean were turning into corpsicles. I started screaming, 'My mother's been murdered!' "

A sergeant rebuked her. "Young lady, we're trying to conduct an investigation here."

Lisa's husband, Jason, twenty-seven, suggested that police test the hands of a possible suspect for gunpowder residue. The technique is fairly common.

"This isn't the movies," he said the detective scoffed.

At the crime scene, technicians removed a large section of wall with part of a bloody palm print. There was a bullet hole in the wall behind a sofa in the paneled den. Another projectile went through a wall, then a window and lodged in a neighbor's screen.

Louise was shot five or six times at close range. Gunpowder had singed her hair.

Z was notified after midnight. A detective telephoned the Dolphin Beach Resort Hotel in St. Petersburg. Tousley, his co-worker, answered.

"Z was asleep. I gave the phone to him. He sat up. He swung his feet out of bed. I heard him say, 'Oh, my God! What do you mean?' He said, 'My wife is dead. Somebody killed my wife.' He was aghast. He seemed to be in a hell of a state of shock."

Z said later, "Someone kept telling me my wife was deceased. I thought it was a drunk. I was going to hang up." Months later, Z said he was still angry. "You've got a man—a major, not a peon—in charge of complete security at that institution. And they didn't even send a state trooper or a policeman" to break the bad news.

Metro police soon called again. Z quotes a detective as saying, "I'm not supposed to tell you this, but one of our suspects is your girlfriend, Jane Mathis."

Z said he told the man, "I don't have a girlfriend. I have a wife, and I don't want to talk anymore."

Detective King spoke to Jane Mathis that night. It would be the only opportunity he ever had. She hired an attorney who instructed her to talk to no one. "She'll stand by her innocence and let the facts speak for themselves," he said.

The day after the murder, Tia and Joy drove to Jane Mathis's house. They say they took a brick and an unloaded gun. They tore the screen and pounded hysterically on the front door. They did not find Jane Mathis.

Z flew back to Miami. His boss, Dr. Ana Gispert, met him at the airport. She drove him straight to police headquarters. "I was hauled in, more or less as a suspect," he told me later, "but they screwed up. They didn't give me my rights."

The mortician asked the daughters to bring white gloves for their mother. "One of the fingers on her right hand was mangled," Lisa says. "They said it would take the whole day to fix her so we could have an open-casket viewing." The family conducted a memorial service at the church where the couple had renewed their wedding vows five months earlier.

The funeral was in Alabama. "It was miserably cold," said only son, Fred, twenty-six. "My dad flew in with my mom's body."

The son did not meet his father at the airport. "I was afraid I would jump on him," he said. "I used to encourage Mom to divorce him. But she was really in love with Dad. That was the whole thing."

Eleanor Brown, Louise's sister, said Z "stayed off to himself at the funeral." The family all knew about Jane Mathis. "No one accused him," she said. "He said the girl didn't do it. She wasn't that kind of girl. I tried to comfort him."

Z placed a small bouquet on his wife's coffin. The card said, *I love you.*

At the funeral, the son said, his father explained that he saw Jane Mathis on the eve of the murder to tell her he "was going to have to quit seeing her."

The day after the murder, Metro detectives arrived at the prison. They wanted to know about Major Z and Jane Mathis. They wanted to examine all the handguns at the prison. The killer had used a .38-caliber weapon. Were any weapons missing? Could anyone have removed a gun, used it and replaced it undetected?

Most prison weapons are stored in a double-locked arsenal. A small number, usually four to six, are kept in the prison control room, in a wooden gun case. None was missing.

Detectives took more than thirty weapons to the crime lab for ballistics tests. Police eventually returned all but one, the murder weapon, a Model 15 Smith and Wesson .38-caliber revolver with a four-inch barrel, serial number 8K45391.

It had cost the taxpayers $93.02 seven years earlier.

Police and the state attorney's office refused to discuss the gun or even publicly acknowledge that they had found the murder weapon. Prison officials talked about it uncomfortably.

"It's embarrassing to the institution," said a former assistant superintendent. "It's a very traumatic thing. We were trying to keep it low-key."

The assistant superintendent said he thought the gun came from the control room at the rear of the main lobby. Sergeant Jane Mathis worked there every day, four P.M. to midnight. Major Z had access to the control room. So did about ten other employees. The guns are inventoried when the shift changes. No one reported any discrepancies. Sergeant Mathis worked until midnight Saturday, January 19.

She was off on Super Bowl Sunday and on Monday, the day of the murder.

Major Z had reported to work Monday morning—before his St. Petersburg trip. He logged out of the prison at 12:52 P.M. Tousley went to pick up a cooler of sandwiches and soft drinks. The two men arranged to meet in fifteen or twenty minutes, near Homestead First National Bank. The bank is six-tenths of a mile—a two-minute drive—from the home of Jane Mathis.

Tousley said he found Z waiting at the intersection. He followed Z for 13.7 miles—to the Carvel shop, where he dropped off a car borrowed from his daughter, Lisa.

Tousley recalled little of their talk during the auto trip across state to St. Petersburg, but he said Z "mentioned something about some keys."

The murder took place that afternoon, presumably while Z was on the road with co-worker Tousley, but the precise time of death is uncertain. Joy last saw her mother about 1:10 P.M. Lisa telephoned at about 1:50 P.M.—and got no answer.

Could Major Z and Sergeant Mathis have seen each other that day—after he left the prison? Major Z denied it.

On the day of the murder Sergeant Mathis walked into the prison about three P.M. She did not belong there. It was her day off. She was not in uniform. She wore a sweater and blue jeans. She said she was there to write a check for $9.80, a monthly premium, to an HMO medical plan. The matter was not urgent. "I had told her to bring in a check sometime that week," said Maribel Ortiz in the personnel office. While she was there, prison officials say, Sergeant Mathis stopped in the control room.

St. Pete hotel records show that Z telephoned Jane Mathis that evening.

"Right from the damn hotel," Z says. "I had nothing to hide." He was worried, he said, about Jane's health. "She had a chest cold—congestion. We discussed the weather."

She cut short the conversation, he said. "She told me she had spilled some paint and had to clean it up." Z said he also tried to call home that evening, but the line was busy. "I hung up and watched TV a little."

Jane Mathis failed to report for work at the prison the next day—or the next. On the third day of her unexplained absence, personnel director Kril Jackson spoke to her mother. "She said her daughter had been questioned by the police and was under a doctor's care for nervousness and strain."

He dispatched an aide to her home with resignation papers.

Jane Mathis signed.

Z never worked a day at the prison again either. His boss took a typed resignation to his home.

Z signed.

The first time the family was allowed to return to the house after the murder, Z searched "frantically for his keys," son-in-law Jason said. "He said he found them under the dishwasher."

Z said he never spoke to Jane Mathis after the murder. He would drive by her house but did not stop. To do so, he said, would "bring hellfire, damnation and police down all over her."

Life after his wife's death was not easy, Z said. Intruders broke into his house, and strangers chased his car and shot out a window. He changed the locks and disconnected the telephone. He was denied unemployment compensation.

The insurance company withheld payment of the hundred thousand dollars. "I'll have to sue the damn insurance companies," Z said. Eventually they paid but not to him.

The money was divided among the dead woman's children.

Z always acknowledged that he and his former lover are the prime suspects. Of himself, he says, "It's not every day you are a murder suspect after an impeccable life: two traffic tickets in fifty-two years. I am innocent. I've seen enough of prison that I don't want to get involved in murder. I've walked down Death Row and seen the electric chair. Murder is not my bag. You have two innocent people here. I have no idea who killed my wife. It wasn't Jane Mathis."

Jane Mathis would not discuss the case. "As far as we're concerned," her lawyer said, "the matter is over. There is no case, absolutely no evidence whatsoever. She wants to go on with her life."

Z said there was no case against anyone: "Just between you and me and the old deep blue sea, I feel that most of what they have is circumstantial evidence."

The state attorney's office agreed.

No one was charged.

The people who loved Mrs. Z never stopped hoping for justice. I grew to know Tia and Lisa and their husbands, Terry and Jason. Joy postponed her wedding after the murder. Eventually she married her fiancé, and they moved to Atlanta. They are all good and wholesome young people.

Tia, the oldest girl, vibrant and levelheaded, often speaks for all of "us kids." Estranged from their father since the murder, they have, in effect, lost both parents.

No murder victim's family has done more to seek justice. Eighteen months after her murder, Mrs. Z's children, grandchildren, sisters, nieces, cousins and other relatives traveled to Miami from Alabama, Georgia, Fort Lauderdale and Leisure City to try to learn why there was no prosecution. Carrying homemade placards and wearing black armbands, they picketed the office of state attorney Janet Reno.

They also picketed the prison—or tried to.

WHO WAS ON DUTY IN THE CONTROL ROOM JAN. 21, 1985? one homemade sign asked.

GUN CONTROL OUT OF CONTROL AT DADE CORRECTIONAL INSTITUTION, said another.

Prison guards denied them access to a road leading to the prison. They promised that an official would come out to talk to them. None ever did—only prison employees, grimly shooting video-camera pictures of the marchers with their signs.

The family also marched on the state capitol, pleading for justice.

They were ignored.

Detectives told them the night of the murder that the case was all but wrapped up, say the children of Mrs. Z, that the killer was known. But prosecutors refuse to press a circumstantial case.

The family even filed a civil suit, against the prison and the state, for not carefully screening employees and for allowing a state owned weapon to fall into the hands of their mother's murderer. A day in court, they hoped, might bring to light evidence that would help a criminal prosecution, but the state stymied their lawyer.

Tia and I talked often. She missed her mom—still does. In a small way, I may have been a substitute, someone for her to turn to. The two blond boys in the pictures are Tia's. They were Mrs. Z's only grandchildren at the time of her death.

She has seven now. One is Amanda, Tia's third child.

Z rented out the family home. His children drive by from time to time. "It will always be my mom's house to us," Tia says.

Many "unsolved cases" are solved in the minds of police who believe they know the guilty party. They want to make an arrest—but prosecutors, ever aware of their conviction records, refuse the case. They insist on more evidence first. Sometimes there is no more.

The most dangerous killers do not commit murder in front of witnesses. They do not wait for police, smoking guns in hand, or sign confessions. It seems unfair not to let a jury decide.

In the dead of winter 1988, nearly three years after the murder, an *Oprah* producer called. A show on unsolved murders was planned, and she asked if I knew of any nagging cases.

First person I called was Tia.

She was suffering from postpartum depression. Amanda had been born on Christmas Eve, and Tia's mom had not been there, as she had been when the boys were born. Her sons' paternal grandfather was near death from cancer. But no blues or bad news could extinguish the spark of hope. The family conferred and concurred. They would do anything to further the case.

I took with me the details of two other murder cases I believed national television exposure could solve. Lisa and Jason also flew to Chicago, at their own expense, to provide moral support. They boarded an earlier flight. By the time we arrived at the Miami airport, with tickets sent by *Oprah*, it was snowing in Chicago and flights were being canceled. Ours was one of them. The show would be taped at nine A.M. next morning. We had to fly out that night to make it in time.

Eastern said nobody was flying into Chicago. Luckily we did not take their word for it and found a Midway flight. As much as I fear and loathe flying, especially through ice and snow, I was relieved. This was a mission.

Tia looked beautiful and was wonderful on the show. Oprah was super. Guests included the parents of a missing girl believed to be a victim of Seattle's Green River killer, a former New York cop whose eleven-year-old daughter was murdered, and the twin brother of a Chicago lawyer who was ambushed by a sniper—all unsolved cases.

Tia talked about her mother's murder, and I spoke about two perplexing mysteries: a small boy found cemented into an apartment-house closet and a dismembered couple found floating.

I was eager for network exposure of the three unidentified corpses from Miami. Identifying the victims would be a giant step toward solving their murders. Oprah knew none of us, yet remembered all our names, all the stories, all the people and places, and had read my book, to boot. She never once stumbled or missed a beat.

Parts of the dismembered couple had surfaced in waters all over Dade County, in April 1985. The man had the letters LR tattooed on his right shoulder and a scar across his back. The woman was brown-haired and petite, with a Caesarean scar.

Somebody out there in America's living rooms had to know their names.

The little boy nobody knew was found by workmen readying an apartment for a new tenant in October 1983. As they removed a cinderblock and concrete cubicle from a closet, it crumbled, exposing the body of a child.

He appeared to be age six or seven and dead for about two years. He had lost two baby teeth, and his second teeth, barely through the gum, had begun to grow in crooked. He would have had a gap-toothed grin.

The former tenant swore he had never seen the child, dead or alive. A man in his sixties, he often allowed friends and acquaintances to use his place and did not specifically recall when the concrete cubicle appeared. He assumed some houseguest had stored belongings inside. Strange as his story seemed, he passed a polygraph test.

Metro Detective John Butchko had contacted the national clearinghouse for missing children, interviewed more than a hundred people and had an expert rebuild the child's face. I took pictures with me.

Somebody had to remember this little boy.

In the case of Mrs. Z, we hoped national coverage would either bring forward new evidence or give police and prosecutors the courage to take action.

We went directly from the TV studio to the airport, all of us lugging Amanda's baggage. Babies do not travel light. The show had aired live in Chicago, and as we boarded, other passengers recognized us. A good omen, I hoped. Excited, I could not wait to reach the newsroom the next day.

Messages were stacked like gifts on Christmas morning. Long computer printouts, names and numbers, people calling from everywhere. What a heady feeling to know that somewhere among them were the answers to these mysteries.

Wrong again.

A young Texas woman wanted me to look into the unsolved murder of her mother, slain when she and her brother were children.

A distraught Michigan couple asked me to investigate the homicide of their daughter, a San Diego, California, businesswoman. There was a suspect, they said, but detectives had done nothing.

Vermont police wanted help in the search for missing newlyweds who had disappeared on their honeymoon.

A tearful Los Angeles widow hoped I could help prove murder and a cover-up in the mysterious death of her husband, killed on the job.

My spirits sank as I returned call after call. No one was offering to help identify *our* victims. All these people, hundreds of them, needed help. There was a world full of pain, tragedy and unfinished business out there. What could I do? I am only a reporter—with enough unsolved murders to keep me busy for life in Miami. No way would my editors sanction time spent on cases outside *The Miami Herald* circulation area, stories with no Florida connection. All the Chicago mission had accomplished was to briefly instill futile hope in the hearts of people in pain.

I never felt so helpless.

No progress was made in the murder of Mrs. Z.

The dead couple is still unidentified. I now suspect they came here from another country.

The little boy was finally identified two years ago—by a stroke of luck.

Maurice was five years old and from Minneapolis. He was waiting for his mother in the car when she was arrested for using a stolen credit card. A woman with his mother got away and drove off with him. Her name was Arlie Phaneus, and she was a prostitute.

When Arlie left for Miami with a man named Nate Mendenhall and several other prostitutes, the mother was still in jail, so they took the boy along. Arlie was jealous because the mother was Nate's former girlfriend. She even objected to stopping for the little boy to use a rest room during the long drive. They came to Miami to buy drugs and decided to stay.

When the mother was released from jail, she reported her son missing and told Minneapolis police who took him. They issued arrest warrants for false imprisonment of a child. Nate Mendenhall was arrested in Miami in a stolen car on September 2, 1981. The warrants were discovered and Minneapolis police notified, but somebody slipped up. Whoever took the call mistakenly reported that the child was no longer missing. The error was fatal to Maurice.

Nobody asked where the boy was, Nate said later. If they had, he would have told them. But no one asked. While Nate was in jail, Arlie killed the child.

A customer let hookers stay in his apartment. He even gave Arlie a key. She took the body there while he was out, bought supplics and constructed the child's tomb herself. She stayed for two weeks. When her host saw body fluids seeping from under the cement, she said she had spilled something. When he noticed the bad smell, he thought it was his clothes. He worked in a gas station.

In 1986, the boy's mother discovered the mistake by Minneapolis authorities and the canceled warrants were reissued. Rearrested in 1987, Nate denied knowing the whereabouts of the child. He was sentenced to three years.

Police in Miami arrested Arlie and asked where the boy was. "In a closet in North Miami," she said.

She blamed Nate, saying he had hit the child, who was dead next morning. Nate stole a car to dispose of the body, she said, but was arrested behind the wheel before he could do so.

Nice try, but no cigar. The truth had been walled up in the closet with the corpse. Police had found a computer-dated store receipt for the building supplies and items used to wrap the body. The date proved that Nate was already in jail when the child died. Arlie pleaded guilty in March 1990 and was sentenced to fifty years in prison.

No way Butchko's diligent detective work could have identified the little boy any sooner. There had been more than one slip-up. The national clearinghouse for missing children had never received his name from Minneapolis. And his little gap-toothed grin meant nothing. When Maurice left Minneapolis, his baby teeth were straight and perfect. Though his adult teeth were growing in crooked, his own mother would not have recognized them.

Danny, ten, and Brandon, seven, take piano lessons, and Tia is learning to play the guitar. She has a lovely bell-clear soprano, just like her mother. Amanda, at two and a half, is astonishingly bright.

Tia still misses her mother. She always will. "Things come up in everyday life, and you want to turn to your own mother," she said last time we talked, "like the questions I want to ask her when the kids get the chicken pox or mumps. I'm twenty-nine years old now, and I will never be too old to need my mother. I need her as much now as when I was fourteen.

"I don't think I could go on if I told myself it will never be solved. So in my heart I believe that someday there's going to be some justice, that Mom's not going to be one of the people whose murder is never solved."

Amen.

For Mrs. Z, and for all of the others.

Chapter 18

AMY

Her name was Amy, and she was a young woman in search of her past. She lacked nothing in her life, yet she felt an irresistible compulsion to reach out to the woman who had given her up for adoption at birth. Her persistent search for her biological mother would unearth murder, tragic secrets and, in the end, joy.

Her story posed two questions: Can a mother-daughter bond exist when the two are strangers? And can it rcmain alive even after death?

Amy's childhood was a happy one: She grew up in East Meadow, Long Island, in a comfortable Jewish home with loving parents. By age five she knew she was adopted. Her parents explained that she was chosen because she was the best, the most beautiful and the most delightful of all children. Made sense to her. But a shadow fell slowly across her life, nonetheless. Between the ages of five and fifteen, Amy occasionally asked questions about her real mother. Her parents, usually honest and open, were uncharacteristically evasive, their stories often conflicting.

Her mother was dead, she was told, struck down by a car. Another time: Her mother was killed in a car that crashed. A third time: Her mother perished in a plane that fell from the sky.

Why were they lying to her? What really happened to her mother? Who was she? Amy daydreamed and fantasized. "I used to think my mother was Marilyn Monroe."

By age sixteen she had become a teenage rebel, a chronic runaway. Her good, hard-working and concerned parents took Amy to a family therapist. To their surprise, the therapist sided with Amy. Had she not been present at the session, she is certain she never would have learned the truth. If Amy wants to discuss her roots, the therapist said, her parents should be forthright.

"Even if it's gruesome?" the adoptive mother asked.

Yes, the therapist said.

That is how Amy learned that her mother had been murdered in Miami.

The parents knew few details. The adoption was arranged before Amy's birth. At the hospital, in Miami Beach, the lawyer handling the details said that the infant's mother was eager to meet the new parents. They declined. They just wanted to take the baby and go. A year later the same lawyer notified them that the woman was dead—murdered.

At age twenty-three, Amy began to actively seek the facts about what happened to her mother. She felt a growing sense of urgency: The people who knew might die before she found them. She zeroed in on the case by locating a decades-old newspaper article in archives at the Miami-Dade Public Library. For a while, Amy worked as a skip tracer for a Long Island law firm. Smart and resourceful, she was good at it, very good. She got fired for spending too much time seeking information about her mother.

She wrote to Dr. Joseph Davis, the Dade County medical examiner. He gave her the name of Miami Homicide Sergeant Mike Gonzalez, who had been lead detective on the now twenty-three-year-old murder. He and Mike, the doctor wrote, were the only people left who would recall her mother's case. "All the others involved in the investigation have long since left office. . . . I suggest you contact Detective Gonzalez, whose memory is well recognized by his peers."

Mike remembered the case as if it had happened yesterday.

Surprised when Amy called and introduced herself, he tried to dissuade her from probing into the past, but she would not be discouraged. He told her what had happened to her mother and sent the information she wanted, along with a note:

Amy,

I have been very reluctant to send you this stuff.

I really don't believe you should relive this ancient tragedy.

Remember that your parents are the ones who raised you and loved you all these years.

It seems to me that it will be very difficult for you to relate to the life and times of Johanna Block.

I hope these reports do not upset you too much. I hope I'm not making a mistake.

Good luck to you—look to the future, not the past.

Sincerely,
Sgt. Mike Gonzalez

The sad and shocking story of her mother's life and death stunned the urbane and polished young woman.

Johanna Block came to America as a German war bride and became a casualty of life in Miami. Happiness eluded her. A judge ordered her hospitalized for mental problems in 1953. By the time she gave birth to Amy, she was an alcoholic barmaid, three times married and divorced.

In the spring of 1961, Johanna Block was thirty-three and about to strike out for a new start in life. She planned to move to Kansas City with friends. She talked about joining Alcoholics Anonymous.

She never got the chance.

On the last night of her life, May 25, 1961, Johanna Block left the Club 41, where she was employed, and walked to her nearby apartment. She had been drinking, and two friends walked her home. They were a woman named Mary Bratt, the daughter of a Miami police captain, and her fiancé, Vernon Edwards, a burly six-foot six-inch house painter. The couple would marry the following month.

Johanna Block failed to answer when friends knocked on her door the following day. A fellow worker stopped by to wake her at one P.M. The door was unlocked, and she stepped inside. Johanna Block lay naked on the floor, strangled with a belt and stabbed. A pair of scissors from her sewing basket protruded from her chest.

A pretty and vivacious woman, Johanna Block always had lots of boyfriends. One ex-husband was an accountant, another was an ex-convict named Walter George Zarzycki, who had owned a jukebox business. Miami police said they had twenty suspects but arrested no one. The slaying joined the ranks of other unsolved mysteries.

Miami's most famous unsolved murder had occurred two years earlier, in 1959. Ethel Little was a gentle fifty-three-year-old churchgoing spinster and legal secretary to a former Miami mayor. Her savage murder became known as the city's most sadistic slaying.

She was found naked, tied spread-eagled to her bed, strangled with a light cord, horribly tortured, raped with a flashlight and sexually mutilated by a killer who sliced off her right breast and hurled it at a mirror in the bedroom of the small cottage where she lived alone.

The only clue left by the killer was a bloody palm print on a windowsill. Police had never found the man who left it.

No detective ever linked the two unsolved murders.

Suddenly, thirteen years later, both were solved by a phone call.

In Decatur, Georgia, in July 1972, the former Mary Bratt picked up a telephone and called the police. Her husband, Vernon Edwards, had been drinking. He was guilt-stricken and depressed. He wanted to confess to two murders in Miami. One of the victims was Ethel Little; the other, Johanna Block.

The windowsill print matched the palm of the hulking 285-pound Edwards. The solution to the famous Ethel Little murder made headlines. Almost as an afterthought, it was mentioned that Edwards had also confessed to the 1961 death of barmaid Johanna Block.

On the night of the murder, after Mary Bratt and Vernon Edwards strolled home with Johanna Block and left her at her apartment, the engaged couple quarreled. Rebuffed and angry, Edwards said he went out and drank some more, then began to think of Johanna Block, drunk, alone and vulnerable. They had never dated. He had never been inside her apartment, but now he went there, with sex in mind. She resisted and started to scream, so he choked her, first with his hands, then with his belt. He thought she was dead, but he had to be sure she would never tell his fiancée. He took the scissors from her sewing kit on the dresser and stabbed her, leaving them in her chest. He searched her room, took what little money she had and left. Hours later, before dawn, he realized that a cigarette lighter with his name engraved on it had fallen from his pocket during the struggle. He returned to the scene of the crime and found it near her body.

A month later he married Mary.

Edwards was sentenced to life in prison for the murder of Ethel Little. He was never even prosecuted for killing Johanna Block. In her case the only evidence against him was his confession, while police had his bloody palm print in the more famous murder. No matter, they reasoned, he would spend life in prison anyway.

Amy wrote to Edwards in prison, hoping to learn more about her mother from the man who had killed her. He never answered. His wife divorced him while he was behind bars. He remarried while still a prisoner.

Life, as defined by our criminal justice system, is short.

Vernon Edwards walked out of prison a free man and drove off with his beaming new bride on July 24, 1990.

I was on leave of absence from the newspaper. Someone else wrote the story about Vernon Edwards's release. The article focused on the Ethel Little case, never mentioning Johanna Block, or her murder.

But she is not forgotten by everyone.

Sergeant Gonzalez sent Amy snapshots from his case file. In one of them, Johanna Block smiles across the years from an old-fashioned kitchen. The other was shot in a five-and-dime photo booth. Amy also found a morgue photo of her mother, a profile. "I had never seen a dead person before," Amy said, "especially my mother. It was horrible. I think my life stopped for a while," she told me later. I was having trouble sleeping, having nightmares."

Now she was even more determined to unlock the long-buried secrets of her mother's life and death. The musty files she had probed for information about her own birth had yielded something else, something that infused her search with new meaning. Before she was born, her mother had given birth to three other children, all boys, born in 1949, 1952 and 1954.

"I want to find them," Amy told me. "We all share a mutual terribleness: our mother's life."

There was one more reason. Amy, now a twenty-five-year-old Long Island housewife, was more than eight months pregnant with her first child. I wrote a news story three days before Christmas, saying, "Amy's Christmas wish is for three strangers. They probably do not know she exists. They are her brothers."

She thought they should know that they would soon be uncles. Hospital records had indicated that Amy's father, name unknown, worked as a jail guard and was married to someone else at the time of her birth. Amy had tried with no luck to find Walter Zarzycki, probably the father of the boys.

The *Herald* story reached readers who remembered the family but no one who knew exactly what had become of Johanna Block's sons. Records reflected that when Walter Zarzycki was informed that his former wife, the mother of his children, had been murdered, he said he had no interest. Johanna Block's funeral was paid for by friends.

She apparently had a lot of them.

I asked a *Miami Herald* librarian to punch the name Zarzycki into her computer system. It spit out a small story that had appeared in the newspaper's Gulf Coast edition. One Raymond Zarzycki, age twenty-nine, was nearly killed in an explosion the prior spring. Riding an all-terrain vehicle along a country trail, he ran over and detonated a buried seismic testing charge placed by a Houston oil-exploration company. The blast hurled him thirty to fifty feet into the air. He suffered leg fractures and powder burns.

He apparently lived in a trailer at the western edge of the Everglades and had no telephone. I sent a telegram:

> IF YOU ARE THE SON OF WALTER ZARZYCKI AND JOHANNA BLOCK, YOUR SISTER AMY, BORN IN 1960 AND PUT UP FOR ADOPTION, IS TRYING TO FIND YOU AND YOUR BROTHERS. SHE IS A CHARMING, DELIGHTFUL WOMAN WHO IS EAGER TO MEET YOU. PLEASE CALL ME COLLECT.

He was, and he did.

"I've had the shakes ever since I got it," he told me. Raymond Zarzycki had worked in agricultural water control until the accident. The explosion had shattered his left leg. He was still recovering, using crutches and a leg brace. His hands trembled as we reached Amy by telephone. So did his voice. The date was January 1. On New Year's Day, a strange woman more than thirteen hundred miles away made Raymond Zarzycki cry.

Amy, in her Long Island living room, laughed a lot, out of sheer joy. Over long-distance telephone, she described her "little nose and pouty lips and a dimple on my chin."

Raymond Zarzycki, barefoot and unshaven, in East Naples, on the fringe of the great Everglades swamp, had them too. The big brother she had never met was the New Year's wish she had feared would never come true.

"I found you!" she cried into a bad telephone connection to Florida.

"I've found you too," Ray said.

"I can't believe I actually succeeded."

"My hands have been shaking since I heard."

Amy, quick and bubbly, talks like New York, where she grew

up. Ray talks southern country, quiet and slow. He grew up attending school with Miccosoukee Indian children out the Tamiami Trail near Frog City.

What they share is roots and the sadness of their mother's life. Raymond and his brother Joseph are the sons of Walter Zarzycki. The third boy must have been by another marriage.

Raymond Zarzycki had no memory of his mother. His father had married again and bought a bar out on the Trail, in the Glades. He later bought a tavern in Naples. He had died several years earlier of natural causes.

He never talked to his sons about the past, Ray said, "never told us we had any kinfolks."

But he and his brother overheard their father and grandmother whispering several times as they grew up. Ray became convinced he had a baby sister somewhere. "I caught a couple of hints. My grandma dropped a few here and there, but I didn't know where to look." When he did search, unaware of the adoption, it was for a sister with the same last name as his.

He had not seen the story eleven days earlier in the *Herald*. But a former classmate had and had sent Amy a picture of Ray's first-grade class and two snapshots of Ray and Joseph scuffling in the grass. The little boy in the school photo bears an astonishing likeness to Amy's pictures at that age.

She had been afraid he would not want to meet her. "I didn't know how you would feel, how you would react," she told Ray.

How did he react? After the telegram, he told Amy, "I told everybody that this was gonna be the best New Year I ever had. I tried so hard to find you. I feel like somebody who's been in the dark for a long, long time. You're part of me. It's great to find someone who is part of you."

"It makes me so happy that somebody was thinking about me, that my brother was looking for me." Excited, her unborn baby kicking vigorously, she agreed, "This will be the best year ever. You should come to live in Long Island."

He was totally unfamiliar with the area. "As long as I could go hunting there," he said uncertainly.

"You don't shoot little animals, do you?" the Long Island housewife asked.

"Yeah," replied the country boy. "I throw 'em in a pan."

Their brother, Joseph, thirty-two, he said, "is a partier." He was last heard from a year earlier in Texas.

Unaware of Johanna Block's third boy, he was startled when Amy said, "You know there are four of us."

The search is not over.

It seemed as though it would be a long time before the brother and sister could meet face to face. Amy's baby was due soon. She and her husband, John, a bartender, were on a tight budget, and Ray, out of work since the explosion, was broke.

"As soon as my boat comes in," he told me, "I'll be up there, or she'll be down here."

"Only money is keeping us apart at this point," Amy said.

I should have known they would see each other far sooner than they expected. When the story of their telephone introduction appeared in the *Herald*, a reader bought Ray a round-trip plane ticket and provided the incidentals, such as a coat, shoes and pocket money for the Florida country boy.

Amy filled me in, with calls, an ecstatic letter and snapshots. Good news from Great Neck. It had to be a bit awkward at first, with Amy nine months pregnant and Ray on crutches. But when he arrived, they stayed up all night talking.

"We both seem to have inherited an inner strength to keep us going and happy," she said. "Finding him was one thing, but having us sit side by side, like we are now, is another."

The story started the New Year right for me too.

Chapter 19

COURAGE

"The quality of a life is not measured by its length, but by the fullness with which we enter into each present moment."

—NATIVE AMERICAN SAYING

True heroes are people who find the courage to fight impossible odds. Some battle savage seas, storms or city streets; others battle simply to stay alive.

The bravest people I have ever known belong to the Southerland family: Ray, a good man and a good cop, full of lightning-fast humor and mischievous grins; his wife, Jane, warm, pretty, and prone to infectious laughter; and their three handsome young sons—the perfect all-American family, which makes their ordeal all the more terrifying.

A killer stalked them for years, the world's deadliest, most merciless killer. They fought back with unmatched courage, dignity and laughter, lots of laughter. They stared death in the face and never flinched. Even when they lost, they were winners.

Midwesterners, Ray and Jane met and married in Terre Haute, Indiana. Good-looking and popular, they enjoyed a solid marriage and three lively little boys, Stephen, six, Jeffrey, three, and Michael, two.

Michael was sniffling from a cold, and Jeffrey seemed pale, so on a sunny day in June their mother trooped all three to the family physician. Jeff, blond, beautiful and big for his age, might be a bit anemic, the doctor thought. He took a blood test.

Diagnosis: acute lymphatic leukemia.

An eighteen-month battle began, to save the tyke who wore a cowboy hat as he trailed after his dad and who laughed a lot, like his mom. Jeff was too young to understand the fight. A child, his parents reasoned, knows only what he sees. If those around him are happy, so is he. "It's contagious," Jane said. "If you're loving and you're smiling and you're kissing, that's his world. That's all he knows and all he needs to know."

So they worked at being as happy and as normal as possible, vowing never to indulge in grief or self-pity.

Doctors tried everything, but there was no remission. Jeff's weight fell, his strength faded. His parents spent long, exhausting nights massaging the tot's painful and swollen body, ravaged by the disease, the chemotherapy and bone-marrow tests.

When doctors said that no more could be done and that Jeff had little time left, the parents decided to take what might be their last vacation together as a family.

They borrowed three hundred dollars, bundled the boys into their little 1961 red Corvair and drove to Florida for a week. They stayed at a beach motel, swam in the Gulf of Mexico and explored a historic fort in St. Petersburg. Then they drove all night, arriving home with six dollars and sunny memories.

Steve's warmest remembrance is that drive home. He sat in the backseat between his two little brothers, who fell asleep, heads nestled against his shoulders.

Two months later, in December 1967, at a Terre Haute clinic, Jeff sat wanly next to his mother as Michael and Stephen romped around the waiting room playing cowboys and Indians. Steve, the cowboy, shot Mike, who playfully collapsed across his mother's lap. As she gently rubbed her youngest son's back in a caress, she detected something that had not been there before—a small lump.

Tests began that day.

A disbelieving doctor delivered the results, reluctant to tell them. How could such a thing happen to the same family twice?

Michael had a rare cancer of the nerve linings of the spine.

They had no time to absorb the bad news. The following day, Ray carried Jeff into the hospital for the last time. Jane softly told her son to "close your eyes and go to sleep." He did so, and died. He was four years old. Jane and Ray had been so sure Jeff would live until Christmas that his presents were already wrapped.

Big brother Steve, nearly eight, wept inconsolably. Throughout Jeff's illness, he took care of Michael. Now that Michael was ill, Steve took care of his parents. In all the times of crisis, he would quickly say, "I'll take care of that, Dad."

Michael, age three, underwent cancer surgery twenty days after Jeff's funeral. "I thought Mike's chances were zero," Ray said. "I thought it was the end." Jane stayed at the Cincinnati Children's Hospital in Ohio with Mike, while Ray worked two jobs in Terre Haute. He would drive to the cemetery at night and play his police-car spotlight across Jeff's hillside grave. Could Mike be saved, he wondered, and if so, would he be crippled?

When Mike's tumor reappeared, surgeons operated again and gave him a 30 percent chance of survival. He endured cobalt treatments until he was five.

Crisis welded the Southerlands together. Ray and Jane had heard of parents growing apart after losing a child. They made a pact: It would never happen to them. When one could not sleep, they stayed up together. They wallpapered the entire kitchen one sleepless night, finishing at dawn.

Ray, a former Marine, finished college in three and a half years, at age twenty-eight. He and Jane cherished memories of their brief vacation in the sun. They loved Florida, and doctors agreed that the climate might improve Michael's fragile health.

They moved to Miami in February 1972. Steve was eleven. Michael, now seven, had beaten cancer. He appeared cured. Chances were good he would stay that way. Ray joined the Metro-Dade Police Department. When a supervisor asked for radar experts, he and another rookie eagerly stepped forward. They discovered on their first assignment that neither knew a thing about radar. Each presumed the other did, but Ray Southerland and Ron Sorensen became a team, best friends for life. Perhaps they got along so well because, unlike many cops, both believed people are basically good. Ray worked as a robbery detective and undercover, but his fondness for young people eventually led him to the Officer Friendly beat, working with school kids.

Mike and Steve excelled in school. Jane sold better dresses at a major department store. They bought a house in the suburbs, and both boys became active in sports. Working together, the parents had reduced $28,000 in outstanding medical bills to $400. The Southerlands were nearly back on their feet.

Then it happened again.

"Did you hear about Ray Southerland's son?" a Dade homicide detective asked casually. "It's a damn shame," he muttered. What he told me could not be worse, or so it seemed then. Steve, the thirteen-year-old son of Police Officer Ray Southerland, was hospitalized, suffering from bone cancer. Then the detective dropped the bombshell: Ray and his wife, Jane, had had three sons—this was the third struck by cancer.

This cannot be true, I thought, scribbling notes. Life is not *that* unfair.

I found Ray Southerland in Cincinnati and learned that it was indeed true. The unspeakable had happened to the same family for the third time. "This one kills me," he said. The tough cop's voice trembled. Steve, a straight-A student and a star athlete, had injured his left leg in a football game. Pain persisted in what appeared to be a pulled muscle. X rays had revealed a tumor.

Ray and Jane had driven all night, rushing Steve to the hospital in Cincinnati. If anyone could perform a miracle they felt it would be the Ohio surgeons who had saved Michael.

"It seems like a nightmare being back here," Ray told me from a hospital pay phone. "It brought back all the bad memories. If ever a boy deserved not to have cancer, it's him. He's a little boy who goes to Sunday School. Nobody has to tell him to go. They were all perfect children, but Steve is something special. He helped us through all the other crisis times. I don't understand it."

Doctors were also baffled. Similar tumors sometimes occur in members of the same family, but the malignancies that stalked the Southerland children were each rare, different and apparently unrelated.

Human tragedy had become medical history.

"This is the first time that this particular group of cancers has occurred in the same family in the United States," Dr. Alvin Mauer said. Mauer, medical director at St. Jude's Hospital, which specializes in childhood cancers, had treated Michael. Now he conferred with Stephen's surgeon. "It could be lightning striking not once, but three times," he said.

"The chances of three children in the same family all developing different, completely unrelated types of cancer are very remote," said Leo Grossman, a Miami Beach pediatrician.

"The odds are astronomical," said another specialist in childhood diseases, "an amazing streak of unbelievably bad luck."

Maybe not luck but something more sinister. "It's terribly important to find if there is some common thread, some common denominator," Dr. Mauer said. "It could help us to better understand cancer and its causes."

The first story appeared on the front page of *The Miami Herald* on March 17, 1974, accompanied by a family portrait, a happy moment from the past, forever frozen in time.

The type of cancer would determine the treatment. Should it be Ewing's tumor, Steve would go back to Florida for radiation and chemotherapy, with a 10 percent chance of survival. If it was osteogenic, they would amputate, but his chances would increase to 20 percent.

"That's enough to give us hope," Ray said. "If we have hope we have everything going for us. We live day by day now."

Diagnosis: osteogenic bone cancer.

Though frightened, Steve agreed that "it was my leg or my life." Ray and Jane kissed his left foot and Steve rolled off to surgery, his spirits high.

"He's one of a kind," his mother said. "We're lucky to have him."

I asked how they would pay the bills. "We don't even look at the monetary side," Ray said. "We both worked and paid it off before."

The newspaper story appeared, and suddenly the Southerlands were no longer alone in their struggle. Reader response was overwhelming. The good people out there constantly restore a reporter's faith in humankind.

Everyone cared. The family's story of bravery in the face of tragedy appeared in newspapers and on radio and TV newscasts. The Southerlands were incredibly appealing. Someone said it was as if the Waltons had cancer. Police in Miami established a fund to help pay mounting medical expenses. The New York Yankees, in spring training in Florida, donated net receipts from a Sunday exhibition game. Michael, now nine, threw out the first ball. Children at a ghetto elementary school where Ray, as Officer Friendly, had warned against the dangers of drug abuse emptied piggy banks, solicited neighbors and plunked down their allowances, raising $585 to help pay medical expenses.

"They are as high as kites," an elated teacher told me. "They're so proud of themselves."

Employees of a Miami restaurant celebrated Steve Southerland Day by donating tips and salaries. Steve's junior high track team won a coveted county championship and sent him the trophy. From San Francisco Bay police officers: $3,800 and a coin-stuffed piggy bank filled by their children. Steve received five thousand pieces of mail from all over the world. "I don't know what to say," Ray said. "People are so wonderful."

Steve responded in character. A day after surgery the spunky teenager gritted his teeth and stood painfully for the first time, on a temporary metal-and-plastic leg.

Told that chemotherapy would make his hair fall out, Steve

said he never liked his straight hair anyway and would like to try a curly wig. His courage endeared him to the staff. He took his first uncertain step a week ahead of schedule, following it with two more before sinking, exhausted, into a wheelchair. When an elevator returned him to his floor, he struggled to his feet, asked a startled nurse to alert his waiting parents and walked slowly down the corridor to join them.

Doctors, nurses and visitors applauded and cheered.

A letter that buoyed his spirits came from Teddy Kennedy, Jr. The son of Senator Edward Kennedy had also lost a leg to cancer. The young Kennedy mentioned a recent Colorado ski trip and invited Steve sailing at Hyannisport when he was able.

Steve answered Kennedy's letter and announced plans to become a lawyer. "My father, in a sense, deals in the law. And that's what I want to do."

Ohio Governor John J. Gilligan sent his car to chauffeur Steve to the opening day of baseball season in Cincinnati. Steve saw Hank Aaron tie Babe Ruth's lifetime record by slamming his 714th home run. He returned to the hospital with a baseball signed by Aaron, talked sports with author George Plimpton, was presented with a football autographed by the Miami Dolphins and received get-well wishes from then-President Richard Nixon.

The Southerlands drew other notable attention. Intrigued researchers from the National Cancer Institute in Bethesda, Maryland, asked them to submit to family testing. Doctors hoped to learn if some genetic factor might have triggered the boys' cancers. The Southerlands agreed without hesitation. "We hope to God they find a link that can save other people," Ray said.

Ever the investigator, Ray advanced a theory, a suspicion, of his own: something that haunted him, something frightening that had happened long ago, on an Indiana autumn afternoon. Ray and Jane, then pregnant with Michael, had taken Steve and Jeff to visit an animal farm. The animals were said to be tame and friendly, but as Ray parked, an ape leaped through the car window and attacked Jeff on his mother's lap, savagely biting and tearing at the tot's left arm as the frantic parents pounded the creature to make him stop.

The sutured wounds became infected, and Jeff, feverish and listless for six weeks, was never really the same again. Soon he was gravely ill with leukemia. Ray read that the mouth of an ape is a fertile breeding ground for viruses. Could some virus transmitted by the animal have caused Jeff's leukemia? And did the illness somehow trigger his brothers' malignancies?

Unlikely, but so is the entire Southerland case history.

Steve vowed to celebrate his May birthday in Miami—"if I have to jog all the way." On April 19, less than a month after surgery, a cheering crowd, including football Dolphins Jim Mandich and Bill Stanfill, welcomed him home at Miami International Airport. When asked how he felt, Steve wisecracked. "I don't have a leg to stand on. But I can't kick, if my knee joint rusts." Delighted to be home, he bantered about football, the weather and his new artificial leg. "They say if it's not paid for in thirty days it will self-destruct," he said, showing off the leg, which had triggered an airport metal detector.

"We always said the only thing that would ever wear out on him is his mouth," his father said.

Talking openly, even cheerfully, about the disease had become Southerland family tradition, along with an indomitable gallows humor. "One thing we can't do is run away from it," Ray said. "There is no place to run."

By his fourteenth birthday, Steve had founded a club for seriously ill youngsters. "Kids are better able to cope with it than parents," he said. "And there are some things they don't want to talk to their parents about."

At school he met daily crises with humor. He called frantically one day. "Dad, can you get down here? My leg's fallen off."

Ray asked which one.

When chemotherapy made him sick in class, Steve's chief concern was what other kids would think. When he fell and a pretty girl caught him, he flirted. "That was fun," he told her. True to his law-school goal, he hit the books and was voted most likely to succeed. His first ambition had been to be a football superstar, but, he said, "one-legged quarterbacks aren't catching on," adding that he was sure to win a gold medal if hopping ever became an Olympic event. He joined the swim team and stayed in shape by wrestling with Michael.

Steve never succeeded in pinning his lithe and quick younger brother. Surprised doctors never expected Michael to be so well-coordinated and athletic after his childhood bout with cancer.

The summer of 1975, the Southerlands packed up their secondhand motor home and set out for the Grand Canyon, determined to cram as many experiences as possible over nine thousand miles and three weeks. The trip was an adventure, since Ray did all the motor home's maintenance work himself. As a result, Jane recalls, "it fell apart all across the West."

They rode down white-water rapids and saw the Petrified Forest, Yellowstone National Park and snow-capped mountains. Two weeks into their dream vacation, at a campground in the shadow of Mount Rushmore, Ray took their small dog out for a walk.

He did not come back.

Concerned, Jane went to find them. She found a curious crowd around a man in convulsions on the ground. It was Ray. He had suffered blackouts twice before; this was by far the worst.

Again, doctors found nothing wrong, attributing the episodes to the stress of his sons' illnesses. He returned to work with his usual zeal. Assigned to a "difficult" junior high, Ray's reception was decidedly cool. This racially mixed two-thousand-member student body wanted nothing to do with a cop. Nevertheless, they were soon calling him "Dad," and the rate of violence dramatically decreased to nearly zero.

By year's end, Steve had grown four inches, finished his chemotherapy and was writing a book about his experiences. The family historian, planner of everything from menus to vacations, he was their cheerleader.

His special spirit would soon be needed more than ever.

Ray, now thirty-eight, remained haunted by the vacation incident. When a Miami medical team introduced a sophisticated new brain scanner, he went for a test, just to be sure. The scan revealed the real reason for Ray's attacks.

Diagnosis: brain tumor.

Ray had always said, "I don't want any of my sons to be quitters."

Steve, now fifteen, gave his father advice: "You're not going to be a quitter. You can meet the challenge, whatever it is. This might be part of a big, heavenly plan, a grand plan to find the cure for cancer." It would also, he quipped, provide at least four new chapters for his book.

Teddy Kennedy, whose son still corresponded with Steve, wrote to Ray: "Were another chapter to be written in President Kennedy's *Profiles in Courage*, it would be about the Southerland family."

Ray was admitted to the National Cancer Institute (NCI) in February 1976. I flew to Washington to be with them. His partner, Ron Sorensen, was also there.

We saw Ray just before surgery, his thick dark hair gone, his head shaved. "I've been wanting to get rid of this dandruff for a long time."

By now it was routine to wisecrack and joke all the way to the operating room. Ray winked at his partner, warning doctors and nurses: "When you open up my head, all the dirty thoughts and undressed ladies are going to come flying out."

During the six-hour wait, Jane sat in the hospital solarium, crocheting an intricate tablecloth. "When we get the time and can afford it," she promised Steve, "we'll have a nervous breakdown."

Ron Sorensen chewed his fingernails to the quick, then played pocket billiards. Steve lost three times, then made a request: "I've already got one handicap—can I have another?"

A surgeon finally emerged, to identify the tumor as the lowest and least deadly of four grades of astrocytoma, a form of slow-growing brain cancer. They had removed it all. Jane called it the "happiest day of my life, like the answer to a prayer. We deserved a break."

She told Ray, still groggy, that the surgery took so long because it took doctors five hours to find his brain.

"I hope this is the last time," said Steve, elated. "The future is pretty optimistic now."

Ray's sole complaint next day was a slight headache and his shaven head. Eight days later, wearing a Kojak hat to cover his baldness, he ignored a waiting wheelchair, strode down a Miami concourse and was engulfed in a hero's welcome. More than a hundred cops, friends, relatives, neighbors and strangers applauded. A woman passerby saw the photographers and squealed, "It's him! It's Telly Savalas!"

Michael, who had painted a gigantic welcome-home sign, dashed through the crowd into Ray's arms. "Made it, didn't I, Tiger?" his dad said. "I knew I'd be back. I had planned to fight like you wouldn't believe."

Bouquets of flowers and lollipops waited, from the school kids who called him Dad. The school band played a concert. Drama students staged plays. Others conducted bake sales, carwashes, plant fairs and ballgames. The kids from the "difficult" school raised $2,592 to help their favorite cop.

Ray underwent cobalt treatments, then passed a six-month checkup with flying colors. "I'm a lucky person," he said. "I don't care what anyone says. Doctors saved two of my children and caught my cancer in time."

That summer, the family piled into their motor home once more. This time their "vacation" destination was the National Cancer Institute, to cooperate with medical detectives seeking clues to the killer's origins. Cancer researchers say their tests may help unlock the secrets of the disease. The Southerlands were X-rayed, photographed and fingerprinted, pushed, pulled, prodded and jabbed. Blood, skin and dexterity were tested and teeth scrutinized. Nearly twenty molecular, chromosome and immunologic tests were performed, many of them unpleasant.

They never balked. They wanted the mystery solved. "There has to be a reason we're the only family like this," Ray said. "Somewhere down the line this thing has to end."

Scientists traced Ray's family tree hoping to learn when the killer first appeared and how often it had struck. They interviewed and tested other family members, including Ray's younger sister, Nancy, age twenty-three, a policeman's wife. Two weeks later, a malignant growth appeared on her calf. Her leg was later amputated.

Scientists learned that Ray's brother, who died at age two, was killed by a brain tumor, not by polio as Ray grew up believing. The anemia that killed his mother was a complication—of breast cancer.

NCI researchers hired a professional genealogist who traced the family back six generations, to 1840, and discovered a lost branch of the Southerland family tree. What he learned excited researchers and supported their theory, ruling out environmental causes and pointing to a genetic defect.

The relatives the genealogist found were strangers to the Southerlands but not to the killer. Cancer took the life of Ray's great-great-grandmother in 1865, when she was in her twenties. The disease killed her son in 1890, when he was in his thirties. His only son died of cancer, which struck three of his daughters. A distant cousin was a leukemia patient at age two. "Things can run in families for genetic or environmental reasons," said Dr. John Mulvihill, chief of the Clinical Genetics Section, Clinical Epidemiology Branch of the NCI. "You can't connect an environmental thread" between such distant family branches. "Certainly what could connect them is their genes."

Enough Southerland blood, tissue and cell samples were harvested and frozen to use in research for years. Doctors are seeking "something different in the cells from the family as compared to other people and sort of an extension that will tell us why other people get the tumors they are getting," Mulvihill said. "There is something in their cells, whether it's genetic or enzymatic, it's something intrinsic in the cell and the way the cell divides."

"It means that cancer literally runs in this family," Jane said. "It's like one great big accident fell on us."

The Southerlands continued to maintain active and happy lives. "I don't want anyone's sympathy," Steve said. "I want their respect."

He earned it. At age seventeen he led a successful petition drive to establish a radiation-therapy center for South Dade cancer patients. He became the first teenager ever honored as Chamber of Commerce Citizen of the Year.

He went to the University of Florida in 1978, but drove 350 miles home most weekends to spend time and go to movies with his kid brother. They ate popcorn, drank Cokes and brought home flowers for their mother.

Michael, at fourteen, planned to be an architect. Cancer-free for nearly ten years, he was a medal-winning swimming champ, an Olympic hopeful who could cut through the water like a fish, leaving Steve, who had taught him to swim, in his wake. However, in late 1978, Michael's perfect backstroke underwent subtle changes.

His side ached when he arched his back. Fearing the worst, his parents whisked him to Cincinnati.

Diagnosis: osteogenic bone cancer, apparently triggered by the radiation treatments that had saved his life a decade earlier.

Doctors planned pioneering surgery never attempted in the United States. Michael knew it was delicate and dangerous. He hung his junior Olympic backstroke medal over his bed. "I'm psyched up for this. No matter how it goes," he told his dad, "pin my medal on me."

He insisted that his mother tape a handwritten sign to his spine before he went to the operating room. A reminder to the surgeons: REMEMBER, I'M A SWIMMER.

This vigil stretched into twelve hours. Surgeons removed a cancerous vertebra, replacing it with metal braces and parts of his ribs.

Michael came home two months later, twenty pounds lighter and half an inch shorter. Pasty and frail, he lay flat across two airline seats, encased in a fifty-pound shoulder-to-knee plaster cast. Painted on the cast was a blue bow tie, vest, red carnation and a pocketwatch permanently set at 3:30, school dismissal time. It was his turn to hide the effects of chemotherapy with a hat.

The press and a crowd was waiting. That too had become tradition. From his supine position, Mike jokingly introduced big brother Steve as "my backbone."

A routine bone scan six weeks later became a cliffhanger. A hot spot, a possible tumor, had appeared above his left knee. Jane flew to Cincinnati to join Mike and Ray. Her flight stopped over in Tampa, and as the jet took off, she glimpsed the twinkling lights of the motel on Tampa Bay where they had spent their last short vacation as a whole family. "I saw that motel and thought, thirteen years later—and I'm still at it," she said. "You'd think someday it would quit."

Doctors decided the frightening image was caused by Michael's immobility—unable to sit or even be tilted. He flew to Cincinnati for chemotherapy so often that he logged more hours in the air than a commercial pilot. In three months he was lifting weights. In four he was walking, first with parallel bars, then a walker, and finally crutches. When he stepped slowly off a Delta jet, the body cast replaced by a plaster jacket bearing a Superman emblem, Miamians gave him a hero's welcome.

Four months later, pain overtook him. The cancer had spread. "I'll fight it to the end," he vowed.

"He's brave," his mother said with a smile. "He's not going to lie down and die. We never say quit, you know."

Ray would grin and shrug his shoulders when asked how he was. "Not so bad. Not bad at all, considering that the whole family has cancer."

Four months later surgeons proposed a last desperate move to save Michael. They would sever his spinal cord, remove seven cancerous vertebrae, then rebuild the cancer-riddled spine with steel rods, plastic and bones from the legs he would never use again.

Michael agreed. Growing up in a wheelchair, he said, beats not growing up at all.

On April 1, 1980, a team of seventeen surgeons operated for seventeen hours. The patient, age fifteen, returned home for the summer, talking about the future. "I want to see Steve finish law school. I want to be married. I want to have kids. I look forward to enjoying every bit of life that I can."

Ray breezed through his fall physical. But when he returned to NCI for a routine checkup in spring 1981, he took growing doubts with him. Something was not right. Miami's fast-talking, articulate Officer Friendly was stumbling over words. His right hand sometimes went numb.

Doctors isolated the problem: a tumor, unrelated to the first, spreading fast through the left side of his brain. On May 5, his forty-third birthday, they told him they would remove as much as they could, but to take it all would strip him of his ability to speak and move.

The crisis was double-barreled. Ray's operation would be at the NCI. Michael was already set for surgery in Cincinnati. Ulcers had cruelly exposed his plastic-and-metal artificial spine.

"In the past we could concentrate our energies on one problem at a time," said Steve, now twenty-one. "Now they are overlapping. This is surely a test of us as human beings."

The family spent a happy weekend at home, full of laughter and reminiscing. In a man-to-man talk Ray told Steve he had no fear of death, that the only pain is leaving the people you love.

Steve took Mike to a movie. They were accustomed by now to the strangers who stared at the boy in the wheelchair pushed by the young man with one leg.

Ray and Jane held hands, took walks and talked for hours.

"I know I've made mistakes in our relationship, and I'm really sorry," she said.

No mistakes, he said. She was the best wife a man could ask for.

He apologized for visiting "all of this" upon her.

No apology, she said. "No matter what happens, I could not have been any happier. I could not have found a man who loved me better or whom I would have loved more."

Both agreed that the happiest time in their lives was when they still had the little red Corvair and three small boys.

She remembered sitting in that car with the kids in the backseat, and telling Ray, "I think I'm about the happiest woman in the world right now. I have everything I want."

Michael and Ray underwent surgery twenty-four hours and five hundred miles apart. Their thirteen-year battle with a killer was now being fought on two fronts, in cities far from the warmth of Miami and home.

Jane spent her ninth Mother's Day at the bedside of a loved one with cancer, this time shuttling between two hospitals.

Father and son each asked about the other when regaining consciousness.

"It's horrendous," said Ray's surgeon, Dr. Paul Kornblith. "They are wonderful people with a superb attitude toward a horrible situation. They are handling as many crises as I have ever seen a family face with a remarkably optimistic approach."

Ray's was the most dangerously malignant of brain tumors, lodged in one of the brain's most inaccessible regions. "They don't come any worse than this one," the physician said.

Michael's doctors said his cancer had spread to his lungs.

"I'm not afraid of Michael's death," Jane said. "I know he's a Christian. He's going to heaven. But it's hard for me to let go."

Michael's final wish, to go home to Miami, was not to be. On a June night, as Jane held his hand, he said, "I love you, Mommy," then called to his pet dog more than a thousand miles away. He was sixteen.

Jane and Steve flew to Washington to break the bad news to Ray. Told two weeks earlier that Michael faced more surgery, his reaction had been anger. Now he did not react at all. The tumor, virulent and rapidly growing, had taken over.

Michael came home to Miami, in a coffin. The crowds who cheered other homecomings were not waiting, but Miamians had not forgotten. The marquee outside a local bank announced: OUR THOUGHTS AND PRAYERS ARE WITH THE SOUTHERLAND FAMILY.

Steve delivered the eulogy.

"A hero is one who faces with courage and strength the indignities of life," he said. "Michael is, and was, a hero."

He was buried on an Indiana hillside, next to his brother Jeff.

"We haven't lost the fight yet," Steve said. "We're going to pull Dad through this."

Ray came home by air ambulance in July—no jokes, no crowds. Steve had promised Ray that outsiders would never see him helpless.

A month later, as Jane held one hand and Steve the other, Ray lost his hard-fought battle with the cruel inheritance that has tormented his family for 141 years.

"He is in heaven with two of his boys," Steve said. "He'll be surprised; he didn't know Michael was there."

As he had hoped, Ray Southerland left a legacy: "The family has made a tremendous contribution to cancer research," said Dr. William Blattner, chief of the study team at NCI. "They also taught me an awful lot about humanity and the courage of individuals."

Steve was reluctant to return to the University of Florida for his senior year and leave his mother alone, but she insisted. His father wanted him to finish college and go to law school.

Back at the 32,000-student campus, he plunged into politics. The UF student-government organization is the largest in the nation. He founded a third party, the University Student Alliance (USA), and campaigned for student-body president. He scored a major upset, edging into a run-off with 33 percent of the vote.

Six feet three inches tall and handsome, Steve worked tirelessly, campaigning on crutches for eighteen-hour stretches. By the end of the campaign, he had worn down several pairs of crutch tips, and his armpits were bloodied. He wore dark shirts so no one could see.

He was the underdog. No candidate had ever won from ten points behind. No nonfraternity member had won in thirty years. No one in a decade had succeeded without the endorsement of the powerful school newspaper. Victory seemed unattainable.

Steve Southerland won.

"I never had any doubt," Jane said proudly, when he called with the news.

Weeping, he said he had done it for Michael and his dad. She knew they were proud too.

The good news, so wonderful for a change, continued. Student president Steve Southerland had two secretaries, controlled a $3.7 million budget, spent fifty hours a week on the job and realized that politics was the love of his life.

He finished his last law-school semester at Oxford, then backpacked through sixteen countries on crutches. Hired by a fifty-five-member Miami law firm, he dated a lovely blond dental assistant. "From the beginning she saw me as a person, a whole person," he said. "That's rare."

That good summer of 1986, Steve, age twenty-six, was prepared to take the bar exam, just two weeks away. But first came the law firm's annual baseball game, Lawyers vs. Summer Clerks, at a Miami park. The clerks were being trounced 9–0, in 91-degree heat. Steve popped out to deep left field his first time at bat.

He played catcher, competing without crutches, hopping around the bases. At the top of the fourth, he said, "All of a sudden I felt my right hand cringing up, then my whole right side. I knew it was a seizure. I never felt so helpless in my whole life."

His collapse stopped the game. "I certainly made an impact," he later said. Lawyers ran for telephones to dial 911. The wife of the senior law partner sped off in her car to find a policeman. His arrival at a local hospital, flanked by two high-powered lawyers, "definitely got their attention." Steve regained consciousness in the emergency room.

Everybody hoped it was heat stroke.

Jane raced to the hospital. Steve had never suffered a seizure before, but he had seen them. "A horrible feeling," he told her. "Poor Dad—now I know what he went through."

Doctors conducted tests. They told Jane first. Nobody had to tell Steve. When he saw her face, he knew. He had seen the look before.

Diagnosis: brain tumor—deep but operable.

"To think that it would come back twelve years later, to haunt you, in a more dangerous place . . . it hit us like a real thunderbolt," he said.

They decided on the hospital in Cincinnati. "Our old stomping grounds," Jane said. "You'd think I'd get better at this, but I'm not."

At question was how to treat him after surgery. Therapy that had once cured his father and brother had killed them later.

Doctors posed a devastating question: How much would Steve sacrifice to live? Was he willing to lose the use of his right leg, his right arm, his ability to speak? The tumor was growing in an area of the brain that controls those functions.

How far did he want them to go?

Steve's options were clear: He needed his right leg. It was the only one he had. "Speech is important for my profession, if I'm going to be a corporate lawyer." He said he could "make do, if necessary, with only one arm." His life, he decided, was worth more than the use of an arm.

Fortunately surgeons found the moon-shaped tumor positioned in a way that made the grim choice unnecessary. Though weakened, his right hand would respond to physical therapy.

Dr. Beatrice Lampkin, an oncologist, has treated the family since 1967. "This indicates once again that there is a cancer gene that can be triggered by things—we don't know what. We hope that studying the Southerlands will shed some light on all of us and our potential for developing cancer."

A week after surgery Steve traded wisecracks with reporters at a hospital press conference. Wearing a fedora to mask his baldness, he said he and his mother had struck a deal. "We're not going to do this again. It's time for her to retire from all this and go on to other adventures."

Five of his firm's young lawyers visited for the weekend. Miamians filled his room with cards and flowers. He had missed the bar exam, but so what. "Before all this happened I thought it was the most important thing in my life. Now just being alive is the most important thing."

He came home to a mob scene, stepping off the plane into a

blizzard of confetti. A huge yellow banner stretched across the terminal. More than fifty colleagues cheered, whistled, and sang "For He's a Jolly Good Fellow." The office had shut down for two hours so everyone could be at the airport. The young associates wore fedoras, like the one Steve wore at his press conference. A fashion step ahead, he was now wearing a blue-and-gold *Top Gun* cap, along with sunglasses, to complete his "Tom Cruise look."

He described the stubble on his shaved-for-surgery scalp as "basic Parris Island Marine." The scar, he said, "looks like a Budweiser Clydesdale stepped on my head." Privately, he confided, "When I left two weeks ago, I thought I would never be back."

Yellow ribbons and balloons decorated the Southerland front yard. He began to regret missing the bar exam and hated waiting until winter. "A brain tumor should be a valid excuse," he said, applying a lawyer's logic. "Why wait six months? I'd like to take it and get it over with—like all this was something that never happened."

He came back strong, but recent brain surgery made it tough to pass the bar, and his flowering romance with the pretty dental assistant faded. The big law firm merged with a bigger one, growing to 680 lawyers. Because he failed the bar twice, the firm followed policy and did not keep Steve Southerland, certainly considered a liability to any group medical plan.

Steve kept plugging.

He finally passed the exam, and I attended the small ceremony when he was sworn in as a member of the bar. With his medical history, what law firm would risk hiring him? So he went solo, sharing space in a low-rent district with two other struggling young lawyers, one black, the other Hispanic.

Jane had married as a teenager and had been Ray's wife for twenty-two years. She seemed content to remain Ray's wife forever. "I believe that's true of most people who have really good marriages," she said. "You don't change your way of thinking because you're widowed."

For almost seven years she focused on her career, general services sales manager at the department store where she once sold dresses, and on her quilting. Her prize quilt won first place at the Dade County Fair.

By fall 1987, I had not seen Jane for some time. When we did meet, she looked so radiant, so absolutely beautiful, that I knew: "You're in love!"

"Well, there is somebody," she said shyly. She and a friend found seats at a crowded Miami boat club Oktoberfest. One was next to Eastern Airlines pilot Bertram Dawson McMillen III. The man is not at all like Ray Southerland, the gregarious prankster who loved life and laughter. The two might not have liked each other. Ray hid his feelings behind grins and practical jokes. Bert is gentle, soft-spoken and sensitive.

A harpist played Persichetti, Handel and Pachelbel at the small June wedding at an elegant old Coral Gables hotel. "Love goes on forever," the pastor said. The only tears were happy ones.

"Now I not only have my mother's love," Steve said, "but the friendship of someone who loves her just as much."

Jane sounded flushed and happy when I called almost a year later. She and Bert were wallpapering the bathroom. Life had not been easy for the newlyweds. Bert was on strike against Eastern. Jane and other longtime employees lost their jobs after Canadian businessman Robert Campeau bought the department-store chain and sent it skidding downhill.

Places, companies and organizations change. So do some people, but not Jane. As buoyant as usual, she was full of good news: Steve was in love, engaged to a college girl, and planning a run for the Florida State Senate. She asked me not to let on that I knew. Steve wanted to tell me himself. When he didn't I hoped it meant he was busy, with more work than he could handle.

The truth came with a call in the night, like the bad ones always do. The deep, familiar voice of Ron Sorensen, Ray Southerland's old partner. "Not good news every time we talk," he said. My heart sank. He was calling about Steve.

"Where?"

"His brain—the left side."

A checkup in Cincinnati—everyone was calling it a spot until the biopsy, but no one had any doubt about what it was.

I grasped at straws. How this could this happen again? "On a scale of one to ten," I demanded, "what are the chances they are wrong?"

He hesitated. "With somebody else I would say, hey, maybe. But not with this family."

"But why, what could have triggered it? Steve doesn't drink, doesn't smoke."

"Who knows . . . we never did find out. It's a shock that here we go again. A shock, but not a surprise."

We promised that someday when one of us had really good news we would break the chain.

I asked Jane. "Why?"

"Because he's a Southerland," she said softly.

Doctors opted for radiation and chemotherapy, despite the inherent long-term risks, hoping to shrink the tumor enough to be excised.

Six months later, in April 1990, I shared lunch with Jane and Steve at a South Dade seafood house. He looked wonderful, back living at home and struggling to keep his small law practice afloat. He wore a baseball cap to conceal the effects of his treatments. His fiancée had ended the engagement before Christmas. She said she might call during the holidays, but she did not.

When I called his office on May 18, to wish him a happy birthday, Steve was in fine spirits. The prognosis had improved, and the treatment had worked. Surgery was again an option. He was going to Cincinnati. "It looks good," he said.

Other good news: Steve had become the youngest member of Miami's Orange Bowl Committee, Jane and Bert were taking him out for a birthday dinner that night, and Bert was about to interview with TWA in St. Louis.

A friend had called earlier to ask if he was depressed at turning thirty.

Not at all. "Turning thirty in this family," Steve Southerland said, "is a major accomplishment."

We talked briefly about survival and the importance of moving forward despite the odds. "I would not trade any of the experiences we've had," he said. "If there is a purpose to all this, it's probably to make other people who deal with crisis know that, despite whatever happens, it's the quality of life you lead, not the quantity."

The surgery went exceptionally well.

Steve Southerland entered the race for Florida State Senate that same summer. Jane looked radiant, her husband beside her, as Steve announced from a wheelchair. His dad's old partner, Ron Sorensen, was there in uniform, our happy occasion at last.

Steve looked vigorous, acknowledging that he was still undergoing physical therapy, but said the tumor had been removed. He playfully vowed to "be back on my foot again soon."

He felt strong, he said, and had no doubt he could serve effectively.

"This is for me a very special moment," he said. "I always felt I should give something back to the community." A tough campaign lay ahead. When someone in the crowd pointed that out, the last of the Southerlands smiled. The uphill race, he said, "will be like any other battle worth fighting."

He fought it well. He raised nine thousand dollars in campaign funds and took 44 percent of the vote from his veteran opponent, who had raised fifty thousand dollars. Forty-four percent was not enough, of course.

Steve's spirit was not dampened. "The best part of the battle is that it taught me a lot about life and taught a lot of people how I feel about life—and making the most of it. Even if you don't succeed, making the effort is a success in itself.

"You should always fight for your dreams."

Steve Southerland is no quitter, nor does he feel sorry for himself. Neither does Jane. "I've had a great life," she said. "Look at people who have five or six kids who've been into drugs and robbery—and even murder. Facing that kind of problem would be really hard for me to handle. Can you imagine having kids on drugs and watching them kill themselves a little at a time?

Mine all fought hard to survive. I had unbelievably good kids. With all they had to go through, I don't remember them ever being bitter. I once apologized to Mike and Steve for bringing them into this world to suffer so. They both said that life was worth it."

As Steve Southerland said, "Just being alive is the most important thing."

Chapter 20

A NEW CHAPTER

Choose a job you love and you'll never have to work a day in your life.

—CONFUCIUS

The world is full of real-life heroes, and I love to tell their stories and chronicle their feats, their adventures and their noble deeds.

I am still hooked on stories, and this singular city, with its rednecks and Rastafarians, Contras and cocaine cowboys, Yahwehs and yahoos, villains and victims. My love affair with Miami, the longest-lasting in my life, endures, as the city and I both grow and change.

Miami is still hot. Sleepy South Beach, once famous for its senior citizens, now throbs through the soft nights with a healthy and youthful energy, more lusty and alive than it has ever been. Hot bodies and the city's sizzling beauty dazzle the world in movies, commercials, fashion photography and stunning photos that capture Miami's true colors, breathtaking blues and shades of gold. Across the Bay, the city seethes with tension, battered by trauma and transition. Sometimes the city heat seems too hot not to burn. Not again. I hold my breath. The world is watching. Miami has been discovered.

To a far lesser degree, I too have been discovered and burn with ideas and stories to tell.

Life is a series of trade-offs; everything exacts a price. The cost of the city's new fame is traffic snarls and parking problems, haze, pollution and destruction of our precious environment and wildlife. The carpetbaggers and profiteers will always be with us.

The struggle never ends—progress at a price. On leave from the *Herald,* I yearn for the fray, the daily battles, the exhilaration of stalking the wild story, the stimulation of the streets, the interaction with sources, strangers and talented newsroom colleagues. I miss the intensity of deadline, focusing in tight on a story and tuning out all the meaningless and mundane irritants of life that make you crazy if you surrender to them.

Working at home, alone, is solitary confinement, but childhood dreams grew out of this self-imposed isolation into reality. Before I could even read, I said that when I grew up I would write books. Fiction was what I had planned before I was swept into that whirlwind called journalism.

In 1990 my first novel was published. I am blessed. How many of us get to do what we dreamed of as children?

I had never written fiction before—though I had been accused of it a few times in the past—and found it to be a source of unexpected satisfaction. We all yearn to be tidy, to wrap up the loose ends and resolve all the perplexing mysteries, but in real life, in journalism, that does not happen. Murders go unsolved; corpses remain unidentified; missing people stay lost forever. They dwell in your dreams.

Write fiction, and you can tell the whole story, solve all the mysteries, tie up the loose ends and see to it that the good guys win.

So unlike real life and so much more satisfying.

Nothing is easy, of course, especially writing fiction in a city where truth is stranger. But once begun, it was a joy to let imagination soar, to see characters spring to life, step forward and clamor to tell their stories.

Afterward, I returned to real people and real life with this book, intending, when finished, to plunge back into journalism and the police beat. But something happened: Certain faces and voices began to haunt my consciousness, imaginary characters with stories to be told. The time came to report once more for work in that big *Herald* newsroom in the sky overlooking Biscayne Bay. I hesitated and picked up my mail only on weekends to avoid the editors and their questions about when I was coming back to the beat. Like someone addicted to secret pleasures, I thought, *Not yet, just one more, just one more book first, another novel.*

So the isolation continues—for one more novel, maybe more. The dual life-styles are a study in contrasts: Reporters battle deadlines, miss regular meals and survive on coffee, action and adrenaline. Authors set their own schedules and work at home, close to the refrigerator, unfortunately.

Police reporters are generally as welcome among strangers as Freddy Krueger in the girls' dorm. It is not unusual for people to slam doors, curse or even run when approached by a reporter.

Authors, however, are invited to literary luncheons and library teas, often by people who would never dream of talking to a police reporter.

In this case, reporter and author are one and the same, not entirely at ease at literary luncheons and teas. I am more comfortable knocking on a stranger's door to inquire if he murdered his wife than making small talk with the literati at a cocktail party.

The life of a reporter is unlike any other. There is something noble and exciting about venturing out into the world in search of the truth. No day is ever the same. Each is an adventure, another crusade. That is how I spent the best years of my life so far, and I want to do it again, but now there is something else that I love as much.

So I try to shut out the sounds of sirens in the night, try to block the news flashes on the latest car bombing, steer clear of the newsroom to avoid being captured, and steel myself against intriguing phone calls from sources. My longtime companion, a portable police scanner, has fallen silent, the batteries long dead. Instead I listen to bird songs and wind chimes, I watch a daredevil mockingbird dive-bomb intruders and the slow-paced mating dance of two love-struck chameleons outside my window. I ponder mountainous clouds, a glowing turquoise sea and sudden summer thunderstorms. No beepers, no emergencies, no three-alarm fires, a news junkie on the wagon.

I work alone, surrounded by heavy-laden fruit trees and brilliant bougainvillea, bright green water, my favorite cat, and a flowing stream of stories, stories, stories, springing up from some inner source.

No news bulletins from downtown. For a writer this is life at its most free.

My days seem like a dream, so far from the familiar din and chaos of the newsroom. The *Herald* lands on my lawn with a plop each morning, minus my byline. I live without the daily link to readers, the lifeblood of communication. But I persist. The news goes on without me as I create my own world in a growing manuscript. It is a long time between deadlines. Sometimes, drowning in the silence, I yearn to surface, emerge from my isolation and travel door to door, delivering my story to total strangers and watching them read it—at gunpoint if necessary.

ACKNOWLEDGMENTS

I am indebted to Marilyn Lane, David M. Thornburgh and Renee Turolla, patient and nurturing friends. Special thanks to the men of Random House, Peter Osnos, Mitchell Ivers and Ken Gellman, for their enthusiastic support, to my agent Michael Congdon for his guidance and friendship, to *The Miami Herald* library staff and Rebecca Smith of the Historical Museum of Southern Florida for their expertise, and to Sergeant David Simmons and all of Miami's heroes for their courage and inspiration.

ABOUT THE AUTHOR

Edna Buchanan came to Miami on vacation from Paterson, New Jersey, and found it like stepping from a gritty black-and-white newsreel into Technicolor and Cinemascope. She fell in love with Miami's bright textures and stark, soulful sunlight.

She settled in Miami Beach and never looked back, working her way up from covering church socials for a small, now defunct newspaper to becoming a Pulitzer Prize–winning crime reporter on the staff of *The Miami Herald*.

Far from the grit of Paterson, she lives in Miami Beach with four cats, at work on a new book, on leave from the maelstrom of her journalism career, in which she has reported more than five thousand violent deaths, three thousand of them murders.

She is still in love with the hard beauty of Miami, a city of sunshine and hurricanes, mayhem and murder—land of the midnight gun.